# Ninja® Foodi™ Pressure Cooker
## THE BIG COOKBOOK

# NINJA® Foodi™

## PRESSURE COOKER

# THE BIG COOKBOOK

## 175 RECIPES AND **3 MEAL PLANS** FOR YOUR FAVORITE **DO-IT-ALL** MULTICOOKER

### Kenzie Swanhart

Photography by Becky Stayner

ROCKRIDGE PRESS

For general information on our other products and services or to obtain technical support, please contact our Customer Care Department within the United States at (866) 744-2665, or outside the United States at (510) 253-0500.

Rockridge Press publishes its books in a variety of electronic and print formats. Some content that appears in print may not be available in electronic books, and vice versa.

TRADEMARKS: Rockridge Press and the Rockridge Press logo are trademarks or registered trademarks of Callisto Media Inc. and/or its affiliates, in the United States and other countries, and may not be used without written permission. All other trademarks are the property of their respective owners. Rockridge Press is not associated with any product or vendor mentioned in this book.

Interior and Cover Designer: Erik Jacobsen
Art Producer: Karen Beard
Editor: Bridget Fitzgerald
Production Editor: Mia Moran
Photography © 2019 Becky Stayner, food styling by Kathleen Phillips and Kellie Gerber Kelley, except © Stocky, p. 14; © Evi Abeler, p. 16 & © Hélène Dujardin, pp. 72 & 130. Author and Ninja Chef Contributor Photos courtesy of © Julien Levesque. Cover recipe: Pork Chops with Green Beans and Scalloped Potatoes, page 277

ISBN: Print 978-1-64611-021-6
eBook 978-1-64611-022-3
R1

*For the Ninja® Foodi™ Family, thank you for loving the Ninja Foodi Pressure Cooker as much as we do!*

Buttermilk Fried
Chicken, page 236

# CONTENTS

The Ninja® Test Kitchen Chefs

## 6 Meatless

Baked Bacon Macaroni
and Cheese, page 257

# INTRODUCTION

**YOU, READING THIS BOOK, ARE THE REASON I DO WHAT I DO. I WANT** to transform the way you cook and make it easier for you to cook a delicious meal for you and your family. I want you to be proud to put dinner on the table!

You are the reason my team and I spend hours upon hours in the Ninja® Test Kitchen, testing prototypes, evaluating every change made to our products, and ensuring that they are the best they can be. No decision is made without thinking about how it will improve your life and your experience in the kitchen.

You are the reason we develop thousands of foolproof recipes that will make you fall in love with cooking. We test every recipe so you have confidence when it is time to cook. Whether you are whipping up a quick breakfast so you can get the kids out the door and off to school, prepping a healthy and nutritious lunch so you can skip the café, or making a delicious dinner so the family can spend time together around the table—my team and I have you covered.

In 2018, we launched the groundbreaking Ninja® Foodi™ Pressure Cooker—the pressure cooker that crisps. This revolution in cooking took the country by storm, flooding social media and selling out at retail stores across the country. We rejoiced in the fact that people across America were about to experience a whole new way of cooking.

The Ninja Foodi combines the speed of a pressure cooker with the quick crisping action of an air fryer to give you TenderCrisp™ Technology. By harnessing pressurized steam to quickly cook and tenderize ingredients, then using the revolutionary crisping lid for a crispy finish, you can make quick, delicious meals from real food. Oh, and did I mention there is only one pot to clean?

Perhaps you have already experienced the revolution that is the Ninja Foodi Pressure Cooker.

Perhaps you are part of the Ninja® Foodi™ Family on social media, sharing your creations and looking for more ways to use your Foodi Pressure Cooker and unlock its full potential.

Perhaps you just purchased a Ninja Foodi Pressure Cooker or received one as a gift and you're not sure where to start.

This book is for you! *The Big Ninja® Foodi™ Pressure Cooker Cookbook* is the ultimate, official cookbook from the Ninja Test Kitchen, packed to the brim with our tips, tricks, and techniques for making the most of the pressure cooker that crisps.

This book delivers 175 foolproof recipes you will want to make at home, including the best recipes from the Ninja Test Kitchen, the Foodi Pressure Cooker staples that will elevate any meal, the Ninja Test Kitchen Chefs' favorite recipes to make at home, and some of our favorite recipes from folks like you.

Get ready for quick and easy recipes for breakfast and brunch, like Broccoli, Ham, and Cheddar Frittata (page 41), Breakfast Burritos (page 48), and Cinnamon Sugar Donuts (page 66). Make snacks and apps including Mexican Street Corn Queso Dip (page 77), Chipotle-Lime Chicken Wings (page 94), and Loaded Potato Skins (page 85), or doable weeknight dinners, such as Bacon Ranch Chicken Bake (page 233), Creamy Turkey and Mushroom Ragu (page 241), and Pork Chops with Green Beans and Scalloped Potatoes (page 277). And let's not forget dessert, like these addicting Sweet and Salty Bars (page 333), Peanut Butter Pie (page 348), and Fried Oreos (page 361). All made in one pot!

With the Ninja Foodi Pressure Cooker, be proud of what you cook!

# 1

# Foodi™ Pressure Cooker Basics

**FOR SO MANY PEOPLE, THERE ARE A FEW UNSPOKEN RULES WHEN** it comes to cooking. It needs to be quick, it needs to be tasty, and it needs to be good for you. However, in the constant hustle and bustle of life, too often we sacrifice at least one of these areas to get the job done and move on to the next thing.

Multi-cookers claim to do it all, and slow cookers have long been touted for their versatility and convenience. After all, they do the work for you: just toss ingredients into the pot and come back to a perfectly cooked meal. Pressure cookers take it a step further, making your food incredibly tender, exceptionally fast.

But what about texture? Tender food is great, but no one wants to eat stews and soups every night. We all crave the crispy and crunchy. What are chicken wings without a crispy exterior? Who wants to eat potpie without a flaky crust?

Enter the Ninja® Foodi™ Pressure Cooker, the pressure cooker that crisps—a revolutionary appliance changing the multi-cooker game. With the Foodi Pressure Cooker, you can make quick, healthy, and delicious meals. As a result, you can spend less time cooking and more time doing all of the other things you need to get done.

This chapter will introduce you to the functions and benefits of this revolutionary appliance and help you choose the one that is right for you. Whether you are new to the Foodi or you are a Foodi fanatic, I will break down cooking with the Ninja® Foodi™ Pressure Cooker, giving you the Ninja Test Kitchen tips and tricks, and helping you unleash its full potential. And, of course, I'll introduce you to the recipes and strategies so you can use it every day.

## FOUR REASONS TO FOODI

For too long we have settled for convenience over flavor. Opting for takeout over a home-cooked meal or leaning on multi-cookers that don't deliver to answer the question, "What's for dinner?" With the Ninja Foodi Pressure Cooker, you no longer have to settle. TenderCrisp™ Technology unlocks unlimited possibilities for breakfast, lunch, dinner, dessert, and more.

### TenderCrisp Technology

TenderCrisp Technology is quite simple. First, use the pressure function to quickly cook and tenderize food with superheated steam. Then, remove the pressure lid and lower the crisping lid to quickly crisp and caramelize for the perfect finishing touch. With TenderCrisp Technology, you can cook quickly and ensure your food is tender inside and crispy on the outside. I'm talking about Garlic-Herb Roasted Chicken (page 214) or Crispy Korean-Style Ribs (page 276)!

### One Pot Meals

With the Foodi Pressure Cooker, you can transform boring, one-texture meals into one-pot wonders. Use the pressure function to quickly cook your favorite casseroles, stews, and chilies. Then top with cheese, biscuits, or a crust. Swap the top and use the crisping lid to broil the cheese, bake the biscuits, or crisp the crust. With everything prepared in one pot, your prep time is cut down, and you only have one pot to clean! Make the recipes that have been handed down from generation to generation—but with this unique twist, you can make them in half the time! Try this Cheesy Chicken and Broccoli Casserole (page 238) or a classic Green Bean Casserole (page 109).

### 360 Meals

Make a delicious, restaurant-inspired meal in one pot. I'm talking a full meal complete with fluffy rice, roasted veggies, and perfectly cooked proteins—each with its own unique texture. Pile grains on the bottom of your cooking pot, add some veggies, pop in the Reversible Rack, and place your proteins on top. Use the recipes throughout the book with the 360 Meal label, or go off book and try your own combination. Some of my favorite 360 Meals include Pork Chops with Green Beans and Scalloped Potatoes (page 277) and Mustard and Apricot-Glazed Salmon with Smashed Potatoes (page 195). Which will you try first?

### Frozen to Crispy

Perhaps the most convenient feature of the Ninja® Foodi™ Pressure Cooker is the ability to cook food straight from frozen. There's no need to wait around for food to thaw. Use pressure to quickly defrost and tenderize frozen meat, then lower the crisping lid to sizzle and crisp the outside. No more uneven defrosting using the microwave or waiting hours for your food to defrost on the counter. Check out freezer-to-table recipes like Salmon with Almonds, Cranberries, and Rice (page 211) and Frozen Chicken and Mozzarella Casserole (page 239).

## CHOOSE THE FOODI FOR YOU

You asked and we listened! After launching the original Ninja Foodi Pressure Cooker in 2018, we have now expanded our offering.

Whether you are a family of four, empty nesters, a single person, newlyweds, or looking to feed a crowd—there is now a Foodi Pressure Cooker for everyone.

On the following page I have outlined the various Foodi Pressure Cooker models to help you choose the Foodi that is right for you. All of the models have TenderCrisp™ Technology, but each comes in a different size with a unique feature set and accessories.

# FOODI™ PRESSURE COOKER MODELS

| NINJA® FOODI™ | MODEL | SIZE | CAPACITY | FUNCTIONS | FEATURES | ACCESSORIES |
|---|---|---|---|---|---|---|
| Ninja Foodi Compact Pressure Cooker | OP101 | 5 Quart | 4 pounds chicken<br><br>2 pounds French fries | Pressure, Steam, Slow Cook, Sear/Sauté, Yogurt, Air Crisp, Bake/Roast | TenderCrisp™ Technology, One Pot Meals, Frozen to Crispy | Cook & Crisp Basket |
| | OP300 | 6.5 Quart | 5 pounds chicken<br><br>2 pounds French fries<br><br>4 chicken breasts | Pressure, Steam, Slow Cook, Sear/Sauté, Yogurt, Air Crisp, Bake/Roast, Broil | TenderCrisp Technology, One Pot Meals, Frozen to Crispy, 360 Meals | Cook & Crisp Basket, Reversible Rack |
| | OP301 | 6.5 Quart | | Pressure, Steam, Slow Cook, Sear/Sauté, Yogurt, Air Crisp, Bake/Roast, Broil | | |
| | OP302 | 6.5 Quart | | Pressure, Steam, Slow Cook, Sear/Sauté, Yogurt, Air Crisp, Bake/Roast, Broil, Dehydrate | | |
| | OP305 | 6.5 Quart | | Pressure, Steam, Slow Cook, Sear/Sauté, Yogurt, Air Crisp, Bake/Roast, Broil, Dehydrate | | |
| Ninja Foodi Deluxe Pressure Cooker | FD401 | 8 Quart | 7 pounds chicken<br><br>4 pounds French fries<br><br>8 chicken breasts | Pressure, Steam, Slow Cook, Sear/Sauté, Yogurt, Air Crisp, Bake/Roast, Broil | TenderCrisp Technology, One Pot Meals, Frozen to Crispy, 360 Meals, 2X Protein Capacity | Cook & Crisp Basket, Deluxe Reversible Rack |
| | FD402 | 8 Quart | | Pressure, Steam, Slow Cook, Sear/Sauté, Yogurt, Air Crisp, Bake/Roast, Broil, Dehydrate | | |

# Scale It Up, Scale It Down

All of the recipes throughout this cookbook were developed using the original Ninja® Foodi™ Pressure Cooker, which has a 6.5-quart cooking pot. But never fear: Most of the recipes throughout the book will work with all of the Ninja Foodi models. Follow my recommendations for how to modify the recipes based on the Foodi you have.

**Scale it up!** If you have the Ninja Foodi Deluxe Pressure Cooker, you can easily modify the recipes throughout this book—plus you can scale the recipes up to feed more people! The Foodi Deluxe has an 8-quart cooking pot and the Deluxe Reversible Rack for two times the protein capacity. Note that some of the recipes may require a bit more cook time or an extra shake of the Cook & Crisp Basket. For best results, check progress throughout cooking, and shake the basket frequently. As a good rule of thumb, you can scale up Pressure recipes like soups, stews, and chilies by as much as 50 percent when using the Foodi Deluxe. You can also fit 50 percent more in the Cook & Crisp Basket.

**Scale it down!** The Ninja Foodi Compact Pressure Cooker is, as the name suggests, compact. So it is perfect for one to two people. Because of the smaller size, some recipes may require a bit less cook time or fewer shakes of the Cook & Crisp Basket. For best results, check progress throughout cooking. As a good rule of thumb, you can scale down Pressure recipes like soups, stews, and chilies by as much as 50 percent when using the Foodi Compact. And for recipes that call for the basket, you will fit about 50 percent fewer ingredients. Also note that the Foodi Compact Pressure Cooker does not come with a Reversible Rack, so you will need to make some 360 Meals in two steps. If you are following a recipe that calls for broiling, choose Air Crisp on the highest temperature setting instead.

# PARTS AND PIECES

**Pressure Release Valve**
Easily release pressure.

**Pressure Lid**
Quickly tenderize and cook ingredients.

**Reversible Rack**
Use to steam, or reverse to broil.

**Cook & Crisp™ Basket**
4-quart nonstick, ceramic-coated basket fits 3 pounds of French fries.

**Crisping Lid**
Use to finish off pressure cooked recipes or to air crisp your food.

**Cooking Pot**
6.5-quart nonstick, ceramic-coated cooking pot fits a 6-pound roast.

**14 Levels of Safety**
Passed rigorous testing to earn UL safety certification, giving you peace of mind.

## Pressure Lid

Use the pressure lid to turn the Ninja® Foodi™ into the ultimate pressure cooker, cooking and tenderizing food faster than you ever thought possible. Turn the valve from the seal to the vent position to steam your favorite fish and veggies or slow cook your favorite stew.

## Crisping Lid

The crisping lid adapts the fan and temperature so that you can Air Crisp, Bake/ Roast, Broil, and Dehydrate. Use the crisping lid after pressure cooking for the ultimate TenderCrisp™ meal or use it on its own for the ultimate Air Crisping experience. On some Ninja® Foodi™ Pressure Cooker models, the crisping lid goes as low as 100ºF so that you can dehydrate fruits, veggies, and meat for yummy snacks with no added sugars.

## Cooking Pot

The Ninja Foodi's cooking pot was specifically designed with an extra wide diameter so that you can sauté vegetables and sear meat without crowding the pot. Go from searing and sautéing to pressure or slow cooking all in the same pot. Since it is covered in a ceramic coating, the cooking pot can handle whatever you want to cook in it. A word of caution: Be sure to use silicone or wooden utensils so as not to scratch the pot.

## Cook & Crisp Basket

The Cook & Crisp Basket is designed to make sure that each bite comes out perfectly golden brown and crispy. Use the Cook & Crisp Basket to Air Crisp crunchy French fries and crispy chicken wings or to dehydrate mangos, apples, and beets. You can use the Cook & Crisp Basket when making TenderCrisp recipes, like finger-licking barbecue or a whole roasted chicken. Like the cooking pot, the Cook & Crisp Basket is ceramic coated for easy cleanup so be sure to use silicone or wooden utensils.

## Reversible Rack

In the lower position, the Reversible Rack allows you to steam veggies and fish quickly and easily. In the higher position, you can broil steaks for a crisp crust or cheesy bread to perfectly golden brown, or you can cook a full meal—protein, starch, and a vegetable—in one pot.

# FOODI PRESSURE COOKER FUNCTIONS

Now that you are acquainted with the Ninja® Foodi™ Pressure Cooker and its parts, let's dive into the nine unique cooking functions and take a look at what you can use them to make.

## Pressure

The Ninja Foodi is a far cry from your grandmother's pressure cooker, but the science behind it is the same—pressurized steam infuses moisture into ingredients and quickly cooks them from the inside out. Pressure cooking is ideal for tenderizing tough cuts of meat, quickly cooking rice, and everything in between. To get started, choose between low and high pressure, set the cook time, make sure the valve is in the SEAL position, and voila! Perfect for Carrot Cake Oats (page 39), Loaded Potato Soup (page 118), or Creamy Tuscan Chicken Pasta (page 234).

## Steam

Steam is the perfect setting for cooking fresh veggies or fish. Simply add water to the cooking pot and place the Reversible Rack in the lower position. Place your food on top of the rack and secure the lid. If you are using the Ninja Foodi Compact Pressure Cooker, use the Cook & Crisp Basket instead of the Reversible Rack.

## Slow Cook

Contrary to pressure cooking, which is used to quickly cook meats, soups, and stews, the slow cooking feature builds flavor by braising food low and slow. If you prefer the convenience of tossing your ingredients into a pot in the morning and coming home to a fully cooked meal, then slow cooking will be your go-to. The Ninja Foodi is equipped with both low and high slow cook settings. Check out this Slow Cooked Chicken in White Wine and Garlic (page 235) or use your favorite slow cooker recipe.

## Sear/Sauté

Use your Ninja Foodi just as you would your stove, alternating between low, medium low, medium, medium high, and high. Easily go from a gentle simmer to a screaming-hot sear. Use this function as a first step before pressure cooking or slow cooking to unlock more flavor from your aromatic ingredients like onions and garlic.

## Air Crisp

Air Crisp is our version of air fry. With Air Crisp you can achieve that crispy, crunchy, golden brown texture we all crave—without all the fat and oil. Use this feature in conjunction with the Cook & Crisp Basket to cook your favorite frozen foods: French fries, onion rings, chicken nuggets, and more. Be sure to shake the basket at least once or twice to ensure the crispiest, most even results, and don't be afraid to sneak a peek under the crisping lid so that you can remove your food when it is crisped to your liking. Try the Ham, Egg, and Cheese Breakfast Pockets (page 58), Rosemary Hush Puppies (page 89), or Fried Oreos (page 361), all crisped to perfection!

## Bake/Roast

The Ninja® Foodi™ Pressure Cooker also works as a mini convection oven, cooking your favorite baked dishes and roasted meats in less time than your oven. Use the bake/roast function to make Curried Chickpea and Roasted Tomato Shakshuka (page 45) or Italian Pasta Potpie (page 259).

## Broil

Broil reaches the hottest temperature of all of the crisping lid settings. Use Broil to add a crispy, cheesy finish to baked pasta dishes or reverse sear your favorite steak for a restaurant-style crisp crust. With Broil, you are cooking your food directly under very high heat, so be sure to open the lid to sneak a peek frequently so that your food is crisped to your liking and not overdone. If you are using the Ninja Foodi Compact Pressure Cooker, it does not have Broil. Instead, choose Air Crisp on the highest temperature setting.

## Dehydrate

Dehydrators can be expensive and take up space in the kitchen. These single-function appliances are usually relegated to the basement after a few uses, but if your Foodi Pressure Cooker has this feature, you can dehydrate fruits, vegetables, meats, herbs, and more without adding another appliance to your collection. Try making the Sweet Potato and Beetroot Chips (page 82) for a healthy homemade snack.

## Yogurt

Yogurt is the newest feature added to the Foodi™ Pressure Cooker. Now you can make homemade yogurt easily with just a few simple ingredients. No need for guesswork here. If you do not have the yogurt feature on your Foodi Pressure Cooker model, there are a number of hacks you can follow to make yogurt in the original Foodi Pressure Cooker.

### Converting the Old Standards

Easily convert your favorite recipes to be used in the Ninja® Foodi™ Pressure Cooker. When converting recipes from a conventional oven, use the Bake/Roast setting and reduce the temperature of the recipe by 25°F. So if your conventional recipes call for baking at 375°F, set your Ninja Foodi to 350°F. You will also likely be able to cut down the cook time. Check food frequently to avoid overcooking and keep notes so you know how to proceed the next time.

You can also use pressure to cook your favorite slow cooker recipes much quicker. A good rule of thumb is recipes that cook 8 hours on low or 4 hours on high in a slow cooker should take 25 to 30 minutes in a pressure cooker. It is also important to check your liquid level and ensure your recipe includes ½ to 1 cup of liquid to get to pressure. And as always, make sure the pressure release valve is in the SEAL position before beginning to build pressure.

# NINJA® TEST KITCHEN FAQ

**Q: How do I know when my food is done?**

A: In the Ninja Test Kitchen we are constantly asked how to get perfect results every time. How can we ensure folks at home have success every time they use the Ninja® Foodi™ Pressure Cooker? All food is created differently but we have put the Foodi through its pacing in the kitchen and developed a ton of charts (page 366) and recipes to guide you through the Foodi.

In addition to following our recommendations, I highly recommend investing in a temperature probe and using it to ensure your proteins are cooked to your desired doneness. While there are a lot of probes available, I find it best to use one with a cable so that you can keep it inserted while cooking and monitor temperature. Note that the temperature probe can only be inserted while cooking with the crisping lid. Always be sure to follow USDA recommendations for doneness.

Last but not least, in addition to monitoring the internal temperature of your food, I always recommend frequently sneaking a peak while cooking. Lift the lid to check on or shake your food. The Foodi Pressure Cooker recovers air temperature quickly so sneak a peek often to ensure your preferred level of crispiness.

**Q: Why do you recommend kosher and sea salt? What if I only have table salt?**

A: Salt is arguably one of the most important ingredients in a number of recipes throughout this cookbook. However, not all salt is created equal. Not only does it differ in size and taste, but also in sodium content. In fact, salt varies not only by type, but also by brand. In the Ninja Test Kitchen, we primarily use kosher salt and sea salt in our recipes. It is important to use the type of salt indicated in each recipe. Note that table salt cannot be substituted for kosher salt and sea salt as it will result in an overly salted dish. If you are sensitive to salt or unsure of how much to use, start with a pinch and season to taste.

**Q: What's the best way to add flavor when pressure cooking?**

A: So often we hear from folks that their pressure cooker recipes were perfectly tender but lacked flavor. This crushes me because there are so many easy tricks to packing your pressure-cooked recipes with flavor.

First and foremost, I always recommend using SEAR/SAUTÉ as a first step to sauté your aromatics before pressure cooking. Sautéing your onions, garlic, and spices in a splash of oil before pressure cooking builds flavor that will be infused into your food during pressure cooking. Searing your meat on the SEAR/SAUTÉ function also helps to build flavor. Remember, color equals flavor, so anytime you can brown and caramelize your food before pressure cooking you are adding another layer of flavor.

Another great tip from the Ninja Test Kitchen is to swap out water in pressure cooker recipes for broth/stock, wine, juice, etc. Use every ingredient in your recipes as a way to add flavor. If you are making pulled pork, add a splash of apple juice. Making pulled chicken? Use chicken stock to ensure that it is packed with flavor. I also love using red wine in my stews to add another depth of flavor.

**Q: How do I know when to manually release pressure?**

A: Releasing the pressure when cooking is complete can be intimidating to people who are new to pressure cooking—especially the manual, quick release. There are two ways to release pressure after the unit beeps, quick release and natural release.

Quick release stops cooking quickly and should be used for ingredients like vegetables so you don't overcook them. To quick release, manually switch the pressure release valve to the VENT position. When doing this, use caution as a jet of steam will be released.

Natural release is when you leave the pressure release switch in the SEAL position when the cook time ends. This lets the pressure release naturally and cooking stops gradually. If a recipe calls for a quick release, you can use a natural release if you prefer, but reduce the cook time so as not to overcook your food.

**Q: I've used my Ninja Foodi to cook a variety of dishes, but the smell of one of those dishes seems to be sticking around. What should I do?**

A: I am happy to report this is an easy fix. A pressure cooker gasket, also known as a sealing ring, is used to keep your Ninja® Foodi™ Pressure Cooker airtight in pressure cooker mode. This gasket can last for a long time; however, some foods can lead to this gasket having an odor over time. To mitigate this, clean the gasket after every use by removing the gasket from the lid and washing it with soap and water. If the odor persists, you can replace the gasket. If you use your pressure cooker frequently, consider investing in two gaskets, one for savory foods and one for sweet.

**Q: The Foodi has so many options for cooking at home. How do I know which is right for me?**

A: If you are new to the Foodi pressure cooking, or pressure cooking in general, it can be intimidating to know what functions to use when. At a basic level, pressure cooking allows you to quickly tenderize ingredients. Pressure cooking is ideal for soups, sauces, stews, and pulled meats. Air Crisp is our version of air fry and is used primarily for crisping foods quickly. Air Crisp is ideal for frozen, breaded ingredients, as well as fresh vegetables.

When in doubt, check the cooking charts on page 366. I also recommend joining the social media pages dedicated to the Ninja® Foodi™. This community is amazing and always has fun, creative ideas for cooking your favorite foods. Oh, and you can always reach out to me on social media as well (@KenzieSwanhart)!

**Q: If I don't have all of the ingredients for a recipe, can I swap the ingredient with something I have?**

A: We get this question all the time in the Ninja Test Kitchen, which is why I have added tips throughout the recipes in the book with ingredient swaps and suggestions. If the recipe you are making doesn't have a recipe swap noted, confirm the swap you want to make will cook in the same amount of time as the original ingredient by checking the cooking charts on page 366.

Some swaps are easier to make than others, like swapping elbows for cavatappi pasta, while other ingredient changes may require adjusting cook times and temperatures. Therefore, I cannot confirm all ingredients swaps will result in success. My advice is to experiment and have fun. After all, that's how we created all these recipes!

## FOODI PRESSURE COOKER KITCHEN

With the Ninja Foodi Pressure Cooker, you don't need a lot to make a delicious meal. By keeping a few simple ingredients in your fridge and pantry, you are sure to be able to throw together a meal in no time. This section will review the staples that will help you get the most out of your Foodi Pressure Cooker, as well as the tools that will unlock the Foodi's full potential.

## Basics: The Foodi Staples

**Bread Crumbs –** These are perfect for topping casseroles and breading chicken. You can buy a prepackaged brand or save some money and make your own. Wheat, white, multi-grain, or rye breads can all be turned into fresh toasted bread crumbs.

**Broth/Stock –** Broths and stocks are an easy way to add extra flavor to any recipe you make using pressure. Simply swap the water in the recipe for vegetable, chicken, or beef broth.

**Canned Tomatoes –** Whole, diced, puréed—tomatoes add acidity, sweetness, and color to a vast array of dishes. It is impractical to assume you will always have fresh tomatoes available, but canned tomatoes provide consistent flavor, especially when fresh tomatoes are out of season. Use canned tomatoes for sauces, stews, and soups.

**Chicken –** From a whole bird to thighs, breasts, or wings—I always have chicken in the fridge (and freezer). It's perfect for creating a quick, healthy meal.

**Garlic –** There are three staples that I use in almost every recipe throughout this book: extra-virgin olive oil, sea salt, and freshly ground pepper. If I had to choose a fourth, it would be garlic. When sautéed before pressure cooking, it adds another layer of flavor.

**Lemons –** There aren't many fresh foods on my list of staples but having lemons available for fresh juice is a must.

**Lentils and Beans –** Relatively inexpensive and super easy to make, lentils and beans add extra protein, fiber, and a bit of bulk to any dish.

**Onions –** Almost every great meal begins with sautéing an onion. Don't worry about keeping all varieties on the counter—a few yellow onions are versatile enough to cook with in most recipes.

**Pasta –** Whether you prefer penne, rigatoni, or cavatappi, having dry pasta in the kitchen means you are always prepared for an impromptu meal. Dry pasta is versatile and can be paired with ragus, soups, and casseroles so you can make a meal with whatever fresh ingredient you have on hand.

**Pie Crust –** Save yourself the time and effort. Refrigerated pie crust can be just as buttery, flaky, and delicious as homemade. Keep a roll in the fridge and you will always be prepared for impromptu casseroles and desserts.

**Rice and Grains –** Rice, oats, and quinoa make a satisfying base for any meal and work for breakfast, lunch, dinner, and dessert. Oats can also be tossed with sugar and butter to turn frozen or fresh fruit into an epic dessert crumble.

**Spices –** I could write a whole section on how to stock your spice cabinet, but there are a few staples you should always have on hand: Sea salt, black pepper, dried basil, garlic powder, ground cinnamon, ground cumin, onion powder, dried oregano, and paprika are our top choices!

## Tools: Set Up for Success

There are a few simple accessories that I recommend for prepping and serving the recipes throughout this book. Many of these tools you likely already own.

**Baking Pans –** The Ninja® Foodi™ Pressure Cooker is so much more than a pressure cooker; it can also be used as a mini convection oven. Baking pans and ramekins are handy for making small batches and unlocking new recipes. Use a cake pan or baking dish to make a Spanish Potato and Chorizo Frittata (page 43) or Coffee Cake (page 362).

**Oven Mitts –** Oven mitts are a must for removing the cooking pot and accessories from the Foodi Pressure Cooker. My favorite are mini silicone mitts because they are easy to maneuver.

**Meat Thermometer –** For best results, use a digital food thermometer to accurately measure internal temperature of protein. Insert the thermometer into centermost, thickest part of protein. If protein is bone-in, insert it very close to (but not touching) the bone.

**Potato Masher –** The Foodi Pressure Cooker not only helps you whip up weeknight dinners, but it is also your best friend when entertaining. Around the holidays, free up the stove and use your Foodi for simple sides like mashed potatoes. Just be sure to use a plastic or silicone potato masher to protect the ceramic coating on the cooking pot.

**Tongs** – Tongs are a quick and convenient way to flip and toss ingredients in the Cook & Crisp Basket. Reach for tongs with a silicone tip.

**Wooden Spoon** – When cooking and serving in and out of the cooking pot, a wooden spoon is a must to protect the ceramic coating. If you don't have a wooden spoon, opt for a silicone one.

## Accessories: Do More with Your Foodi Pressure Cooker

In addition to the accessories that came with your Ninja® Foodi™ Pressure Cooker, there are a few additional accessories you can purchase so that you can truly get the most out of your Foodi. All of these accessories are available by going to NinjaKitchen.com.

 **Dehydrate Rack –** This rack is specifically designed to expand the amount of food you can dehydrate at once. Arrange ingredients in a single layer and carefully place the rack in the cooking pot. Follow the Dehydrate Chart (page 386) to create your own custom jerky, vegetable chips, dried fruit snacks, and more.

 **Glass Lid –** With this new accessory, there is no second guessing with how your food is cooking. The glass allows you to check on your food as it steams and slow cooks without removing the lid. I also love using the glass lid with the Keep Warm setting as a buffet. Great for holidays or keeping dinner warm until the whole family is home to enjoy together!

 **Loaf Pan –** This specially designed loaf pan fits perfectly on the Reversible Rack. The ideal baking accessory for quick breads, it works equally as well for your favorite meatloaf recipe. Plus, the loaf pan has ceramic coating and is nonstick for easy cleaning.

 **Multi-Purpose Pan –** Perfect for baking everything from desserts to casseroles, the Multi-Purpose Pan is the must-have accessory for any Ninja Foodi fanatic and can be used across most Ninja Foodi products. If you follow me on Instagram, you know the skillet cookie is my favorite recipe to make in the Multi-Purpose Pan, but you can also make cobblers, frittatas, and casseroles.

 **Multi-Purpose Sling –** Aluminum foil is a hack used in many recipes for removing accessories and roasts from pressure cookers. The multi-purpose sling is a more durable, reusable option, and is great for that whole roasted chicken or the Multi-Purpose Pan.

 **Tube Pan –** A tube pan is very similar to a Bundt pan but it has detachable sides like a springform pan, making it easy to remove foods. Use this pan for everything from cheesecakes and delicate desserts to cornbread and casseroles.

## ABOUT THIS BIG COOKBOOK

The following chapters are filled with the best recipes from the Ninja Test Kitchen, the recipes we love to make at home. There are also some from home cooks and Foodi fanatics! All were chosen to inspire you to use the Ninja® Foodi™ Pressure Cooker to elevate your everyday meals. They use common ingredients to create incredible meals, many of which can be made in 30 minutes or less.

As you begin, remember to read through each recipe completely and gather all the ingredients you need in advance. A little prep work before you begin to cook will save you time in the long run.

### Menu Planning

In addition to providing you with a plethora of delicious recipes, my goal is to help you strategize and meal plan using your pressure cooker to make cooking and leftovers easier, tastier, and more creative—with less work. The Foodi can transform the way you cook, and in the next chapter, I will offer sample meal plans to help jump-start your Foodi adventure and show you how using different cooking functions can help you reimagine breakfast, lunch, and dinner all week long.

### Ninja Test Kitchen Recipes

Perhaps my favorite thing about coming to work every day is the amazing team I get to work with in the Ninja Test Kitchen. While I have the privilege of representing the Ninja Test Kitchen at a variety of events, on home shopping channels, and, of course, by penning this collection of the ultimate Ninja Foodi Pressure Cooker recipes, I am only able to do so because of my team.

The Ninja Test Kitchen is comprised of a team of diverse chefs, each with a unique background, who spend hours upon hours testing prototypes, building intelligent programs, and evaluating every change made to our products. From increasing the temperature of the heating element, to adding nonstick coatings, and even determining the number of ingredients in each recipe, no decision is made without thinking about how it will improve your life and your experience in the kitchen.

Our goal is to make mistakes so that you don't have to. Not only do we find joy in transforming the way you cook, we also develop the recipes that allow you to fall in love with our products.

I am so excited to introduce you to the Ninja Test Kitchen chefs throughout this book! You will also see that I've included recipes from the whole team. Each chef's name is included on the recipes they developed, and you can learn more about each chef and their background on page 415.

## Ninja® Foodi™ Family Recipes

Chances are you have seen the Ninja® Foodi™ Pressure Cooker flooding your social media feed. The Ninja Foodi revolution created an amazing online community, and I could not be prouder of how the Foodi Pressure Cooker is inspiring folks to get back in the kitchen and have fun cooking.

The Foodi family is made up of amazing home cooks and food bloggers, and I love seeing what they make every day in their Foodi Pressure Cookers. When putting together this book, I knew I had to share some of these recipes with you. So that's what I did. We chose some of the best recipes from across the web and tried them out in the Ninja Test Kitchen. These recipes are included throughout the book and include a short intro from me or from the person who developed them.

As you experiment with your Foodi Pressure Cooker and cook your way through the book, join the Facebook communities and use hashtags on Instagram to show off your amazing creations.

## Ingredients, Labels, and Tips

In order to help you choose the recipe that is right for you, I have included dietary labels (Dairy-Free, Gluten-Free, Nut-Free, Vegetarian, or Vegan) on every recipe. You will also note labels for recipes that are Under 30 Minutes, 5-Ingredient, Family Favorite, and 360 Meals that include a protein, starch, and vegetable. All recipes also include nutritional information.

Last but not least, I have included my best tips, tricks, and recommendations for making the most out of every recipe:

**Substitution Tips** – These are my favorite ingredient substitutions for a particular recipe and can be used to customize a recipe based on your dietary preferences or what you have on hand.

**Variation Tips** – These are my recommendations for how to put a twist on the dish and truly make it your own.

**Ingredient Info** – Here I will highlight interesting information about a particular ingredient that you might not know.

**Hack It** – The difference between a good cook and a great cook is the secret hacks they use to make the recipe even easier. These are my tricks for easy prep, cook, and cleanup.

**Make More, Make Less** – I've outlined some specific recommendations for recipes that require a function not available on all Foodi models but will help you get a similar result.

# 2

# Foodi™ Pressure Cooker Meal Planning

**FOOD SHOULDN'T BE COMPLICATED, BUT TOO OFTEN WE GET** stuck deciding what to cook and wind up resenting mealtime. If you are looking to save time, make better choices, and have a less hectic mealtime, you need to plan your meals.

Meal planning means different things to different people, but to me it means making weeknight cooking easier. Whether you make meals in advance, batch cook and freeze, or prep in advance, a little bit of planning can make your weeks a little tastier and a lot less stressful.

Take a few minutes each week to think about your meals for the week ahead. Read through recipes, make a shopping list, and keep in mind that there is no one right way to meal prep—it's about what works best for you.

With the Ninja® Foodi™ Pressure Cooker, not only is dinner a breeze but you can now plan and prep all meals with ease.

To help you along the way, I have designed three week-long meal plans to guide you through breakfast, lunch, and dinner—with a few sweet treats added in. These are meant to be flexible, so if a particular recipe doesn't appeal to you, swap it out for another—after all, this book has 175 recipes to choose from. Just be sure to update your shopping list so you have everything you need. To download and print these meal plans and lists, visit www.callistomediabooks.com/BigNinjaFoodiCookbook.

## MEAL PLAN 1: AROUND THE WORLD

My husband Julien and I love to travel, not only to see and experience new places but to experiment with and try new foods as well. This meal plan was inspired by our love for travel. With recipes from around the world, you are sure to be flavor-fulfilled every day. From Tuscan-inspired Italian favorites to Cuban cuisine, I have included some of my favorite regional dishes, with an emphasis on dinners that serve several people so that you can capitalize on leftovers. Use this meal plan to inspire a week of global cuisine.

### Prep Plan

This globally inspired menu gives you a handful of opportunities to make some recipes ahead of time—over the weekend or if you have free time during the week. The Southern Grits Casserole (page 50) and Spanish Potato and Chorizo Frittata (page 43) are great breakfast options and can be easily reheated on the busiest mornings. Cajun Turkey Breast (page 242) and Fluffy Quinoa (page 311) can also be prepared in advance and heated up as needed for lunch and dinner.

## Leftovers

When it comes to leftovers for the week, use these easy tips:

- Store leftovers in airtight containers in the refrigerator or, for the Cheese Babka, store in an airtight container in a cabinet or on the counter.
- Cut your leftover Southern Grits Casserole into slices and refrigerate. For best results, reheat in the Cook & Crisp Basket according to the recipe note.
- Reheat the Italian Sausage, Potato, and Kale Soup in the Ninja Foodi on the SEAR/SAUTÉ setting on LO.
- Reheat other leftovers through a method of your choice.

## Menu

| | BREAKFAST | LUNCH | DINNER | DESSERT |
|---|---|---|---|---|
| **Monday** | Breakfast Burritos (page 48) | Fish Finger Sandwich (page 185) | Creamy Tuscan Chicken Pasta (page 234) | Cheese Babka (page 335) |
| **Tuesday** | Chilaquiles (page 54) | Leftover Creamy Tuscan Chicken Pasta | Italian Sausage, Potato, and Kale Soup (page 119) | Tres Leches Cake (page 357) |
| **Wednesday** | Southern Grits Casserole (page 50) | Leftover Italian Sausage, Potato, and Kale Soup | Ropa Vieja (page 291) | Coconut Rice Pudding (page 334) |
| **Thursday** | Spanish Potato and Chorizo Frittata (page 43) | Leftover Ropa Vieja | Lamb Tagine (page 296) | Leftover Cheese Babka |
| **Friday** | Leftover Southern Grits Casserole | Leftover Lamb Tagine | Jerk Chicken Thighs with Sweet Potato and Banana Mash (page 225) | Leftover Coconut Rice Pudding |
| **Saturday** | Curried Chickpea and Roasted Tomato Shakshuka (page 45) | New England Lobster Rolls (page 190) | Cajun Turkey Breast (page 242) with Baked Sweet Potato (page 317) | Leftover Tres Leches Cake |
| **Sunday** | Chocolate Hazelnut Toaster Pastries (page 63) | Leftover Cajun Turkey Breast with Fluffy Quinoa (page 311) | Fresh Kielbasa and Braised Sweet and Sour Cabbage (page 255) | Leftover Coconut Rice Pudding |

## Shopping List

### Produce

- Avocado (1)
- Bananas (2)
- Bell peppers, green (2)
- Bell peppers, red (4)
- Bell peppers, yellow (1)
- Cabbage, red (1 head)
- Celery stalks (1)
- Cilantro (1 bunch)
- Garlic cloves (15)
- Jalapeño (1)
- Kale (6 cups)
- Lemons (2)
- Lettuce, butter (4 leaves)
- Onion, white (1)
- Onion, yellow (6)
- Potato, Russet (5)
- Potato, sweet (7)

### Dairy

- Butter, unsalted (2 sticks)
- Cheese, Cheddar, shredded (3 cups)
- Cheese, cotija (½ cup)
- Cheese, feta (8 ounces)
- Cheese, Mexican blend, shredded (1 cup)
- Cream cheese (8 ounces)
- Cream, heavy whipping (1½ cups)
- Eggs (38)
- Milk, whole (4¼ cups)
- Sour cream (1 tablespoon)

### Meat, Poultry, and Fish

- Beef, chuck roast (2½ pounds)
- Chicken thighs, boneless, skin-on (4)
- Chorizo, link (1)
- Chorizo, ground (1 pound)
- Cod fillets, 4 (5- to 6-ounce)
- Lamb stew meat (2 pounds)
- Lobster tails 4 (4-ounce)
- Sausage, breakfast (1 pound)
- Sausage, Italian, hot, ground (1½ pounds)
- Sausage, Italian, sweet, ground (1 pound)
- Sausage, kielbasa, link, fresh (1½ pounds)
- Turkey breast, boneless, skinless, 1 (4-pound)

### Canned and Bottled Goods

- Agave nectar (2 tablespoons)
- Beans, black (½ cup)
- Beer, ale (8 ounces)
- Chickpeas, 2 (15.5-ounce) cans
- Chocolate hazelnut spread (¼ cup)
- Chocolate sprinkles
- Coconut milk, full-fat, 2 (15-ounce) cans
- Cooking spray
- Curry paste, red (1 tablespoon)
- Evaporated milk (16-ounce can)
- Jerk marinade, spicy (½ cup)
- Mayonnaise (¼ cup)

- Oil, canola
- Olive oil, extra-virgin
- Olives, green with pimentos (1 cup)
- Pico de gallo
- Red enchilada sauce, 2 (10-ounce) cans
- Stock, beef (1 cup)
- Stock, chicken (7 cups)
- Sweetened condensed milk (16-ounce can)
- Tartar sauce
- Tomato paste (10-ounce can)
- Tomatoes, crushed (16-ounce can)
- Tomatoes, fire-roasted, crushed (28-ounce can)
- Vanilla icing
- Vinegar, apple cider (⅓ cup)
- Vinegar, white (1 tablespoon)
- Wine, white, dry (½ cup)

### Frozen and Refrigerated

- Corn (1 cup)
- Guacamole
- Pie crust (1)

### Grains and Nuts

- Almonds, toasted (1 cup)
- Apricots, dried (1 cup)
- Bread, sandwich (4 slices)
- Couscous (1 cup)
- Grits, stone-ground (2 cups)
- Hot dog buns, split-top (4)
- Rice, arborio (¾ cup)
- Taco shells, hard (10)
- Tortilla, flour 4 (10-inch)

### Pantry Items

- Allspice, ground (⅛ teaspoon)
- Bay leaves (2)
- Black pepper, freshly ground
- Cajun seasoning (2 tablespoons)
- Caraway seeds (2 teaspoons)
- Celery seed (¼ teaspoon)
- Chili powder (½ tablespoon)
- Cornstarch (1 cup)
- Crushed red pepper flakes (2 teaspoons)
- Cumin, ground (1½ tablespoons)
- Flour, all-purpose (3½ cups)
- Italian seasoning (2 tablespoons)
- Oregano (2 teaspoons)
- Paprika (1 teaspoon)
- Ras el hanout (2 tablespoons)
- Salt, sea
- Salt, kosher
- Sugar, granulated (1⅔ cups)
- Vanilla extract (1 teaspoon)
- Yeast, dry active (.31-ounce packet)
- Yellow cake mix (1 box)

## MEAL PLAN 2: COZY COMFORTS

From chilly winter nights to long, stressful weeks, sometimes you just crave comfort food. This meal plan was inspired by comfort food favorites and takeout fake-out meals so you can enjoy the flavors you love at home. Cozy up with cheesy casseroles and hearty stews. Cure your sweet tooth with desserts like cakes, pies, or donuts. This meal plan is sure to improve a long, stressful week or keep you warm during a week full of snowstorms.

### Prep Plan

There are a ton of opportunities to use your Ninja® Foodi™ Pressure Cooker over the weekend to get you and your family ready for the week. Make the Italian Pasta Potpie (page 259) in advance and you'll have two meals to start your Monday off on the right foot. All the breakfast items on this menu except for the Cinnamon Sugar Donuts (page 66) are great make-ahead options.

### Snacks

Looking for snack ideas to round out the week that keep the cozy theme going? Try these:

- Three-Layer Taco Dip (page 76)
- Loaded Potato Skins (page 85)
- Rosemary Hush Puppies (page 89)
- Honey-Garlic Chicken Wings (page 93)
- Pull Apart Cheesy Garlic Bread (page 110)

# Menu

| | BREAKFAST | LUNCH | DINNER | DESSERT |
|---|---|---|---|---|
| **Monday** | Cinnamon Roll Monkey Bread (page 70) | Italian Pasta Potpie (page 259) | Cheesy Chicken and Broccoli Casserole (page 238) | Red Velvet Cheesecake (page 352) |
| **Tuesday** | Carrot Cake Oats (page 39) | Leftover Cheesy Chicken and Broccoli Casserole | Lasagna Soup (page 144) | Coconut Cream "Custard" Bars (page 337) |
| **Wednesday** | Chocolate Chip and Banana Bread Bundt Cake (page 69) | Leftover Lasagna Soup | Leftover Italian Pasta Potpie | Peanut Butter Pie (page 348) |
| **Thursday** | Leftover Cinnamon Roll Monkey Bread | Cauliflower Enchiladas (page 167) | Pasta Primavera (page 171) | Leftover Red Velvet Cheesecake |
| **Friday** | Leftover Carrot Cake Oats | Goulash (Hungarian Beef Soup) (page 115) | Spicy Kimchi and Tofu Fried Rice (page 163) | Leftover Coconut Cream "Custard" Bars |
| **Saturday** | Leftover Chocolate Chip and Banana Bread Bundt Cake | Garlic Bread Pizza (page 180) | Coconut Shrimp with Pineapple Rice (page 204) | Leftover Peanut Butter Pie |
| **Sunday** | Cinnamon Sugar Donuts (page 66) | Crispy Korean-Style Ribs (page 276) | Simple Chicken Parmesan (page 227) | Fried Oreos (page 361) |

# Shopping List

## Produce

- Apples (2)
- Bananas (3)
- Basil (1 bunch)
- Bell peppers, red (2)
- Broccoli (1 head)
- Carrots (4)
- Cauliflower (1 head)
- Cilantro (½ cup)
- Garlic cloves (18)
- Ginger, minced (2 tablespoons)
- Lemons (1)
- Lime (3)
- Onion, red (1)
- Onion, yellow (4)
- Parsley (1 bunch)
- Potatoes, gold (1½ pounds)
- Scallions (2)
- Yellow squash (1)
- Zucchini (1)

## Dairy

- Butter, unsalted (3 sticks)
- Buttermilk (½ cup)
- Cheese, Cheddar, shredded (2 cups)
- Cheese, Mexican blend, shredded (1½ cups)
- Cheese, mozzarella, shredded (4 cups)
- Cheese, mozzarella, slices (6)
- Cheese, Parmesan, grated (1½ cups)
- Cream, heavy whipping (1½ cups)
- Cream cheese, 4 (8-ounce) packages
- Eggs (14)
- Milk, whole (2⅔ cups)
- Ricotta cheese (3 cups)
- Sour cream (¼ cup)

## Meat, Poultry, and Fish

- Beef stew meat (2 pounds)
- Baby back ribs (3-pound rack)
- Chicken breasts, 4 (8-ounce)
- Chicken cutlets, 4 (6-ounce)
- Sausage, Italian (1 pound)
- Sausage, Italian, links, 4 (4-ounce)
- Shrimp (10 ounces)

## Canned and Bottled Goods

- Almond milk, unsweetened vanilla (4 cups)
- Condensed Cheddar cheese soup (10.5-ounce can)
- Cooking spray
- Honey (¼ cup)
- Kimchi (½ cup)
- Maple syrup (½ cup)
- Marinara sauce, 2 (25-ounce) jars
- Oil, canola
- Oil, sesame (2 tablespoons)
- Olive oil, extra-virgin
- Peanut butter, creamy (⅓ cup)
- Pineapple, diced (20-ounce can)
- Red enchilada sauce (10-ounce can)
- Soy sauce (⅔ cup)
- Stock, chicken (3½ cups)
- Stock, beef (2 cups)
- Stock, vegetable (1 cup)
- Tomato-basil sauce (¾ cup)

- Tomato paste (2 tablespoons)
- Tomatoes, diced (14.5-ounce can)
- Vinegar, rice (2 tablespoons)
- Vinegar, white (½ teaspoon)

## Frozen and Refrigerated

- Cinnamon rolls, 2 (12.5-ounce) tubes
- Garlic bread (6 slices)
- Meatballs, cooked (12-ounce bag)
- Peas and carrots (½ cup)
- Pie crust (1)
- Tofu, extra-firm (8 ounces)
- Whipped cream topping (14-ounce tub)

## Grains and Nuts

- Almonds, chopped (½ cup)
- Bread crumbs, panko (½ cup)
- Bread crumbs, seasoned (1 cup)
- Buttered crackers (2 cups)
- Coconut, unsweetened, shredded (½ cup)
- Coconut flakes (½ cup)
- Cookies, Oreo (1 package)
- Cookies, peanut butter (10)
- Flour tortillas, 5 (8-inch)
- Lasagna noodles (8 ounces)
- Oats (2 cups)
- Pancake mix (½ cup)
- Penne pasta (1-pound box)
- Rice, Texmati® brown (1 cup)
- Rice, white, long-grain (1 cup)
- Rigatoni pasta (1-pound box)

## Pantry Items

- Baking powder (½ teaspoon)
- Baking soda (1 teaspoon)
- Basil (1½ teaspoons)
- Black pepper, freshly ground
- Cayenne pepper (1 tablespoon)
- Chocolate, dark (4 tablespoons)
- Chocolate chips (1 cup)
- Chocolate peanut butter cups (1)
- Chili pepper (1 teaspoon)
- Cinnamon (4½ teaspoons)
- Cocoa powder, unsweetened (2 tablespoons)
- Crushed red pepper flakes (¼ teaspoon)
- Cumin, ground (2 teaspoons)
- Cranberries, dried (1 cup)
- Flour, all-purpose (6⅓ cups)
- Oregano (1½ teaspoons)
- Paprika (1 teaspoon)
- Paprika, smoked (2 tablespoons)
- Parsley (1½ teaspoons)
- Red food coloring (1 tablespoon)
- Rosemary (¼ teaspoon)
- Salt, kosher
- Salt, sea
- Sesame seeds
- Sugar, confectioners' (1 tablespoon)
- Sugar, dark brown (½ cup)
- Sugar, granulated (1¼ cups)
- Thyme (½ teaspoon)
- Vanilla extract (5 teaspoons)
- Vanilla pudding, instant (1 packet)

## MEAL PLAN 3: EXTRA EASY

This extra easy meal plan is filled with some of the easiest and quickest recipes. When time is tight, I always reach for recipes that require little prep so I can toss the ingredients in the Ninja® Foodi™ Pressure Cooker and walk away. If you have an extra busy week or just need a break, reach for this meal plan and let the Ninja Foodi handle dinner so you can handle life. The best part, these recipes are all one pot meals so cleanup is a breeze. Toss the pot and accessories in the dishwasher and get back to the things that matter most.

### Prep Plan

While this meal plan is meant to provide easy meals that can be ready quickly, there's no harm in getting a head start over the weekend. Create your Baked Bacon Macaroni and Cheese (page 257) on Sunday so you have lunch ready to go for Monday. You can also make the Homemade Vanilla Yogurt (page 65) and Tex-Mex Chicken Tortilla Soup (page 135) in advance.

## Desserts

These sweet treats are made with minimal ingredients and come together in no time to complete your extra easy week:

- Sugar Cookie Pizza (page 332)
- Bacon Blondies (page 347)
- Apple Crisp (page 343)
- Hazelnut Cheesecake (page 353)

## Menu

| | BREAKFAST | LUNCH | DINNER |
|---|---|---|---|
| **Monday** | Waffle Bread Pudding with Maple-Jam Glaze (page 60) | Baked Bacon Macaroni and Cheese (page 257) | Southwest Chicken Bake (page 240) |
| **Tuesday** | Homemade Vanilla Yogurt (page 65) | Leftover Southwest Chicken Bake | Crab Cake Casserole (page 209) |
| **Wednesday** | Leftover Waffle Bread Pudding with Maple-Jam Glaze | Leftover Crab Cake Casserole | Tex-Mex Chicken Tortilla Soup (page 135) |
| **Thursday** | Breakfast Burritos (page 48) | Leftover Tex-Mex Chicken Tortilla Soup | Veggie Loaded Pasta (page 165) |
| **Friday** | Leftover Homemade Vanilla Yogurt | Leftover Veggie Loaded Pasta | Frozen Chicken and Mozzarella Casserole (page 239) |
| **Saturday** | Sweet Potato Hash and Eggs (page 53) | Bacon-Wrapped Hot Dogs (page 249) | Low Country Boil (page 189) |
| **Sunday** | Cinnamon Bun Oatmeal (page 37) | Coconut and Shrimp Bisque (page 127) | Beef Stroganoff (page 294) |

# Shopping List

## Produce

- Avocados (3)
- Bell peppers, green (1)
- Bell peppers, red (4)
- Celery (2 stalks)
- Cherry tomatoes (1 cup)
- Cilantro (1 bunch)
- Corn (3 ears)
- Garlic cloves (3)
- Jalapeño (1)
- Limes (4)
- Mushrooms, cremini (4 cups)
- Onion, red (3)
- Onion, yellow (4)
- Potatoes, Red Bliss (2 pounds)
- Spinach (4 cups)
- Scallions (2 bunches)
- Sweet potatoes (3 pounds)
- Thyme (2 sprigs)

## Dairy

- Butter, unsalted (3 sticks)
- Cheese, Cheddar, shredded (5 cups)
- Cheese, Gouda (8 ounces)
- Cheese, Mexican blend, shredded (1 cup)
- Cheese, Parmesan, shredded (¼ cup)
- Cream, heavy whipping (1 cup)
- Cream cheese (2 ounces)
- Eggs (10)
- Eggs, brown (6)
- Milk, whole (½ gallon)
- Sour cream (½ cup)
- Yogurt, plain with active live cultures (3 tablespoons)

## Meat, Poultry, and Fish

- Bacon (8 strips)
- Beef stew meat (2 pounds)
- Chicken breasts, 4 (8-ounce)
- Chorizo, ground (1 pound)
- Hot dogs, beef (4)
- Sausage, smoked (14-ounce package)
- Shrimp, 21-30 count (2 pounds)

## Canned and Bottled Goods

- Black beans, 3 (15-ounce) cans
- Coconut milk, full-fat (14-ounce can)
- Corn, 2 (15-ounce) cans
- Crab meat, lump, 3 (8-ounce) cans
- Evaporated milk (5-ounce can)
- Honey (½ cup)
- Maple syrup (⅓ cup)
- Marinara sauce (23-ounce jar)
- Mayonnaise (¼ cup)
- Mustard, Dijon (¼ cup)
- Oil, canola
- Olive oil, extra-virgin
- Pico de gallo
- Raspberry jam (⅓ cup)
- Red curry paste (¼ cup)
- Red enchilada sauce (10-ounce can)
- Sauerkraut (1 cup)
- Soy sauce (2 tablespoons)
- Stock, chicken (6 cups)
- Tomatoes, fire-roasted with chiles, 2 (10-ounce) cans
- Tomato paste (10-ounce can)

## Frozen and Refrigerated

- Chicken breasts, 4 (6-ounce)
- Guacamole
- Mozzarella sticks, 2 (11-ounce) boxes
- Peas (1 cup)
- Waffles, 2 (12-ounce) boxes

## Grains and Nuts

- Bread crumbs, panko (2 cups)
- Butter crackers (5-ounce sleeve)
- Egg noodles (1 pound)
- Flour tortillas, 4 (10-inch)
- Hot dog buns, bakery (4)
- Oats, rolled (½ cup)
- Oats, steel-cut (1 cup)
- Pasta, elbow (1-pound box)
- Pasta, rigatoni (1-pound box)
- Rice, basmati (1½ cups)
- Rice, white (1 cup)

## Pantry Items

- Black pepper, freshly ground
- Cinnamon (½ teaspoon)
- Cornstarch (2 tablespoons)
- Creole seasoning (2½ tablespoons)
- Flour, all-purpose (½ cup)
- Mustard, ground (1 tablespoon)
- Nutmeg (1 teaspoon)
- Paprika, smoked (2 teaspoons)
- Raisins (¾ cup)
- Salt, kosher
- Salt, sea
- Sugar, brown (⅔ cup)
- Sugar, confectioners' (2 tablespoons)
- Sugar, granulated (⅓ cup)
- Taco seasoning (2 packets)
- Vanilla extract (2½ teaspoons)

# 3

# Breakfast & Breads

# Cinnamon Bun Oatmeal

SERVES 6

*Nothing warms me up on a chilly morning quite like a bowl of warm oatmeal, and this is my favorite version. Packed with spicy cinnamon, topped with a buttery crumble topping, and finished with a sticky sweet icing, this oatmeal dish emulates all of the flavor of your favorite baked good. Plus, the oats are full of fiber to keep you feeling satisfied all morning.*

**NUT-FREE, VEGETARIAN, UNDER 30 MINUTES**

**PREP TIME:** 15 minutes
**TOTAL COOK TIME:**
26 minutes

**APPROX. PRESSURE BUILD:**
10 minutes
**PRESSURE COOK:**
11 minutes
**PRESSURE RELEASE:**
5 minutes, then Quick
**AIR CRISP:** 10 minutes

**SUBSTITUTION TIP:** If you prefer old-fashioned oats, you can substitute an equal amount of them for the steel-cut oats and reduce pressure cook time to 6 minutes. You can also add more water if you prefer a thinner oatmeal.

1 cup gluten-free
    steel-cut oats

3½ cups water

¼ teaspoon sea salt

1 teaspoon nutmeg

2 teaspoons
    cinnamon, divided

½ cup all-purpose flour

½ cup rolled oats

⅔ cup brown sugar

⅓ cup cold unsalted
    butter, cut into pieces

2 tablespoons
    granulated sugar

¾ cup raisins

2 ounces cream cheese,
    at room temperature

2 tablespoons
    confectioners' sugar

1 teaspoon whole milk

1. Place the steel-cut oats, water, salt, nutmeg, and 1 teaspoon of cinnamon in the pot. Assemble pressure lid, making sure the pressure release valve is in the SEAL position.

2. Select PRESSURE and set to HI. Set time to 11 minutes. Select START/STOP to begin.

3. In a medium bowl, combine the flour, rolled oats, brown sugar, butter, remaining 1 teaspoon of cinnamon, and granulated sugar until a crumble forms.

4. When pressure cooking is complete, allow pressure to naturally release for 5 minutes. After 5 minutes, quick release any remaining pressure by moving the pressure release valve to the VENT position. Carefully remove lid when unit has finished releasing pressure.

5. Stir the raisins into the oatmeal. Cover and let sit 5 minutes to thicken.

6. Evenly spread the crumble topping over the oatmeal. Close crisping lid.

7. Select AIR CRISP, set temperature to 400°F, and set time to 10 minutes. Select START/STOP to begin.

CONTINUED ▶

# Cinnamon Bun Oatmeal continued

8. In a small bowl, whisk together the cream cheese, confectioners' sugar, and milk. Add more milk or sugar, as needed, to reach your desired consistency.

9. When crumble topping is browned, cooking is complete. Open lid and serve the oatmeal in individual bowls topped with a swirl of cream cheese topping.

*Per serving: Calories: 454; Total Fat: 16g; Saturated Fat: 9g; Cholesterol: 37mg; Sodium: 117mg; Carbohydrates: 73g; Fiber: 5g; Protein: 8g*

# Carrot Cake Oats by Caroline Schliep

SERVES 8

**Chef says:** *My mom makes the most fantastic carrot cake, and I love oatmeal. So naturally the chef in me wanted to put these two things together to remind me of the comforts of home. And who wouldn't jump at the chance to make breakfast taste like a dessert? This warm and healthy morning treat uses a mix of whole grains, shredded carrots, fruit, and spices to serve up a bowlful of extraordinary flavors and textures that is sure to start you off on your day.*

**DAIRY-FREE, GLUTEN-FREE, VEGAN, UNDER 30 MINUTES**

**PREP TIME:** 10 minutes
**TOTAL COOK TIME:** 13 minutes

**APPROX. PRESSURE BUILD:** 7 minutes
**PRESSURE COOK:** 3 minutes
**PRESSURE RELEASE:** 10 minutes, then Quick

**VARIATION TIP:** For a bit of added sweetness, swap the maple syrup with brown sugar.

2 cups oats
1 cup water
4 cups unsweetened vanilla almond milk
2 apples, diced
2 cups shredded carrot

1 cup dried cranberries
½ cup maple syrup
2 teaspoons cinnamon
2 teaspoons vanilla extract

1. Place all the ingredients in the pot. Assemble pressure lid, making sure the pressure release valve is in the SEAL position.

2. Select PRESSURE and set to LO. Set time to 3 minutes. Select START/STOP to begin.

3. When pressure cooking is complete, allow pressure to naturally release for 10 minutes. Then quick release remaining pressure by moving the pressure release valve to the VENT position. Carefully remove lid when unit has finished releasing pressure.

4. Stir oats, allowing them to cool, and serve with toppings such as chopped walnuts, diced pineapple, or shredded coconut, if desired.

*Per serving: Calories: 252; Total Fat: 3g; Saturated Fat: 0g; Cholesterol: 0mg; Sodium: 112mg; Carbohydrates: 54g; Fiber: 6g; Protein: 4g*

# Broccoli, Ham, and Cheddar Frittata by Craig White

**SERVES 6**

**Chef says:** *Adding cheese to broccoli is a great way to get your kids to eat their veggies. Hiding it in a cheese-covered frittata is the next level. Air crisping the broccoli adds depth and nuttiness to this Italian staple. The ham was invited to this party by his buddy cheese, and this is a great recipe if hosting brunch or lunch events.*

**GLUTEN-FREE, NUT-FREE**

**PREP TIME:** 15 minutes
**TOTAL COOK TIME:**
40 minutes

**AIR CRISP:** 15 minutes
**BAKE/ROAST:** 15 minutes

**ACCESSORIES:** Cook &
Crisp Basket

**INGREDIENT INFO:** The most common type of broccoli is the Calabrese broccoli, which is named after its place of origin: Calabria, Italy. I recommend trying different broccolis or other brassicas, such as Brussels sprouts, cauliflower, and kohlrabi, in this recipe. If you really want to get your kids excited about vegetables, get your hands on some Romanesco broccoli. Its fractal shape makes it one of the coolest looking vegetables around.

1 head broccoli, cut into 1-inch florets

1 tablespoon canola oil

Kosher salt

Freshly ground black pepper

12 large eggs

¼ cup whole milk

1½ cups shredded white Cheddar cheese, divided

3 tablespoons unsalted butter

½ medium white onion, diced

1 cup diced ham

1. Place Cook & Crisp Basket in the pot. Close crisping lid. Select AIR CRISP, setting temperature to 390°F, and set time to 5 minutes. Select START/STOP to begin preheating.

2. In a large bowl, toss the broccoli with the oil and season with salt and pepper.

3. Once unit is preheated, open lid and add the broccoli to basket. Close crisping lid.

4. Select AIR CRISP, set temperature to 390°F, and set time to 15 minutes. Select START/STOP to begin.

5. In a separate large bowl, whisk together the eggs, milk, and 1 cup of cheese.

6. After 7 minutes, open lid. Remove basket and shake the broccoli. Return basket to pot and close lid to continue cooking.

7. After 8 minutes, check the broccoli for desired doneness. When cooking is complete, remove broccoli and basket from pot.

8. Select SEAR/SAUTÉ and set to HI. Select START/STOP to begin.

9. After 5 minutes, add the butter. Melt for 1 minute, then add the onion and cook for 3 minutes, stirring occasionally.

CONTINUED ▶

# Broccoli, Ham, and Cheddar Frittata continued

10. Add the ham and broccoli and cook, stirring occasionally, for 2 minutes.

11. Add the egg mixture, season with salt and pepper, and stir. Close crisping lid.

12. Select BAKE/ROAST, set temperature to 400ºF, and set time to 15 minutes. Select STOP/START to begin.

13. After 5 minutes, open lid and sprinkle the remaining ½ cup of cheese on top. Close lid to continue cooking.

14. When cooking is complete, remove pot from unit and let the frittata sit for 5 to 10 minutes before serving.

Per serving: *Calories: 404; Total Fat: 30g; Saturated Fat: 14g; Cholesterol: 430mg; Sodium: 671mg; Carbohydrates: 10g; Fiber: 3g; Protein: 27g*

# Spanish Potato and Chorizo Frittata

**SERVES 4**

*I think of this frittata as a formula more than an actual recipe because it can be made with whatever ingredients you have on hand. It's a smart, quick choice for breakfast or an effortless dinner on nights when you don't know what to cook. This version is based on a Spanish frittata and is filled with hearty potatoes and smoky chorizo.*

**GLUTEN-FREE, NUT-FREE, UNDER 30 MINUTES**

**PREP TIME:** 10 minutes
**TOTAL COOK TIME:** 20 minutes

**APPROX. PRESSURE BUILD:** 10 minutes
**PRESSURE COOK:** 20 minutes
**PRESSURE RELEASE:** Quick

**ACCESSORIES:** Ninja Multi-Purpose Pan, Reversible Rack

**VARIATION TIP:** Swap the potato and corn for other veggies like broccoli, spinach, and onions, but stay away from those that will release water, like tomatoes, zucchini, and mushrooms.

4 eggs
1 cup milk
Sea salt
Freshly ground black pepper
1 potato, diced
½ cup frozen corn
1 chorizo sausage, diced
8 ounces feta cheese, crumbled
1 cup water

1. In a medium bowl, whisk together the eggs and milk. Season with salt and pepper.

2. Place the potato, corn, and chorizo in the Multi-Purpose Pan or an 8-inch baking pan. Pour the egg mixture and feta cheese over top. Cover the pan with aluminum foil and place on the Reversible Rack. Make sure it's in the lower position.

3. Pour the water into the pot. Assemble pressure lid, making sure the pressure release valve is in the SEAL position.

4. Select PRESSURE and set to HI. Set time to 20 minutes. Select START/STOP to begin.

5. When pressure cooking is complete, quick release the pressure by moving the pressure release valve to the VENT position. Carefully remove lid when unit has finished releasing pressure.

6. Remove the pan from pot and place it on a cooling rack for 5 minutes, then serve.

*Per serving: Calories: 361; Total Fat: 24g; Saturated Fat: 13g; Cholesterol: 232mg; Sodium: 972mg; Carbohydrates: 17g; Fiber: 2g; Protein: 21g*

# Sweet Potato, Sausage, and Rosemary Quiche by Meg Jordan

**SERVES 6**

*Chef says:* *Quiches can be intimidating for the home cook. How do you get a not-soggy crust and a properly cooked egg mixture? This recipe pre-browns the crust before adding the eggs—giving you a quiche your family won't want to put down.*

NUT-FREE

PREP TIME: 10 minutes
TOTAL COOK TIME:
38 minutes

SEAR/SAUTÉ: 10 minutes
BAKE/ROAST: 23 minutes

ACCESSORIES: Ninja
Multi-Purpose Pan,
Reversible Rack

*Per serving: Calories: 344;
Total Fat: 22g; Saturated Fat: 7g;
Cholesterol: 194mg; Sodium: 743mg;
Carbohydrates: 22g; Fiber: 2g;
Protein: 14g*

**6 eggs**

**¼ cup sour cream**

**½ pound ground
Italian sausage**

**1 tablespoon fresh
rosemary, chopped**

**2 medium sweet potatoes,
cut into ½-inch cubes**

**2 teaspoons kosher salt**

**½ teaspoon freshly
ground black pepper**

**1 store-bought
refrigerated pie crust**

1.  In a medium bowl, whisk together the eggs and sour cream until well combined. Set aside.

2.  Select SEAR/SAUTÉ and set to HI. Select START/STOP to begin. Let preheat for 5 minutes.

3.  Add the sausage and rosemary and cook, stirring frequently, for about 5 minutes. Add the sweet potatoes, salt, and pepper and cook, stirring frequently, for about 5 minutes. Transfer this mixture to a bowl.

4.  Place the pie crust in the pan, using your fingers to gently push onto the bottom and sides of the pan. Place pan with pie crust on the Reversible Rack, making sure it is in the lower position. Place rack with pan in pot. Close crisping lid.

5.  Select BAKE/ROAST, set temperature to 400°F, and set time to 8 minutes. Select START/STOP to begin.

6.  Stir the sausage and sweet potatoes in to the egg mixture.

7.  When cooking is complete, open lid and pour the egg mixture into the browned crust. Close crisping lid.

8.  Select BAKE/ROAST, set temperature to 360°F, and set time to 15 minutes. Select START/STOP to begin.

9.  When cooking is complete, carefully remove pan from pot. Let cool for 10 minutes before removing from pan.

# Curried Chickpea and Roasted Tomato Shakshuka by Craig White

**SERVES 6**

*Chef says: If shakshuka is on a brunch menu, I am probably ordering it. And if I am at brunch, it means I probably had a late night out with friends the night before. This baked egg dish is one of my late-night recovery cures. I added the chickpeas as they are a great source of vitamin B6, and industry legend has it that vitamin B6 is a great hangover helper. Either way, make sure you have plenty of crusty bread to sop up all of the spicy tomato-y goodness.*

DAIRY-FREE, GLUTEN-FREE, NUT-FREE, VEGETARIAN, UNDER 30 MINUTES

PREP TIME: 10 minutes
TOTAL COOK TIME: 30 minutes

APPROX. PRESSURE BUILD: 10 minutes
PRESSURE COOK: 10 minutes
PRESSURE RELEASE: Quick
BAKE/ROAST: 10 minutes

HACK IT: Making the shakshuka base ahead of time allows the flavors to meld and get friendly with each other. It also saves you time when you're entertaining: All you'll have to do is reheat and cook the eggs. And after a late night out, you're going to want to do the least amount of work possible.

- 2 tablespoons extra-virgin olive oil
- 2 red bell peppers, diced
- 1 small onion, diced
- 2 garlic cloves, minced
- 1 tablespoon red curry paste
- 1 tablespoon tomato paste
- 1 (28-ounce) can crushed fire-roasted tomatoes
- 1 (15.5-ounce) can chickpeas, rinsed and drained
- Kosher salt
- Freshly ground black pepper
- 6 large eggs
- 2 tablespoons chopped cilantro

1. Select SEAR/SAUTÉ and set to HI. Select START/STOP to begin. Add the olive oil and let preheat for 5 minutes.

2. Add the bell peppers, onion, and garlic and cook for 3 minutes, stirring occasionally.

3. Add the curry and tomato pastes and cook for 2 minutes, stirring occasionally.

4. Add the crushed tomatoes, chickpeas, and season with salt and pepper and stir. Assemble pressure lid, making sure the pressure release valve is in the SEAL position.

5. Select PRESSURE and set to HI. Set time to 10 minutes. Select START/STOP to begin.

6. When pressure cooking is complete, quick release the pressure by turning the pressure release valve to the VENT position. Carefully remove the lid when the unit has finished releasing pressure.

7. With the back of a spoon, make six indents in the sauce. Crack an egg into each indent. Close crisping lid.

CONTINUED ▶

# Curried Chickpea and Roasted Tomato Shakshuka continued

8. Select BAKE/ROAST, set temperature to 350ºF, and set time to 10 minutes (or until eggs are cooked to your liking). Select START/STOP to begin.

9. When cooking is complete, open lid. Let cool 5 to 10 minutes, then garnish with the cilantro and serve. If desired, serve with crusty bread, chopped scallions, feta cheese, and/or pickled jalapeños.

*Per serving: Calories: 258; Total Fat: 12g; Saturated Fat: 3g; Cholesterol: 186mg; Sodium: 444mg; Carbohydrates: 27g; Fiber: 6g; Protein: 11g*

# Breakfast Burritos by Caroline Schliep

**SERVES 4**

*Chef says:* Ever since my dad's best friend introduced him to authentic Tex-Mex cuisine, he was hooked. One of his favorites is chorizo and eggs, which eventually became one of his staple weekend breakfast dishes. On Sunday mornings, my dad would get up (early per usual) and cook for our family. The delicious smell of chorizo frying up would waft up the stairs and wake us up in no time, making this recipe very near and dear to my heart. I took his recipe and put my own twist on it to make these utterly delicious breakfast burritos.

**NUT-FREE, 360 MEAL, UNDER 30 MINUTES**

**PREP TIME:** 10 minutes
**TOTAL COOK TIME:** 30 minutes

**SEAR/SAUTÉ:** 10 minutes
**AIR CRISP:** 16 minutes

**ACCESSORIES:** Cook & Crisp Basket

**SUBSTITUTION TIP:** Can't find chorizo? Use your favorite ground breakfast sausage.

1 pound ground chorizo
½ onion, diced
½ red bell pepper, diced
1 small jalapeño, minced
½ cup canned black beans, rinsed and drained
Kosher salt
Freshly ground black pepper
6 eggs, beaten
4 (10-inch) flour tortillas
1 cup shredded Mexican blend cheese
1 cup cilantro, minced
Guacamole, for serving
Pico de gallo, for serving

1. Select SEAR/SAUTÉ and set temperature to MED. Let preheat for 5 minutes.

2. Add the chorizo, breaking up the meat with a silicone spatula until cooked through, 3 to 5 minutes. Add the onions, bell pepper, jalapeño, black beans, and season with salt and pepper. Cook until onions are translucent, about 3 minutes.

3. Add the eggs and cook, stirring frequently, until they have reached your desired consistency. When cooking is complete, transfer the mixture to a large bowl.

4. Lay a tortilla on a flat surface and load with ¼ cup of cheese, ¾ cup of egg mixture, and ¼ cup of cilantro. Roll the burrito by folding the right and left sides over the filling, then roll the tortilla over itself from the bottom forming a tight burrito. Repeat this step three more times with the remaining tortillas, cheese, egg mixture, and cilantro.

5. Place two burritos seam-side down in the Cook & Crisp Basket and place basket in pot. Close crisping lid.

6. Select AIR CRISP, set temperature to 390ºF, and set time to 16 minutes. Select START/STOP to begin.

7. After 8 minutes, open lid and remove the burritos from basket. Place the remaining two burritos seam-side down in the basket. Close lid and continue cooking for the remaining 8 minutes.

8. When cooking is complete, let the burritos cool for a few minutes. Serve with the guacamole and pico de gallo.

*Per serving: Calories: 693; Total Fat: 36g; Saturated Fat: 14g; Cholesterol: 345mg; Sodium: 1732mg; Carbohydrates: 48g; Fiber: 5g; Protein: 44g*

# Southern Grits Casserole by Chelven Randolph

## SERVES 8

*Chef says:* A classic Southern breakfast dish that makes a complete meal into a casserole, this dish is perfect for making ahead of time and being reheated. To do so, allow to cool completely and slice into portions. When ready to reheat, place a portion into the Cook & Crisp Basket and Air Crisp for 7 to 10 minutes.

**GLUTEN-FREE, NUT-FREE, VEGETARIAN**

**PREP TIME:** 15 minutes
**TOTAL COOK TIME:**
45 minutes

**APPROX. PRESSURE BUILD:**
10 minutes
**PRESSURE COOK:**
10 minutes
**PRESSURE RELEASE:**
15 minutes, then Quick
**BAKE/ROAST:** 25 minutes

**SUBSTITUTION TIP:** If you do not have stone ground grits, no worries. Cornmeal works just as well.

3 cups water

2 cups milk or heavy (whipping) cream, divided

2 cups stone ground grits

Kosher salt

Freshly ground black pepper

4 tablespoons unsalted butter

1 pound cooked breakfast sausage, casing removed and chopped

6 eggs

2 cups shredded Cheddar cheese

1. Pour the water, 1½ cups of milk, and grits in the pot. Season with salt and pepper. Stir well. Assemble pressure lid, making sure the pressure release valve is in the SEAL position.

2. Select PRESSURE and set to HI. Set time to 10 minutes. Select START/STOP to begin.

3. When pressure cooking is complete, allow pressure to naturally release for 15 minutes. Then quick release remaining pressure by moving the pressure release valve to the VENT position. Carefully remove lid when unit has finished releasing pressure.

4. Stir in the butter and sausage.

5. In a large bowl, whisk together the eggs and remaining ½ cup of milk. Fold the eggs and cheese into the grits. Close crisping lid.

6. Select BAKE/ROAST, set temperature to 375ºF, and set time to 25 minutes. Select START/STOP to begin.

7. Once cooking is complete, open lid. Let cool for 10 minutes before slicing to serve.

*Per serving: Calories: 551; Total Fat: 36g; Saturated Fat: 17g; Cholesterol: 218mg; Sodium: 692mg; Carbohydrates: 31g; Fiber: 3g; Protein: 27g*

# Spinach and Gruyère Cheese Quiche

SERVES 6

*Flip breakfast on its head with this unique twist on an old favorite. I love the combination of spinach and Gruyère, but you can adapt this recipe with whatever you have on hand, such as swapping in Cheddar or Swiss, piling on the vegetables with broccoli, peppers, or tomatoes, or adding protein with diced ham or bacon. Paired with a premade crust, this is the perfect quick and easy breakfast for any day of the week.*

**NUT-FREE, VEGETARIAN, UNDER 30 MINUTES**

**PREP TIME:** 10 minutes
**TOTAL COOK TIME:**
20 minutes

**SEAR/SAUTÉ:** 11 minutes
**BROIL:** 10 minutes

8 eggs
½ cup milk
1 teaspoon sea salt
1 teaspoon freshly ground black pepper
1 cup shredded Gruyère cheese

1 tablespoon extra-virgin olive oil
1 yellow onion, chopped
2 garlic cloves, minced
2 cups fresh spinach
1 refrigerated piecrust, at room temperature

1. Select SEAR/SAUTÉ and set to HI. Select START/STOP to begin. Allow the pot to preheat for 5 minutes.

2. In a large mixing bowl, whisk together the eggs, milk, salt, and pepper. Stir in the Gruyère cheese.

3. Put the oil, onion, and garlic in the preheated pot and stir occasionally for 5 minutes. Add the spinach and cook sauté another 5 minutes.

4. Pour the egg mixture over the vegetables and gently stir for 1 minute (this will allow the egg mixture to temper well and ensure that it cooks evenly under the crust).

5. Lay the piecrust evenly on top of the filling mixture, folding over the edges if necessary. Make a small cut in the center of the piecrust so that steam can escape during baking.

6. Close the crisping lid. Select BROIL and set the time to 10 minutes. Select START/STOP to begin. Check the crust after 5 minutes to check for desired crispness.

7. When cooking is complete, remove the pot and place it on a heat-resistant surface. Let the quiche rest for 5 to 10 minutes before serving.

*Per serving: Calories: 303; Total Fat: 21g; Saturated Fat: 7g; Cholesterol: 236mg; Sodium: 584mg; Carbohydrates: 16g; Fiber: 1g; Protein: 14g*

# Sweet Potato Hash and Eggs by Chelven Randolph

*Chef says:* Hash of all types is widely popular throughout the South. It is a great way to incorporate veggies and starch to round out a meal. Although it is great for breakfast, it can also be served as a side for lunch or dinner—simply omit the eggs. Serve it hot or cold like a potato salad.

GLUTEN-FREE, NUT-FREE, VEGETARIAN, 360 MEAL, FAMILY FAVORITE

PREP TIME: 20 minutes
TOTAL COOK TIME:
35 minutes

APPROX. PRESSURE BUILD:
10 minutes
PRESSURE COOK: 2 minutes
PRESSURE RELEASE: Quick
SEAR/SAUTÉ: 10 minutes
AIR CRISP: 10 minutes

ACCESSORIES: Cook &
Crisp Basket

VARIATION TIP: If you want to make this dish a bit heartier or incorporate more protein, sauté ½ pound of breakfast sausage or chopped bacon. If you are not a fan of sweet potatoes, use peeled white potatoes instead.

3 pounds sweet potatoes, diced

2 cups water

2 tablespoons unsalted butter

1 yellow onion, diced

3 garlic cloves, minced

1 red bell pepper, diced

1 green bell pepper, diced

1 bunch scallions, sliced

2 teaspoons smoked paprika

Kosher salt

Freshly ground black pepper

6 brown eggs

1. Place the sweet potatoes in the Cook & Crisp Basket. Pour the water in pot and insert basket. Assemble the pressure lid, making sure the pressure release valve is in the SEAL position.

2. Select PRESSURE and set to HI. Set timer for 2 minutes. Select START/STOP to begin.

3. When pressure cooking is complete, quick release the pressure by turning the pressure release valve to the VENT position. Carefully remove lid when the unit has finished releasing pressure.

4. Remove basket with sweet potatoes. Pour out any remaining water from the pot.

5. Select SEAR/SAUTÉ and set to MED. Let preheat for 3 minutes.

6. Add the butter, onion, garlic, and bell peppers. Cook for 5 minutes. Add the sweet potatoes, scallions, and paprika and stir. Cook for 5 minutes, stirring occasionally. Season with salt and pepper. Crack the eggs on top of the hash, equally spaced apart. Close crisping lid.

7. Select AIR CRISP, set temperature to 325ºF, and set time to 10 minutes. Select START/STOP to begin.

8. When cooking is complete, open lid and serve immediately.

Per serving: *Calories: 376; Total Fat: 13g; Saturated Fat: 5g; Cholesterol: 338mg; Sodium: 304mg; Carbohydrates: 51g; Fiber: 8g; Protein: 16g*

# Chilaquiles by Sam Ferguson

***Chef says:*** *I distinctly remember the morning we were on vacation on Lake Tahoe and my mother-in-law introduced me to homemade chilaquiles. As someone who really doesn't like eating eggs for breakfast, her chilaquiles surprised me because of how flavorful and un-eggy they were—the enchilada sauce, tortillas, and garnishes transform the dish from a boring egg breakfast into a super tasty delight.*

**GLUTEN-FREE, NUT-FREE, VEGETARIAN, UNDER 30 MINUTES**

**PREP TIME:** 10 minutes
**TOTAL COOK TIME:** 25 minutes

**SEAR/SAUTÉ:** 10 minutes
**BAKE/ROAST:** 14 minutes

**INGREDIENT INFO:** Enchilada sauce is a convenient, versatile ingredient that packs a ton of flavor. You can use it with soups, stews, pastas, and breakfasts.

2 tablespoons canola oil

1 white onion, chopped

1 green bell pepper, chopped

2 (10-ounce) cans red enchilada sauce

10 hard taco shells (one 4.6-ounce box)

6 eggs

Kosher salt

Freshly ground black pepper

½ cup crumbled cotija cheese

2 tablespoons minced cilantro

1 avocado, pitted, peeled, and thinly sliced

1. Select SEAR/SAUTÉ and set to HI. Select START/STOP to begin. Let preheat for 5 minutes.

2. Add the oil, onion, and bell pepper. Cook for 5 minutes, stirring occasionally.

3. Reduce SEAR/SAUTÉ to MED and select START/STOP to continue cooking. Add the enchilada sauce and stir, cooking for 5 minutes until sauce thickens slightly. Coarsely crumble the taco shells into the pot, then stir.

4. Crack the eggs over the mixture in the pot, making sure they are evenly distributed across the surface. Season the eggs with salt and pepper. Close crisping lid.

5. Select BAKE/ROAST, set temperature to 350°F, and set time to 14 minutes. Select START/STOP to begin.

6. After 12 minutes, check eggs for doneness. It may be necessary to cook the eggs for up to an additional 2 minutes for the egg whites to completely set.

7. When cooking is complete, open lid and garnish the eggs with the cotija cheese, cilantro, and avocado. Serve.

*Per serving: Calories: 298; Total Fat: 20g; Saturated Fat: 4g; Cholesterol: 164mg; Sodium: 806mg; Carbohydrates: 23g; Fiber: 4g; Protein: 8g*

# Bacon and Gruyère Egg Bites by Meg Jordan

**SERVES 6**

***Chef says:*** *I'm usually strapped for time in the morning and was searching for a breakfast recipe that I could take on the go that wasn't a sugary pastry. These egg bites combine two of my favorite things—bacon and cheese—for a filling breakfast that I can pop in my backpack before I head to work in the Ninja® Test Kitchen.*

**GLUTEN-FREE, NUT-FREE, UNDER 30 MINUTES**

**PREP TIME:** 10 minutes
**TOTAL COOK TIME:** 26 minutes

**SEAR/SAUTÉ:** 5 minutes
**APPROX. PRESSURE BUILD:** 7 minutes
**PRESSURE COOK:** 10 minutes
**PRESSURE RELEASE:** 6 minutes, then Quick
**AIR CRISP:** 5 minutes

**ACCESSORIES:** Ninja Silicone Mold

**SUBSTITUTION TIP:** Not a meat eater? Sauté your favorite vegetables such as peppers, broccoli, or onions instead of bacon for a meat-free option.

5 slices bacon, cut into ½-inch pieces

5 eggs

1 teaspoon kosher salt

¼ cup sour cream

1 cup shredded Gruyère cheese, divided

Cooking spray

1 cup water

1 teaspoon chopped parsley, for garnish

1. Select SEAR/SAUTÉ and set temperature to HI. Select START/STOP and let preheat for 5 minutes.

2. Add the bacon and cook, stirring frequently, about 5 minutes, or until the fat is rendered and bacon starts to brown. Transfer the bacon to a paper towel-lined plate to drain. Wipe the pot clean of any remaining fat.

3. In a medium bowl, whisk together the eggs, salt, and sour cream until well combined. Fold in ¾ cup of cheese and the bacon.

4. Spray egg molds or Ninja Silicone Mold with the cooking spray. Ladle the egg mixture into each mold, filling them halfway.

5. Pour the water in the pot. Carefully place the egg molds in the pot. Assemble pressure lid, making sure the pressure release valve is in the SEAL position.

6. Select PRESSURE and set to LO. Set time to 10 minutes. Select START/STOP to begin.

7. When pressure cooking is complete, natural release the pressure for 6 minutes, then quick release the remaining pressure by moving the pressure release valve to the VENT position.

CONTINUED ▶

# Bacon and Gruyère Egg Bites continued

8. Carefully remove the lid. Using mitts or a towel, carefully remove egg molds. Top with the remaining ¼ cup of cheese, then place the mold back into the pot. Close the crisping lid.

9. Select AIR CRISP, set temperature to 390°F, and set time to 5 minutes. Select START/STOP to begin.

10. Once cooking is complete, carefully remove the egg molds and set aside to cool for 5 minutes. Using a spoon, carefully remove the egg bites from the molds. Top with chopped parsley and serve immediately.

Per serving: *Calories: 230; Total Fat: 18g; Saturated Fat: 8g; Cholesterol: 175mg; Sodium: 557mg; Carbohydrates: 2g; Fiber: 0g; Protein: 16g*

# Ham, Egg, and Cheese Breakfast Pockets

**SERVES 4**

*Julien and I are constantly on the go, so we are always looking for make-ahead break-fast solutions that we can take with us. I've made a variety of breakfast pockets over the years, and this version has been on repeat as of late. Make a batch the night before and simply reheat in the morning before you head out the door.*

**NUT-FREE, UNDER 30 MINUTES, FAMILY FAVORITE**

**PREP TIME:** 10 minutes
**TOTAL COOK TIME:** 29 minutes

**SEAR/SAUTÉ:** 5 minutes
**AIR CRISP:** 12 minutes

**ACCESSORIES:** Cook & Crisp Basket

**VARIATION TIP:** Load these breakfast pockets with your favorite breakfast sandwich toppings. Simply sub the ham for sausage or bacon, or add in some fresh veggies.

5 large eggs, divided
1 tablespoon extra-virgin olive oil
Sea salt
Freshly ground black pepper
1 (8-ounce) tube refrigerated crescent rolls
4 ounces thinly sliced ham
1 cup shredded Cheddar cheese
Cooking spray

1. Select SEAR/SAUTÉ and set to MD:HI. Select START/STOP and let preheat for 5 minutes.

2. Lightly whisk 4 eggs in a medium bowl.

3. Once unit has preheated, add the oil and beaten eggs. Season with salt and pepper. Whisk the eggs until they just begin to set, cooking until soft and translucent, 3 to 5 minutes. Remove the eggs from the pot and set aside.

4. In a small bowl, whisk the remaining egg.

5. Remove the crescent rolls from the tube and divide them into 4 rectangles. Gently roll out each rectangle until it is 6-by-4 inches. Top one half of each rectangle with ham, cheese, and scrambled eggs, leaving about a ½-inch border.

6. Brush the edges of the filled dough with water. Fold over the rectangle and press firmly to seal. Brush the top of each pocket with the egg.

7. Place Cook & Crisp Basket in pot. Coat 2 pastries well on both sides with cooking spray and arrange them in the basket in a single layer. Close crisping lid.

8. Select AIR CRISP, set temperature to 375°F, and set time to 12 minutes. Select START/STOP to begin.

9. After 6 minutes, open lid, remove basket, and use silicone-tipped tongs to flip the breakfast pockets. Lower basket back into pot and close lid to continue cooking, until golden brown.

10. When cooking is complete, check for your desired crispiness. Place the pockets on a wire rack to cool. Repeat steps 7, 8, and 9 with the remaining 2 pastries.

**Per serving:** *Calories: 501; Total Fat: 34g; Saturated Fat: 12g; Cholesterol: 278mg; Sodium: 1131mg; Carbohydrates: 24g; Fiber: 0g; Protein: 24g*

# Waffle Bread Pudding with Maple-Jam Glaze by Sam Ferguson

**SERVES 6**

***Chef says:*** *This is a reimagination of all my favorite breakfast ingredients and flavors—waffles, maple syrup, and raspberry jam. I like to take any leftover bread pudding and griddle it with melted butter using the Ninja® Foodi™ Pressure Cooker's SEAR/SAUTÉ function.*

**NUT-FREE, VEGETARIAN, UNDER 30 MINUTES**

**PREP TIME:** 15 minutes
**TOTAL COOK TIME:** 25 minutes

**APPROX. PRESSURE BUILD:** 10 minutes
**PRESSURE COOK:** 15 minutes
**PRESSURE RELEASE:** Quick
**BROIL:** 10 minutes

**ACCESSORIES:** Ninja Multi-Purpose Pan, Reversible Rack

**VARIATION TIP:** This recipe will work great with any bread, not just waffles. Try substituting frozen packaged French toast, croissants, or plain bread.

2 whole eggs

4 egg yolks

1 cup heavy (whipping) cream

½ teaspoon ground cinnamon

¼ cup granulated sugar

1 teaspoon vanilla extract

20 waffles (two 12-ounce boxes), cut in sixths

1 cup water

⅓ cup desired jam (I prefer raspberry)

⅓ cup maple syrup

1. In a large mixing bowl, combine the eggs, egg yolks, cream, cinnamon, sugar, and vanilla. Whisk well to combine. Add the waffle pieces and toss very well to incorporate. The waffles should be completely soaked through with cream sauce, with some extra residual cream sauce at the bottom of the bowl.

2. Place the waffle mixture in the Ninja Multi-Purpose Pan or 8-inch round baking dish. Press down gently to ensure ingredients are well packed into the pan. Cover the pan tightly with plastic wrap.

3. Add the water to the pot. Place the pan on the Reversible Rack and place rack in pot. Assemble pressure lid, making sure the pressure release valve is in the SEAL position.

4. Select PRESSURE and set to HI. Set time to 15 minutes. Select START/STOP to begin.

5. Place the jam and maple syrup in a small bowl and mix well to combine.

6. When pressure cooking is complete, quick release the pressure by moving the pressure release valve to the VENT position. Carefully remove lid when unit has finished releasing pressure.

7. Remove rack from pot, then remove the plastic wrap from the pan. Pour the jam and syrup mixture over top of waffles. Place rack and pan back in pot. Close crisping lid.

8. Select BROIL and set time to 10 minutes. Select START/STOP to begin.

9. When cooking is complete, open lid and remove rack from pot. Serve the bread pudding warm.

*Per serving: Calories: 640; Total Fat: 30g; Saturated Fat: 12g; Cholesterol: 265mg; Sodium: 765mg; Carbohydrates: 82g; Fiber: 3g; Protein: 12g*

# Chocolate Hazelnut Toaster Pastries

SERVES 4

*When I wrote the first cookbook for the Ninja® Foodi™ Pressure Cooker, I was blown away by the response to my Strawberry Toaster Pastries. Folks were amazed that you could make tasty, flaky treats for breakfast (or dessert!) in next to no time. In this version I've swapped out the fruity strawberries for sweet, creamy chocolate hazelnut spread for an ultimate indulgence any time of the day.*

**VEGETARIAN, FAMILY FAVORITE, 5 INGREDIENT**

**PREP TIME:** 15 minutes
**TOTAL COOK TIME:** 14 minutes

**AIR CRISP:** 14 minutes

**ACCESSORIES:** Cook & Crisp Basket

**VARIATION TIP:** Switch up the filling in these toaster pastries to add your own twist. Try adding bananas with the chocolate hazelnut spread or swap out the spread in place of my Simple Strawberry Jam (page 309) or your favorite fruit preserves.

All-purpose flour

1 refrigerated piecrust, at room temperature

¼ cup chocolate hazelnut spread

Cooking spray

Vanilla icing, for frosting

Chocolate sprinkles, for topping

1. Place the Cook & Crisp Basket in the pot and close crisping lid. Select AIR CRISP, set temperature to 350ºF, and set time to 5 minutes. Press START/STOP to preheat.

2. On a lightly floured surface, roll out the piecrust into a large rectangle. Cut the dough into 8 rectangles.

3. Spoon 1 tablespoon of chocolate hazelnut spread into the center of each of 4 dough rectangles, leaving a ½-inch border. Brush the edges of the filled dough rectangles with water. Top each with one of the remaining 4 dough rectangles. Press the edges with a fork to seal.

4. Once unit is preheated, carefully place two pastries in the basket in a single layer. Coat each pastry well with cooking spray. Close crisping lid.

5. Select AIR CRISP, set temperature to 350ºF, and set time to 7 minutes. Select START/STOP to begin.

6. Once cooking is complete, check for your desired crispiness. Place the pastries on a wire rack to cool. Repeat steps 4 and 5 with the remaining 2 pastries.

7. Frost the pastries with vanilla icing, then top with sprinkles.

*Per serving: Calories: 334; Total Fat: 17g; Saturated Fat: 3g; Cholesterol: 0mg; Sodium: 271mg; Carbohydrates: 43g; Fiber: 0g; Protein: 1g*

# Homemade Vanilla Yogurt

**SERVES 6**

*This year we launched the first Ninja® Foodi™ Pressure Cooker with a yogurt function. The response was so positive we decided to roll it out across all of the Foodi Pressure Cookers so that everyone can enjoy creamy, tangy homemade yogurt. This is my base recipe for making yogurt, but you can also customize the flavor and sweetener based on your personal preference. For a classic plain yogurt, omit the vanilla and honey or serve with fruit preserves for a fruit-based option.*

**GLUTEN-FREE, NUT-FREE, VEGETARIAN, 5 INGREDIENT**

**PREP TIME:** 5 minutes
**TOTAL COOK TIME:** 8 hours
**CHILL TIME:** 8 to 12 hours

**YOGURT:** 9 hours

**HACK IT:** If you prefer a thicker, Greek-style yogurt, strain it through cheesecloth overnight in the fridge, placing it over a large bowl while draining.

½ **gallon whole milk**

3 **tablespoons plain yogurt with active live cultures**

½ **tablespoon vanilla extract**

½ **cup honey**

1. Pour the milk into the pot. Assemble pressure lid, making sure the pressure release valve is in the VENT position.

2. Select YOGURT and set time to 8 hours. Select START/STOP to begin.

3. After the milk has boiled, the display will read COOL.

4. Once cooled, the unit will beep and display ADD & STIR. Remove pressure lid. Add the plain yogurt and whisk until fully incorporated. Reassemble pressure lid, making sure the pressure release valve is still in the VENT position.

5. When incubating is complete after 8 hours, transfer the yogurt to a glass container or bowl, cover, and refrigerate for a minimum of 8 hours.

6. Once the yogurt has chilled, stir in the vanilla and honey until well combined. Cover and place the glass bowl back in the refrigerator or divide the yogurt into airtight glass jars. The yogurt may be refrigerated up to 2 weeks.

*Per serving: Calories: 286; Total Fat: 11g; Saturated Fat: 6g; Cholesterol: 33mg; Sodium: 133mg; Carbohydrates: 38g; Fiber: 0g; Protein: 11g*

# Cinnamon Sugar Donuts

**SERVES 4**

*These donuts are the perfect bite-size treats to enjoy with your morning cup of coffee or with a scoop of vanilla ice cream as a sweet treat at the of end the day. The air-fried dough is rolled in warm cinnamon and sweet sugar crystals, so each bite is like a warm hug.*

**NUT-FREE, VEGETARIAN, UNDER 30 MINUTES, FAMILY FAVORITE**

**PREP TIME:** 10 minutes
**TOTAL COOK TIME:** 10 minutes

**AIR CRISP:** 10 minutes

**ACCESSORIES:** Cook & Crisp Basket

**VARIATION TIP:** To put a different twist on these donut bites, swap out the cinnamon sugar coating for confectioners' sugar or icing and sprinkles.

⅔ **cup all-purpose flour, plus additional for dusting**

3 **tablespoons granulated sugar, divided**

½ **teaspoon baking powder**

¼ **teaspoon, plus ½ tablespoon cinnamon**

¼ **teaspoon sea salt**

2 **tablespoons cold unsalted butter, cut into small pieces**

¼ **cup plus 1½ tablespoons whole milk**

**Cooking spray**

1. In a medium bowl, mix together the flour, 1 tablespoon of sugar, baking powder, ¼ teaspoon of cinnamon, and salt.

2. Use a pastry cutter or two forks to cut in the butter, breaking it up into little pieces until the mixture resembles coarse cornmeal. Add the milk and continue to mix together until the dough forms a ball.

3. Place the dough on a lightly floured work surface and knead it until a smooth ball forms, about 30 seconds. Divide the dough into 8 equal pieces and roll each piece into a ball.

4. Place the Cook & Crisp Basket in the pot. Close crisping lid. Select AIR CRISP, set temperature to 350ºF, and set time to 3 minutes. Press START/STOP to begin.

5. Once preheated, coat the basket with cooking spray. Place the dough balls in the basket, leaving room between each. Spray them with cooking spray. Close crisping lid.

6. Select AIR CRISP, set temperature to 350ºF, and set time to 10 minutes. Press START/STOP to begin.

7. In a medium bowl, combine the remaining 2 tablespoons of sugar and ½ tablespoon of cinnamon.

8. When cooking is complete, open lid. Place the dough balls in the bowl with the cinnamon sugar and toss to coat. Serve immediately.

*Per serving: Calories: 192; Total Fat: 7g; Saturated Fat: 4g; Cholesterol: 17mg; Sodium: 126mg; Carbohydrates: 31g; Fiber: 1g; Protein: 3g*

# Chocolate Chip and Banana Bread Bundt Cake

**SERVES 8**

*Have you ever bought a bunch of bananas only for them to ripen faster than you can eat them? One of my favorite things to do with those "extra" bananas is to bake a cake. This is a decadent breakfast treat that is sure to please a crowd.*

NUT-FREE, VEGETARIAN, FAMILY FAVORITE

---

**PREP TIME:** 15 minutes
**TOTAL COOK TIME:** 40 minutes

---

**BAKE/ROAST:** 40 minutes

---

**ACCESSORIES:** Ninja Tube Pan, Reversible Rack

---

**VARIATION TIP:** Try swapping the chocolate chips for walnuts or fresh blueberries.

2 cups all-purpose flour
1 teaspoon baking soda
¼ teaspoon cinnamon
¼ teaspoon sea salt
1 stick (½ cup) unsalted butter, at room temperature
½ cup dark brown sugar
¼ cup granulated sugar
2 eggs, beaten
1 teaspoon vanilla extract
3 ripe bananas, mashed
1 cup semisweet chocolate chips
Cooking spray

1.  Close crisping lid. Select BAKE/ROAST, set temperature to 325ºF, and set time to 5 minutes. Select START/STOP to begin preheating.

2.  In a medium bowl, stir together the flour, baking soda, cinnamon, and salt.

3.  In a large bowl, beat together the butter, brown sugar, and granulated sugar. Stir in the eggs, vanilla, and bananas.

4.  Slowly add the dry mixture to wet mixture, stirring until just combined. Fold in chocolate chips.

5.  Use cooking spray to grease the Ninja Tube Pan or a 7-inch Bundt pan. Pour the batter into the pan.

6.  Once preheated, place pan on the Reversible Rack in the lower position. Close crisping lid.

7.  Select BAKE/ROAST, set temperature to 325ºF, and set time to 40 minutes. Select START/STOP to begin.

8.  After 30 minutes, open lid and check doneness by inserting a toothpick into the cake. If it comes out clean, it is done. If not, continue baking until done.

9.  When cooking is complete, remove pan from pot and place on a cooling rack for 30 minutes before serving.

*Per serving: Calories: 484; Total Fat: 21g; Saturated Fat: 13g; Cholesterol: 71mg; Sodium: 238mg; Carbohydrates: 70g; Fiber: 4g; Protein: 6g*

# Cinnamon Roll Monkey Bread

**SERVES 8**

*On a chilly weekend morning, is there anything more comforting than the smell of fresh baked cinnamon rolls? Sticky, spicy, and covered in delicious icing, I can't think of a better way to kick off the weekend. In fact, this recipe is a go-to in our family every holiday. Whether we are watching the Thanksgiving Day parade or opening presents under the tree, this semi-homemade recipe is quick and easy, so we spend less time in the kitchen and more time with each other.*

**NUT-FREE, VEGETARIAN, UNDER 30 MINUTES, FAMILY FAVORITE, 5 INGREDIENT**

**PREP TIME:** 5 minutes
**TOTAL COOK TIME:** 20 minutes

**BAKE/ROAST:** 20 minutes

**VARIATION TIP:** I love to top this monkey bread with walnuts and maple syrup before serving, but you can also bake walnuts right into the bread. Simply add them in step 2.

4 eggs
¼ cup whole milk
1 teaspoon vanilla extract
½ teaspoon cinnamon

Cooking spray
2 (12.5-ounce) tubes refrigerated cinnamon rolls with icing, quartered

1. In a medium bowl, whisk together the eggs, milk, vanilla, and cinnamon.

2. Lightly coat the pot with cooking spray, then place the cinnamon roll pieces in the pot. Pour the egg mixture over the dough. Close crisping lid.

3. Select BAKE/ROAST, set temperature to 350°F, and set time to 20 minutes. Select START/STOP to begin.

4. When cooking is complete, remove pot from unit and place it on a heat-resistant surface. Remove lid. Let cool for 5 minutes, then top with the icing from the cinnamon rolls and serve.

*Per serving: Calories: 327; Total Fat: 12g; Saturated Fat: 4g; Cholesterol: 83mg; Sodium: 710mg; Carbohydrates: 46g; Fiber: 1g; Protein: 7g*

# 4

# Sides, Snacks & Apps

# Louisiana Crab Dip by Chelven Randolph

**SERVES 8**

**Chef says:** *This dip is one of the first seafood dishes I ever learned to make. It is simple and straightforward but full of flavor. My mom would make this dish for family gatherings, and it was always the first appetizer to be eaten. The beauty of this dish is it's equally delicious hot as it is cold. Whether you make it and serve it immediately, or refrigerate it and serve it later, it's sure to be a crowd pleaser. Serve it with your favorite buttered crackers or sliced carrots and celery!*

**GLUTEN-FREE, NUT-FREE**

**PREP TIME:** 15 minutes
**TOTAL COOK TIME:**
50 minutes

**SEAR/SAUTÉ:** 5 minutes
**BAKE/ROAST:** 40 minutes

**VARIATION TIP:** Try this recipe with claw & knuckle lobster meat instead of crab meat for an awesome New England twist to this delicious dish.

2 tablespoons
  unsalted butter

3 garlic cloves, minced

½ cup mayonnaise

1 pound (16 ounces) whipped
  or room temperature
  cream cheese

2 teaspoons
  Worcestershire sauce

3 teaspoons hot sauce

3 teaspoons freshly
  squeezed lemon juice

2 teaspoons
  Creole seasoning

¾ cup Parmesan cheese

1 pound lump crab meat

1. Select SEAR/SAUTÉ and set to MED. Select START/STOP to begin. Let preheat for 3 minutes.

2. Add the butter and garlic and sauté for 2 minutes.

3. Add the mayonnaise, cream cheese, Worcestershire sauce, hot sauce, lemon juice, Creole seasoning, and Parmesan cheese. Stir well.

4. Add the crab meat and lightly fold to incorporate. Close crisping lid.

5. Select BAKE/ROAST, set temperature to 350°F, and set time to 40 minutes. Select START/STOP to begin

6. When cooking is complete, open lid. Let cool for 10 minutes before serving.

*Per serving: Calories: 391; Total Fat: 39g; Saturated Fat: 18g; Cholesterol: 114mg; Sodium: 976mg; Carbohydrates: 4g; Fiber: 0g; Protein: 16g*

# Three-Layer Taco Dip by Meg Jordan

**SERVES 6**

***Chef says:*** *I love going to parties to hang out with friends . . . and to eat dip. A good dip is my kryptonite. I love Mexican cuisine and wanted to create a recipe that combines layers of flavor. The creaminess of the beans, melted cheese, and crunch of the iceberg lettuce will have your friends coming back for more. Serve with tortilla chips and let the party begin!*

**GLUTEN-FREE, NUT-FREE, VEGETARIAN, UNDER 30 MINUTES**

**PREP TIME:** 10 minutes
**TOTAL COOK TIME:** 15 minutes

**APPROX. PRESSURE BUILD:** 10 minutes
**PRESSURE COOK:** 5 minutes
**PRESSURE RELEASE:** Quick
**BROIL:** 10 minutes

- 2 (15.5-ounce) cans pinto beans, rinsed and drained
- 1 white onion, chopped
- 8 garlic cloves, chopped
- 1 (14.5-ounce) can diced tomatoes
- 1 serrano chile, seeded and chopped
- 1 teaspoon kosher salt
- 2 teaspoons ground cumin
- 2 teaspoons chili powder
- 2 cups shredded Mexican blend cheese
- 1 cup shredded iceberg lettuce

1. Place the beans, onions, garlic, tomatoes, chile, salt, cumin, and chili powder in the pot. Assemble pressure lid, making sure the pressure release valve is in the SEAL position.

2. Select PRESSURE and set to HI. Set time to 5 minutes. Select START/STOP to begin.

3. When pressure cooking is complete, quick release the pressure by moving the pressure release valve to the VENT position. Carefully remove lid when unit has finished releasing pressure.

4. Using a silicone spatula, stir the mixture in the pot. Sprinkle shredded cheese across the top of the bean mixture. Close crisping lid.

5. Select BROIL and set time to 10 minutes. Select STOP/START to begin.

6. When cooking is complete, open lid. Let cool for 5 minutes, then add the shredded lettuce. Serve immediately.

*Per serving: Calories: 327; Total Fat: 14g; Saturated Fat: 9g; Cholesterol: 46mg; Sodium: 612mg; Carbohydrates: 33g; Fiber: 10g; Protein: 19g*

# Mexican Street Corn Queso Dip by Craig White

SERVES 8

***Chef says:*** *Mexican street corn, or elote, is one of my favorite foods on a stick. The only problem with this delicious Mexican delicacy is that it's very messy and not what I would consider "first date food" as it always winds up on your face. Transforming it into a dip alleviates the stresses of worrying about how much mayonnaise is on your cheek. Enjoy this dip with corn tortilla chips, some mezcal, and muchos amigos.*

**GLUTEN-FREE, NUT-FREE, VEGETARIAN, UNDER 30 MINUTES**

**PREP TIME:** 10 minutes
**TOTAL COOK TIME:** 20 minutes

**BAKE/ROAST:** 20 minutes

**SUBSTITUTION TIP:** Feta cheese is an excellent substitution for cotija if you can't find it. Both are crumbly and give this dip the salty kick it needs.

- 1 (8-ounce) package cream cheese, quartered
- 6 ounces cotija cheese, crumbled, 2 ounces reserved for topping
- 1 (10-ounce) can fire-roasted tomatoes with chiles
- ½ cup mayonnaise
- Zest of 2 limes
- Juice of 2 limes
- 2 (8-ounce) packages shredded Mexican cheese blend, divided
- 1 garlic clove, grated
- 1 (14.75-ounce) can cream corn
- 1 cup frozen corn
- Kosher salt
- Freshly ground black pepper

1. Pour the cream cheese, 4 ounces of cotija cheese, tomatoes with chiles, mayonnaise, lime zest and juice, one 8-ounce package Mexican cheese blend, garlic, cream corn, and frozen corn in the pot. Season with salt and pepper and stir. Close crisping lid.

2. Select BAKE/ROAST, set temperature to 375ºF, and set time to 20 minutes. Select START/STOP to begin.

3. After 10 minutes, open lid and sprinkle the dip with the remaining 2 ounces of cotija cheese and remaining 8-ounce package of Mexican blend cheese. Close crisping lid and continue cooking.

4. When cooking is complete, the cheese will be melted and the dip hot and bubbling at the edges. Open lid and let the dip cool for 5 to 10 minutes before serving. Serve topped with chopped cilantro, hot sauce, and chili powder, if desired.

*Per serving: Calories: 538; Total Fat: 45g; Saturated Fat: 22g; Cholesterol: 109mg; Sodium: 807mg; Carbohydrates: 18g; Fiber: 2g; Protein: 20g*

# Mexican Street Corn

**by Doug Malvo, Ninja® Foodi™ Family Member**

*Kenzie says:* I love Mexican street corn, and it is one recipe I am always asked about, which is why it came as no surprise that this recipe from Doug Malvo blew up on Facebook when he posted it a while back! If you love this recipe, try the Mexican Street Corn Queso Dip (page 77) that Craig developed.

GLUTEN-FREE, NUT-FREE, UNDER 30 MINUTES, VEGETARIAN

---

**PREP TIME:** 10 minutes
**TOTAL COOK TIME:** 14 minutes

---

**AIR CRISP:** 12 minutes
**BROIL:** 2 minutes

---

**ACCESSORIES:** Cook & Crisp Basket

---

**SUBSTITUTION TIP:** Can't find cotija cheese? Try Parmesan cheese instead!

---

**Find Doug on Facebook:** Ninja Foodi Nation—By cooking with Doug

**3 ears corn, husked, rinsed, and dried**

**Olive oil spray**

**¼ cup sour cream**

**¼ cup mayonnaise**

**¼ cup crumbled cotija cheese, plus more for garnish**

**1 teaspoon freshly squeezed lime juice**

**½ teaspoon garlic powder**

**¼ teaspoon chili powder, plus more as needed**

**Fresh cilantro leaves, for garnish**

**½ teaspoon salt**

**½ teaspoon freshly ground black pepper**

1. Select AIR CRISP, set the temperature to 400°F, and set the time to 5 minutes to preheat. Select START/STOP to begin.

2. Lightly mist the corn with olive oil and place the corn in the Cook & Crisp Basket. Close the crisping lid.

3. Select AIR CRISP, set the temperature to 400°F, and set the time to 12 minutes. Select START/STOP to begin. After 7 minutes, flip the corn. Close the crisping lid and cook for 5 minutes more.

4. While the corn cooks, in a small bowl, stir together the sour cream, mayonnaise, cotija cheese, lime juice, garlic powder, and chili powder until blended.

5. When cooking is complete, carefully remove the corn and brush or spoon the sauce onto it. Sprinkle with cilantro, cotija cheese, and more chili powder.

6. If desired, return the corn to the basket. Close the crisping lid. Select BROIL and set the time for 2 minutes. Select START/STOP to begin.

7. Serve hot, seasoned with salt and pepper, as needed.

*Per serving: Calories: 280; Total Fat: 15g; Saturated Fat: 6g; Cholesterol: 25mg; Sodium: 701mg; Carbohydrates: 35g; Fiber: 4g; Protein: 7g*

# Zucchini Chips

**by Justine Howell, Ninja® Foodi™ Family Member**

**SERVES 6**

**Kenzie says:** *This air fryer zucchini chips recipe was created by Justine from The Typical Mom blog when the zucchini plant in her garden went crazy! She had several to use each day and was inspired by her family's love of fried zucchini. Knowing she could make a healthier version in her Ninja Foodi, she went on a quest to create the best healthy snack. These chips are now a family favorite!*

FAMILY FAVORITE,
NUT-FREE, UNDER
30 MINUTES, VEGETARIAN,
5 INGREDIENT

**PREP TIME:** 15 minutes
**TOTAL COOK TIME:**
13 minutes per batch

**AIR CRISP:** 13 minutes

**ACCESSORIES:** Cook &
Crisp Basket

Find Justine
@thetypical_mom
and on Facebook:
The Typical Mom

1 large egg, beaten
¾ cup panko bread crumbs
1 teaspoon Old Bay seasoning
1 teaspoon garlic salt
½ teaspoon kosher salt

2 large zucchini, ends trimmed cut into ¼- to ½-inch rounds (the thinner the crispier)
Olive oil spray

1. Place the Cook & Crisp Basket into the unit. Select AIR CRISP, set the temperature to 350ºF, and set the time to 5 minutes to preheat. Select START/STOP to begin.

2. Place the beaten egg in a shallow bowl. In another shallow bowl, stir together the panko, Old Bay seasoning, garlic salt, and kosher salt.

3. One at a time, dip the zucchini rounds into the egg and into the panko mixture, coating all sides. Working in batches as needed, place the coated zucchini chips in the Cook & Crisp Basket in a single layer so they do not overlap. Coat the pieces with cooking spray and place them into the preheated Cook & Crisp Basket.

4. Select AIR CRISP, set the temperature to 350ºF, and set the time to 13 minutes. Select START/STOP to begin. After 10 minutes, flip the zucchini. Close the crisping lid and cook for 3 minutes more, or longer for crispier results.

5. Remove and repeat with the second batch.

*Per serving: Calories: 59; Total Fat: 2g; Saturated Fat: 0g; Cholesterol: 31mg; Sodium: 374mg; Carbohydrates: 9g; Fiber: 2g; Protein: 3g*

# Hand-Cut French Fries

**SERVES 4**

*Hand-cut fries take a little bit of time and technique to get the best result, but trust me—they're worth it. By soaking the potatoes first, you're able to remove some of the excess starch on the strips and get a crispy exterior. You'll never want to default to the frozen variety again.*

**DAIRY-FREE, GLUTEN-FREE, NUT-FREE, VEGAN, UNDER 30 MINUTES, FAMILY FAVORITE, 5 INGREDIENT**

**PREP TIME:** 15 minutes, plus 30 minutes to soak
**TOTAL COOK TIME:** 25 minutes

**AIR CRISP:** 25 minutes

**ACCESSORIES:** Cook & Crisp Basket

**VARIATION TIP:** There are so many easy ways to elevate simple spuds into fancy frites. Toss them with your favorite spices, herbs, or oils. Try spicing things up with cumin, chili powder, and a pinch of cayenne pepper or toss with a drizzle of truffle oil, rosemary, and grated Parmesan cheese.

1 pound Russet or Idaho potatoes, cut in 2-inch strips

3 tablespoons canola oil

1. Place potatoes in a large bowl and cover with cold water. Let soak for 30 minutes. Drain well, then pat with a paper towel until very dry.

2. Place Cook & Crisp Basket in pot. Close crisping lid. Select AIR CRISP, set temperature to 390°F, and set time to 5 minutes. Select START/STOP to begin preheating.

3. In a large bowl, toss the potatoes with the oil.

4. Once unit is preheated, open lid and add the potatoes to the basket. Close lid.

5. Select AIR CRISP, set temperature to 390°F, and set time to 25 minutes. Select START/STOP to begin.

6. After 10 minutes, open lid, then lift basket and shake fries or toss them with silicone-tipped tongs. Lower basket back into pot and close lid to continue cooking.

7. After 10 minutes, check for desired crispness. Continue cooking up to 5 minutes more, if necessary.

8. When cooking is complete, serve immediately with your favorite dipping sauce.

*Per serving: Calories: 171; Total Fat: 11g; Saturated Fat: 1g; Cholesterol: 0mg; Sodium: 7mg; Carbohydrates: 18g; Fiber: 3g; Protein: 2g*

# Sweet Potato and Beetroot Chips

**MAKES 1 CUP**

*Not only is the Ninja® Foodi™ Pressure Cooker the pressure cooker that crisps—it is also a dehydrator! This added feature makes it easy to make healthy, homemade snacks like jerky, dried fruit, and veggie chips. Just pop your ingredients in and walk away. Although you can use the standard Foodi Pressure Cooker to make enough snacks for one or two, you can also upgrade to the Ninja Dehydrator Rack to really unlock the full potential of this feature. This recipe is one of my favorites for simple Sweet Potato and Beetroot Chips. You can even recreate your favorite potato chip flavors by adding cinnamon, onion powder, smoked paprika, or any combination of seasonings of your choice in step 3.*

**DAIRY-FREE, GLUTEN-FREE, NUT-FREE, VEGAN, 5 INGREDIENT**

**PREP TIME:** 15 minutes
**TOTAL COOK TIME:** 8 hours

**DEHYDRATE:** 8 hours

**ACCESSORIES:**
Reversible Rack

**HACK IT:** Use a mandoline to ensure that the beet and sweet potato are sliced evenly into consistent ⅛-inch slices.

½ **small beet, peeled and cut into ⅛-inch slices**

½ **small sweet potato, peeled and cut into ⅛-inch slices**

½ **tablespoon extra-virgin olive oil**

½ **teaspoon sea salt**

1. In a large bowl, toss the beet slices with half the olive oil until evenly coated. Repeat, in a separate bowl, with the sweet potato slices and the rest of the olive oil (if you don't mind pink sweet potatoes, you can toss them together in one bowl). Season with salt.

2. Arrange the beet slices flat in a single layer in the bottom of the pot. Arrange the sweet potato slices flat in a single layer on the Reversible Rack in the lower position. Place rack in pot and close crisping lid.

3. Select DEHYDRATE, set temperature to 135ºF, and set time to 8 hours. Select START/STOP to begin.

4. When dehydrating is complete, remove rack from pot. Transfer the beet and sweet potato chips to an airtight container.

*Per serving: Calories: 221; Total Fat: 7g; Saturated Fat: 1g; Cholesterol: 0mg; Sodium: 1057mg; Carbohydrates: 36g; Fiber: 6g; Protein: 4g*

# Loaded Potato Skins by Caroline Schliep

**SERVES 4**

***Chef says:*** *Delicious yet easy to make, these potato skins are to die for. They are hollowed out and loaded—and I mean loaded—with fresh chives, diced ham, and cheese, of course. And you could never forget the dollop of sour cream on top. All of which makes them a perfect accompaniment to steak and pork chops. Or serve them on their own as an appetizer for a Super Bowl party or even a classy dinner party with your friends.*

**GLUTEN-FREE, NUT-FREE**

**PREP TIME:** 5 minutes
**TOTAL COOK TIME:**
45 minutes

**AIR CRISP:** 35 minutes
**BROIL:** 5 minutes; 5 minutes

**ACCESSORIES:**
Reversible Rack

**VARIATION TIP:** Load on the veggies and add broccoli to the mashed mix.

2 large Russet
   potatoes, cleaned

1 tablespoon extra-virgin
   olive oil

Kosher salt

Freshly ground black pepper

¾ cup shredded sharp
   Cheddar cheese

3 tablespoons
   unsalted butter

¼ cup milk

¼ cup sour cream, plus
   more for serving

1 bunch chives, sliced

4 slices of ham, cubed

1. Using a fork, poke holes in each potato. Rub each potato with the olive oil and season the skin with salt and pepper. Place the potatoes on the Reversible Rack in the lower position and place in the pot. Close the crisping lid.

2. Select AIR CRISP, set temperature to 390ºF, and set time to 35 minutes. Select START/STOP to begin.

3. When cooking is complete, open lid and use tongs to transfer the potatoes to a cutting board.

4. Cut the potatoes in half lengthwise. Using a spoon, scoop out the flesh into a large bowl, leaving about ¼ inch of flesh on the skins. Set aside.

5. Sprinkle the hollowed-out potato skins with ¼ cup of cheese and place them back in the pot on the rack. Close crisping lid.

6. Select BROIL and set time to 5 minutes. Select START/STOP to begin.

7. Add the butter, milk, and sour cream to the bowl with the flesh. Season with salt and pepper and mash together. Use a spatula to fold in ¼ cup of cheese, one-quarter of the chives, and ham into the potato mixture.

CONTINUED ▶

# Loaded Potato Skins continued

8. When cooking is complete, open lid. Using tongs, carefully transfer the potato skins to the cutting board. Evenly distribute the mashed potato mixture into each potato skin and top with the remaining ¼ cup of cheese. Return the loaded potato skins to the rack. Close crisping lid.

9. Select BROIL and set time to 5 minutes. Select START/STOP to begin.

10. When cooking is complete, open lid. Carefully remove the potatoes. Cut them in half and garnish with the remaining chives. Serve with additional sour cream, if desired.

Per serving: *Calories: 402; Total Fat: 24g; Saturated Fat: 14g; Cholesterol: 68mg; Sodium: 561mg; Carbohydrates: 32g; Fiber: 5g; Protein: 14g*

# Potato Samosas by Meg Jordan

***Chef says:*** *My first exposure to making Indian food was in culinary school. I was so mesmerized by the depth of flavors. I became hooked and started cooking more Indian dishes at home. My favorite Indian appetizer, potato samosas, are typically deep fried, but this version takes them to a healthier level without skimping on crisping or flavor.*

**NUT-FREE, VEGETARIAN**

**PREP TIME:** 20 minutes
**TOTAL COOK TIME:**
31 minutes

**SEAR/SAUTÉ:** 10 minutes
**APPROX. PRESSURE BUILD:**
7 minutes
**PRESSURE COOK:** 1 minute
**PRESSURE RELEASE:** Quick
**AIR CRISP:** 20 minutes

**ACCESSORIES:** Cook &
Crisp Basket

**VARIATION TIP:** Change the stuffing to ground or braised meat to turn these samosas into a take on Mexican empanadas.

2 tablespoons canola oil

4 cups Russet potatoes, peeled and cut into ½-inch cubes

1 small yellow onion, diced

1 cup frozen peas

1½ teaspoons kosher salt

2½ teaspoons curry powder

1 cup vegetable stock

1 (½ package) frozen puff pastry sheet, thawed

1 egg beaten with 1 teaspoon water

1.  Select SEAR/SAUTÉ and set temperature to HI. Select START/STOP to begin. Let preheat for 5 minutes.

2.  Add the oil and let heat for 1 minute. Add the potatoes, onions, and peas and cook, stirring frequently, about 10 minutes. Add the salt and curry powder and stir to coat the vegetables with it. Add the vegetable stock. Assemble pressure lid, making sure the pressure release valve is in the SEAL position.

3.  Select PRESSURE and set to LO. Set time to 1 minute. Select START/STOP to begin.

4.  When pressure cooking is complete, quick release the pressure by turning the pressure release valve to the VENT position. Carefully remove the lid when the unit has finished releasing pressure.

5.  Transfer the potato mixture to a medium bowl. Let fully cool, about 15 minutes.

6.  Lay out the puff pastry sheet on a cutting board. Using a rolling pin, roll out the sheet into a 12-by-10-inch rectangle. Cut it in 4 strips lengthwise, then cut the strips into thirds for a total of 12 squares.

7.  Place 2 tablespoons of potato mixture in center of a pastry square. Brush the egg wash onto edges, and then fold one corner to another to create a triangle. Use a fork to seal edges together. Repeat with the remaining potato mixture and pastry squares.

CONTINUED ▶

# Potato Samosas continued

8. Insert Cook & Crisp Basket into unit. Close crisping lid. Select AIR CRISP, set temperature to 390°F, and set time to 20 minutes. Select START/STOP to begin. Let preheat for 5 minutes.

9. Once unit has preheated, working in batches, place 3 samosas in the basket. Close lid to begin cooking.

10. After 5 minutes, open lid and use silicone-tipped tongs to remove the samosas. Repeat with the remaining batches of samosas.

11. Once all samosas are cooked, serve immediately.

*Per serving: Calories: 449; Total Fat: 24g; Saturated Fat: 9g; Cholesterol: 47mg; Sodium: 639mg; Carbohydrates: 53g; Fiber: 7g; Protein: 10g*

# Rosemary Hush Puppies

**SERVES 6**

*Earlier this year Julien and I went to a wedding in beautiful Mystic, Connecticut, and one of the restaurants we stopped at had the most incredible herb-flavored hush puppies. I wanted to recreate this taste using the Air Crisp feature on the Foodi™ Pressure Cooker, incorporating one of my favorite flavors—rosemary. I hope you enjoy these as much as we do!*

**NUT-FREE, VEGETARIAN, UNDER 30 MINUTES**

**PREP TIME:** 15 minutes
**TOTAL COOK TIME:**
20 minutes

**AIR CRISP:** 15 minutes

**ACCESSORIES:** Cook & Crisp Basket

**VARIATION TIP:** Put your own twist on this recipe by folding in herbs and seasoning into the batter. Try adding a pinch of cayenne or sliced jalapeño for a little spice.

1 cup yellow cornmeal
¾ cup all-purpose flour
1½ teaspoons baking powder
¼ teaspoon granulated sugar
¼ teaspoon sea salt
½ onion, finely chopped
1 tablespoon dried rosemary
1 large egg, lightly beaten
¾ cup whole milk
Cooking spray

1. In a large bowl, combine the cornmeal, flour, baking powder, sugar, and salt. Stir in the onions and rosemary.

2. In a small bowl, whisk together the egg and milk. Pour the wet ingredients into the dry ingredients and mix until combined.

3. Place Cook & Crisp Basket in pot. Close crisping lid. Select AIR CRISP, set temperature to 390ºF, and set time to 5 minutes. Select START/STOP to begin preheating.

4. Form the mixture into 12 small, round balls.

5. Once unit has preheated, open lid. Place 6 dough balls in the basket in a single layer. Coat well with cooking spray. Close lid.

6. Select AIR CRISP, set temperature to 390ºF, and set time to 10 minutes. Select START/STOP to begin.

7. After 5 minutes, open lid, then lift the basket and flip the hush puppies with silicone-tipped tongs. Coat well with cooking spray and lower basket back into pot. Close lid and continue cooking.

8. When cooking is complete, check for desired crispness. Place the hush puppies on a plate and repeat steps 5, 6, and 7 with the remaining hush puppies. Serve warm.

*Per serving: Calories: 198; Total Fat: 3g; Saturated Fat: 1g; Cholesterol: 34mg; Sodium: 114mg; Carbohydrates: 37g; Fiber: 3g; Protein: 6g*

# Chicken Bites

**SERVES 4**

*This is a great recipe that people of all ages can enjoy because you can eat these little bites in so many ways. Put them out as an appetizer at your next get-together with a selection of dipping sauces, chop them up and use them to top a big salad, or just enjoy them on their own.*

**NUT-FREE, UNDER 30 MINUTES, FAMILY FAVORITE, 5 INGREDIENT**

**PREP TIME:** 15 minutes
**TOTAL COOK TIME:** 8 minutes

**AIR CRISP:** 13 minutes

**ACCESSORIES:** Cook & Crisp Basket

½ cup Italian seasoned bread crumbs

2 tablespoons grated Parmesan cheese

¼ teaspoon sea salt

¼ teaspoon freshly ground black pepper

1 boneless, skinless chicken breast, cut into 1-inch pieces

½ cup unsalted butter, melted

Cooking spray

1. Place Cook & Crisp Basket in pot. Close crisping lid. Select AIR CRISP, set temperature to 390°F, and set time to 5 minutes. Select START/STOP to begin preheating.

2. In a medium bowl, combine the bread crumbs, Parmesan cheese, salt, and pepper. In a separate medium bowl, toss the chicken in the butter until well coated. Move a few of the chicken pieces to the breadcrumb mixture and coat. Repeat until all the chicken is coated.

3. Once unit is preheated, open lid and place the chicken bites in the basket in a single layer. Coat well with cooking spray. Close lid.

4. Select AIR CRISP, set temperature to 390°F, and set time to 8 minutes. Select START/STOP to begin.

5. After 4 minutes, open lid, then lift basket and flip the chicken bites with silicone-tipped tongs. Coat well with cooking spray. Lower basket back into pot and close lid to continue cooking.

6. After 4 minutes, check for desired crispness. Cooking is complete when the internal temperature of the chicken reads at least 165°F on a food thermometer.

*Per serving: Calories: 279; Total Fat: 25g; Saturated Fat: 15g; Cholesterol: 84mg; Sodium: 246mg; Carbohydrates: 5g; Fiber: 0g; Protein: 10g*

# Cheesy Fried Risotto Balls

**SERVES 6**

*This recipe is a favorite both in my family and in the test kitchen. There is something irresistible about the creamy, cheesy rice paired with the crispy, crunchy exterior that will keep you coming back for more. If you love mushrooms, sauté them with the onion in step 2—and feel free to stir in some frozen peas after pressure cooking for a little green! Have fun and make this recipe your own.*

**NUT-FREE, VEGETARIAN, FAMILY FAVORITE**

**PREP TIME:** 20 minutes
**TOTAL COOK TIME:** 45 minutes

**SEAR/SAUTÉ:** 5 minutes
**APPROX. PRESSURE BUILD:** 6 minutes
**PRESSURE COOK:** 7 minutes
**PRESSURE RELEASE:** 10 minutes, then Quick
**AIR CRISP:** 20 minutes

½ cup extra-virgin olive oil, plus 1 tablespoon
1 small yellow onion, diced
2 garlic cloves, minced
5 cups vegetable broth
½ cup white wine
2 cups arborio rice
½ cup shredded mozzarella cheese
½ cup shredded fontina cheese
½ cup grated Parmesan cheese, plus more for garnish
2 tablespoons chopped fresh parsley
1 teaspoon sea salt
1 teaspoon freshly ground black pepper
2 cups fresh bread crumbs
2 large eggs

1.  Select SEAR/SAUTÉ and set to MD:HI. Select START/STOP to begin. Allow the pot to preheat for 5 minutes.

2.  Add 1 tablespoon of oil and the onion to the preheated pot. Cook until soft and translucent, stirring occasionally. Add the garlic and cook for 1 minute.

3.  Add the broth, wine, and rice to the pot; stir to incorporate. Assemble the pressure lid, making sure the pressure release valve is in the SEAL position.

4.  Select PRESSURE and set to HI. Set the time to 7 minutes. Press START/STOP to begin.

5.  When pressure cooking is complete, allow pressure to naturally release for 10 minutes. After 10 minutes, quick release any remaining pressure by turning the pressure release valve to the VENT position. Carefully remove the lid when the unit has finished releasing pressure.

6.  Add the mozzarella, fontina, and Parmesan cheeses, the parsley, salt, and pepper. Stir vigorously until the rice begins to thicken. Transfer the risotto to a large mixing bowl and let cool.

CONTINUED ▶

# Cheesy Fried Risotto Balls  continued

7. Meanwhile, clean the pot. In a medium mixing bowl, stir together the bread crumbs and the remaining ½ cup of olive oil. In a separate mixing bowl, lightly beat the eggs.

8. Divide the risotto into 12 equal portions and form each one into a ball. Dip each risotto ball in the beaten eggs, then coat in the breadcrumb mixture.

9. Arrange half of the risotto balls in the Cook & Crisp Basket in a single layer.

10. Close the crisping lid. Select AIR CRISP, set the temperature to 400°F, and set the time to 10 minutes. Select START/STOP to begin.

11. Repeat steps 9 and 10 to cook the remaining risotto balls.

*Per serving: Calories: 722; Total Fat: 33g; Saturated Fat: 9g; Cholesterol: 84mg; Sodium: 1160mg; Carbohydrates: 81g; Fiber: 4g; Protein: 23g*

# Honey-Garlic Chicken Wings

*Sweet honey and fragrant garlic come together to make a sticky wing sauce that you won't be able to get enough of. My favorite thing about this recipe is how easily everything comes to life using the Foodi™ Pressure Cooker—you get moist AND crispy wings using the crisping lid and then build your sauce right in the cooking pot. Add some crushed red pepper flakes to give your next batch a little zing.*

**GLUTEN-FREE, NUT-FREE, 5 INGREDIENT**

**PREP TIME:** 10 minutes
**TOTAL COOK TIME:** 43 minutes

**AIR CRISP:** 30 minutes
**SEAR/SAUTÉ:** 13 minutes

**ACCESSORIES:** Cook & Crisp Basket

**VARIATION TIP:** For classic buffalo chicken wings, follow the cook time for this recipe but skip the seasoning. Once the wings are cooked and crispy, toss them with a few tablespoons of buffalo sauce.

**2 pounds fresh chicken wings**
**¾ cup potato starch**
**Cooking spray**
**¼ cup unsalted butter**
**4 tablespoons minced garlic**
**¼ cup honey**
**¼ teaspoon sea salt**

1. Insert Cook & Crisp Basket into pot and close crisping lid. Select AIR CRISP, set temperature to 390ºF, and set time to 5 minutes. Select START/STOP to begin preheating.

2. Pat the chicken wings dry. In a large bowl, toss the chicken wings with potato starch until evenly coated.

3. Once unit has preheated, place the wings in the basket. Close lid.

4. Select AIR CRISP, set temperature to 390ºF, and set time to 30 minutes. Select START/STOP to begin.

5. After 15 minutes, open lid, then lift the basket and shake the wings. Coat with cooking spray. Lower basket back into the pot. Close lid and continue cooking until the wings reach your desired crispiness.

6. Cooking is complete when the internal temperature of the meat reads at least 165ºF on a food thermometer.

7. Remove basket from pot. Cover with aluminum foil to keep warm.

8. Select SEAR/SAUTÉ and set to MD:LO. Select START/STOP to begin.

9. Add the butter and garlic and sauté until fragrant, about 3 minutes. Add the honey and salt and simmer for about 10 minutes, adding water as needed to thin out the sauce.

10. Place the wings in a large bowl. Drizzle with the sauce and toss the chicken wings to coat. Serve.

*Per serving: Calories: 654; Total Fat: 33g; Saturated Fat: 14g; Cholesterol: 320mg; Sodium: 302mg; Carbohydrates: 53g; Fiber: 1g; Protein: 39g*

# Chipotle-Lime Chicken Wings

*Bring the heat the next time you make wings with the smoky flavor of chipotle chiles. Balanced out with some zesty lime flavor, these are perfect when hosting friends and family for the next big game—or a snack you make anytime using frozen wings you have in your freezer.*

**DAIRY-FREE, GLUTEN-FREE, NUT-FREE, UNDER 30 MINUTES**

**PREP TIME:** 10 minutes
**TOTAL COOK TIME:** 28 minutes

**APPROX. PRESSURE BUILD:** 10 minutes
**PRESSURE COOK:** 5 minutes
**PRESSURE RELEASE:** Quick
**AIR CRISP:** 15 minutes

**ACCESSORIES:** Cook & Crisp Basket

**VARIATION TIP:** Using fresh wings instead of frozen? Follow the instructions in the Air Crisp Chart on page 376.

½ cup water

2 pounds frozen chicken wings

¼ cup extra-virgin olive oil

2 tablespoons chipotle chiles in adobo sauce, chopped

Juice of 2 limes

Zest of 1 lime

1 tablespoon minced garlic

Sea salt

Freshly ground black pepper

1. Pour the water in the pot. Place the wings in the Cook & Crisp Basket and insert basket in pot. Assemble pressure lid, making sure the pressure release valve is in the SEAL position.

2. Select PRESSURE and set to HI. Set time to 5 minutes. Select START/STOP to begin.

3. In a large bowl mix together the olive oil, chipotles in adobo sauce, lime juice, lime zest, and garlic. Season with salt and pepper.

4. When pressure cooking is complete, quick release the pressure by turning the pressure release valve to the VENT position. Carefully remove lid when unit has finished releasing pressure.

5. Transfer the chicken wings to the large bowl and toss to coat. Place the wings back in the basket. Close crisping lid.

6. Select AIR CRISP, set temperature to 375°F, and set time to 15 minutes. Select START/STOP to begin.

7. After 7 minutes, open lid, then lift the basket and shake the wings. Lower the basket back into pot. Close lid and continue cooking until the wings reach your desired crispiness.

*Per serving: Calories: 560; Total Fat: 45g; Saturated Fat: 11g; Cholesterol: 152mg; Sodium: 942mg; Carbohydrates: 2g; Fiber: 1g; Protein: 38g*

# Chicken and Vegetable Egg Rolls

by Aurelia McCollom, Ninja® Foodi™ Family Member

**SERVES 16**

*Aurelia says:* I've been making these since 1980. The egg rolls were originally made in our wok fried in oil. Time for an upgrade to healthier cooking!

DAIRY-FREE, NUT-FREE, UNDER 30 MINUTES

---

**PREP TIME:** 20 minutes
**TOTAL COOK TIME:**
10 minutes per batch

---

**SEAR/SAUTÉ:** 14 minutes
**AIR CRISP:** 10 minutes

---

**ACCESSORIES:** Cook & Crisp Basket

---

**SUBSTITUTION TIP:** Swap out the chicken for pork or seafood.

---

**Find Aurelia on Facebook: Ninja Foodi & All Ninja Multi-Cooker Systems+Recipes— since 2013!**

2 tablespoons sherry
2 tablespoons soy sauce
2 tablespoons beef broth
2 tablespoons cornstarch
½ teaspoon salt
½ teaspoon granulated sugar
½ teaspoon ground ginger
3 tablespoons canola oil
8 scallions, chopped
½ cup chopped mushrooms
3 cups shredded cabbage

½ cup shredded carrot
½ cup bean sprouts, washed
2 cups chopped cooked chicken
1 (16-ounce) package egg rolls wrappers
1 egg, beaten
Cooking spray
Hot mustard, for dipping
Sweet and sour sauce, for dipping

1. In a small bowl, stir together the sherry, soy sauce, beef broth, cornstarch, salt, sugar, and ginger until combined and the sugar dissolves. Set aside.

2. Select SEAR/SAUTÉ and set temperature to HI. Select START/STOP to begin and allow to preheat for 5 minutes.

3. Add the canola oil to the cooking pot and allow to heat for 1 minute. Add the scallions and mushrooms and sauté for 2 to 3 minutes, stirring well, until the vegetables just begin to soften.

4. Add the cabbage, carrot, and bean sprouts, stirring to incorporate well. Decrease the temperature to MD:LO. Cook the vegetables for about 7 minutes, until cabbage and carrots are softened.

5. Stir in the chicken. Add the sauce and cook, stirring constantly, until the sauce thickens the filling, about 3 minutes. Select START/STOP to end the function. Transfer the filling to a bowl to cool. Wash the pot and return it to the cooker.

CONTINUED ▶

# Chicken and Vegetable Egg Rolls continued

6. Place the Cook & Crisp Basket in the Foodi pot.

7. Select AIR CRISP, set the temperature to 390ºF, and set the time to 5 minutes to preheat. Select START/STOP to begin.

8. Working one at a time, using a small silicone spatula, moisten the 4 sides of an egg roll wrapper with the beaten egg. Place 3 tablespoons of the filling on the center of the egg roll wrapper. Fold an edge over the mixture and tuck it under the point. Fold the edges in and continue rolling. Press the end point over the top of the roll to seal. Continue with the remaining wrappers and filling.

9. Place 3 egg rolls in the basket, making sure they don't touch each other. Coat the egg rolls in on cooking spray, then close the crisping lid.

10. Select AIR CRISP, set the temperature to 390ºF, and set the time to 10 minutes. After 5 minutes, open the crisping lid, flip the egg rolls, and spritz the other side with cooking spray. Close the crisping lid and cook for the remaining 5 minutes.

11. Using tongs, carefully transfer the egg rolls to a wire rack to cool for least 6 minutes before serving.

12. Repeat step 8 with the remaining egg rolls. Keep in mind that the unit is already hot, which may decrease the cooking time. Monitor closely for doneness.

13. Serve with the hot mustard and sweet and sour sauce for dipping.

Per serving: *Calories: 166; Total Fat: 6g; Saturated Fat: 1g; Cholesterol: 24mg; Sodium: 364mg; Carbohydrates: 20g; Fiber: 1g; Protein: 9g*

# Crispy Delicata Squash

*Delicata squash has a super smooth flesh and an edible, delicate skin—making it easy to prep for cooking. I've seasoned it simply with olive oil and salt, and then I crisped up the edges while keeping the interior creamy, giving you a variety of textures in each bite.*

DAIRY-FREE, GLUTEN-FREE, NUT-FREE, VEGAN, UNDER 30 MINUTES, 5 INGREDIENT

PREP TIME: 10 minutes
TOTAL COOK TIME: 15 minutes

AIR CRISP: 15 minutes

ACCESSORIES: Cook & Crisp Basket

1 large delicata squash, seeds removed and sliced

1 tablespoon extra-virgin olive oil

¼ teaspoon sea salt

1. Place Cook & Crisp Basket in pot. Close crisping lid. Select AIR CRISP, set temperature to 390ºF, and set time to 5 minutes. Select START/STOP to begin preheating.

2. In a large bowl, toss the squash with the olive oil and season with salt.

3. Once unit has preheated, place the squash in the basket. Close crisping lid.

4. Select AIR CRISP, set temperature to 390ºF, and set time to 15 minutes. Select START/STOP to begin.

5. After 7 minutes, open the lid, then lift the basket and shake the squash. Lower the basket back into pot. Close lid and continue cooking until the squash achieves your desired crispiness.

*Per serving: Calories: 75; Total Fat: 4g; Saturated Fat: 1g; Cholesterol: 0mg; Sodium: 117mg; Carbohydrates: 10g; Fiber: 2g; Protein: 2g*

# Charred Broccoli with Mustard Cream Sauce

*Broccoli is one of my favorite vegetables, and I love making it in my Ninja® Foodi™ Pressure Cooker to add some great texture to the florets. Long gone are the days of simple and soft steamed broccoli with dinner. Drizzle some mustard cream sauce over the top for a tangy, elevated veggie side dish.*

GLUTEN-FREE, NUT-FREE, VEGETARIAN, UNDER 30 MINUTES, FAMILY FAVORITE, 5 INGREDIENT

PREP TIME: 10 minutes
TOTAL COOK TIME:
13 minutes

AIR CRISP: 13 minutes

ACCESSORIES: Cook & Crisp Basket

VARIATION TIP: Swap out the broccoli for other green veggies like green beans or asparagus by following the cook times outlined in the Air Crisp Chart on page 376.

2 heads broccoli, trimmed into florets

2 tablespoons extra-virgin olive oil

Sea salt

½ cup heavy (whipping) cream

2 tablespoons brown mustard

1 tablespoon freshly squeezed lemon juice

1. Place Cook & Crisp Basket in pot. Close crisping lid. Select AIR CRISP, set temperature to 390°F, and set time to 5 minutes. Select START/STOP to begin preheating.

2. In a large bowl, toss the broccoli with the oil. Season with salt.

3. Once unit has preheated, open lid and place the broccoli in the basket. Close crisping lid.

4. Select AIR CRISP, set temperature to 390°F, and set time to 13 minutes. Select START/STOP to begin.

5. In a medium bowl, whisk together the heavy cream, brown mustard, and lemon juice. Season with salt.

6. After 5 minutes, open lid, then lift basket and shake the broccoli or toss them with silicone-tipped tongs. Lower basket back into pot and close lid to continue cooking.

7. After 5 minutes, check for desired crispness. Continue cooking up to 3 minutes more if necessary.

8. When cooking is complete, serve the broccoli topped with the mustard cream sauce.

*Per serving: Calories: 421; Total Fat: 19g; Saturated Fat: 8g; Cholesterol: 41mg; Sodium: 206mg; Carbohydrates: 16g; Fiber: 6g; Protein: 7g*

# Horseradish Roasted Carrots

**SERVES 4**

*Carrots are my favorite vegetable. When I was a kid, I actually ate so many carrots that my skin became tinted orange, I kid you not. I've cut back since but love to find new ways to highlight this ingredient whether in a meal or as a side dish. The carrots are the star of the show in this recipe, and the horseradish is a great contrast to their sweetness.*

**DAIRY-FREE, GLUTEN-FREE, NUT-FREE, VEGETARIAN, UNDER 30 MINUTES, 5 INGREDIENT**

**PREP TIME:** 5 minutes
**TOTAL COOK TIME:** 10 minutes

**APPROX. PRESSURE BUILD:** 10 minutes
**PRESSURE COOK:** 2 minutes
**PRESSURE RELEASE:** Quick
**BROIL:** 6 minutes

**INGREDIENT INFO:** Carrots are an excellent source of vitamin A, providing more than 200 percent of your daily requirement in just one carrot.

1 pound carrots, peeled and cut into 1-inch pieces
½ cup vegetable stock
2 tablespoons grated horseradish

¾ cup mayonnaise
½ teaspoon kosher salt
½ teaspoon freshly ground black pepper
Minced parsley, for garnish

1. Place the carrots and stock in the pot. Assemble pressure lid, making sure the pressure release valve is in the SEAL position.

2. Select PRESSURE and set to HI. Set time to 2 minutes. Select START/STOP to begin.

3. When pressure cooking is complete, quick release the pressure by turning the pressure release valve to the VENT position. Carefully remove lid when unit has finished releasing pressure.

4. In a small bowl, combine the horseradish, mayonnaise, salt, and pepper. Add mixture to the cooked carrots and stir carefully. Close crisping lid.

5. Select BROIL and set time to 6 minutes. Select START/STOP to begin.

6. After 3 minutes, open lid to check doneness. If further browning desired, close lid and continue cooking.

7. When cooking is complete, garnish with parsley and serve immediately.

*Per serving: Calories: 323; Total Fat: 30g; Saturated Fat: 5g; Cholesterol: 15mg; Sodium: 632mg; Carbohydrates: 13g; Fiber: 2g; Protein: 1g*

# Cauliflower Gratin by Craig White

***Chef says:*** *Creating a great side dish like this can really set off the rest of your meal. Sure you nailed the temp on that bone-in ribeye, but what did you serve it with? Place that steak down next to a golden-brown cauliflower gratin, and now we're talking.*

**NUT-FREE, VEGETARIAN, UNDER 30 MINUTES**

**PREP TIME:** 10 minutes
**TOTAL COOK TIME:** 28 minutes

**APPROX. PRESSURE BUILD:** 10 minutes
**PRESSURE COOK:** 5 minutes
**PRESSURE RELEASE:** Quick
**SEAR/SAUTÉ:** 8 minutes
**BAKE/ROAST:** 20 minutes

**ACCESSORIES:**
Reversible Rack, Ninja Multi-Purpose Pan

**SUBSTITUTION TIP:** Switch up the cheeses. Have Cheddar? Use Cheddar! Love mozzarella? Me too.

2 cups water
1 large head cauliflower, cut into 1-inch florets
3 tablespoons unsalted butter
3 tablespoons all-purpose flour
1½ cups whole milk
1 cup heavy (whipping) cream
2 tablespoons capers, drained
1 tablespoon fresh thyme
Kosher salt
Freshly ground black pepper
¾ cup shredded Swiss cheese
¼ cup grated Parmesan cheese

1. Pour the water in the pot. Place the Reversible Rack in the lower position in the pot. Place the cauliflower on the rack. Assemble pressure lid, making sure the pressure release valve is in the SEAL position.

2. Select PRESSURE and set to HI. Set time to 5 minutes. Select START/STOP to begin.

3. When pressure cooking is complete, quick release the pressure by turning the pressure release valve to the VENT position. Carefully remove lid when the unit has finished releasing pressure.

4. Remove rack and place the cauliflower in the Ninja Multi-Purpose Pan or 8-inch baking dish. Drain the water from the pot and wipe it dry. Reinsert pot into base.

5. Select SEAR/SAUTÉ and set temperature to HI. Select START/STOP to begin. Let preheat for 5 minutes.

6. Add the butter. Once melted, add the onion and cook 3 minutes. Add the flour and cook, stirring constantly, 1 minute.

7. Add the milk, cream, capers, and thyme. Season with salt and pepper. Bring to a boil and cook, about 4 minutes.

8. Pour the sauce over the cauliflower. Place the pan onto the Reversible Rack, making sure the rack is in the lower position. Place the rack with pan in the pot. Close crisping lid.

9.  Select BAKE/ROAST, set temperature to 400ºF, and set time to 20 minutes. Select START/STOP to begin.

10. After 15 minutes, open lid and sprinkle the cauliflower with the Swiss and Parmesan cheeses. Close lid and continue cooking.

11. Once cooking is complete, open lid. Let the gratin sit for 10 minutes before serving.

*Per serving: Calories: 341; Total Fat: 27g; Saturated Fat: 17g; Cholesterol: 91mg; Sodium: 263mg; Carbohydrates: 16g; Fiber: 4g; Protein: 11g*

# Sweet Potato Gratin by Sam Ferguson

**SERVES 6**

***Chef says:*** *This dish makes me think of my home state of Maine in the fall—my mom used to make a potato gratin similar to this one that I remember enjoying with my family on Sunday afternoons while watching the Patriots.*

VEGETARIAN, UNDER
30 MINUTES, FAMILY
FAVORITE

PREP TIME: 5 minutes
TOTAL COOK TIME:
15 minutes

SEAR/SAUTÉ: 10 minutes
APPROX. PRESSURE BUILD:
7 minutes
PRESSURE COOK: 1 minute
PRESSURE RELEASE: Quick
BROIL: 5 minutes

VARIATION TIP: Although
the sweetness of the sweet
potatoes helps accentuate
the flavors of this dish,
the gratin can be made
with any potato you'd
like to use.

2 tablespoons unsalted butter

3 tablespoons
all-purpose flour

2 cups heavy (whipping)
cream, warmed
in microwave

2 teaspoons kosher salt

1 teaspoon pumpkin pie spice

¼ cup water

3 large sweet potatoes,
peeled and cut in half,
then cut into half-moons
¼-inch thick

1¼ cups shredded Cheddar
cheese, divided

½ cup chopped walnuts or
pecans, or slivered almonds

1. Select SEAR/SAUTÉ and set to MD:HI. Select START/STOP to begin. Let preheat for 5 minutes.

2. Add the butter. Once melted, add the flour and stir together until a thick paste forms, about 1 minute. (The combination of butter and flour is called a roux). Continue cooking the roux for 2 minutes, stirring frequently with a rubber-coated whisk. Slowly add the warm cream while continuously whisking so there are no lumps, about 3 minutes. The cream should be thickened.

3. Add the salt and pumpkin pie spice and whisk to incorporate. Whisk in the water and let the mixture simmer for 3 minutes.

4. Place the potatoes in the pot. Assemble pressure lid, making sure the pressure release valve is in the SEAL position.

5. Select PRESSURE and set to LO. Set time to 1 minute. Select START/STOP to begin.

6. When pressure cooking is complete, quick release pressure by moving the pressure release valve to the VENT position. Carefully remove lid when unit has finished releasing pressure.

7. Add ¼ cup of cheese and stir gently to incorporate, being careful not to break up the cooked potatoes.

CONTINUED ▶

# Sweet Potato Gratin continued

Ensure mixture is flat, then cover top with remaining 1 cup of cheese. Sprinkle the nuts over the cheese. Close crisping lid.

8. Select BROIL and set time to 5 minutes. Select START/ STOP to begin.

9. When cooking is complete, open lid and let the gratin cool for 10 minutes before serving.

*Per serving: Calories: 536; Total Fat: 47g; Saturated Fat: 27g; Cholesterol: 143mg; Sodium: 409mg; Carbohydrates: 20g; Fiber: 3g; Protein: 10g*

# Green Bean Casserole by Chelven Randolph

*Chef says: Green bean casserole is a classic dish that is perfect for colder days. Usually associated with a canned side dish at Thanksgiving, this version uses fresh green beans, giving it a bit more texture and crunch.*

NUT-FREE, VEGETARIAN

PREP TIME: 15 minutes
TOTAL COOK TIME:
46 minutes

APPROX. PRESSURE BUILD:
10 minutes
PRESSURE COOK: 5 minutes
PRESSURE RELEASE: Quick
BAKE/ROAST: 30 minutes

ACCESSORIES:
Reversible Rack

VARIATION TIP: If you're in a pinch, you can substitute 2 cans of drained green beans in place of fresh green beans. Just skip the pressure cooking. For a creamier casserole, add ½ cup of shredded Cheddar cheese with the fried onions in step 5.

1 cup water

2 pounds fresh green beans, cleaned and trimmed

1 cup vegetable or chicken stock

½ cup milk

1 (10.5-ounce) can condensed cream of mushroom soup

2 teaspoons soy sauce

2 cups fried onion strings, divided

Kosher salt

Freshly ground black pepper

1. Pour the water into the pot. Place the Reversible Rack in the lower position in the pot and add the green beans. Assemble pressure lid, making sure the pressure release valve is in the SEAL position.

2. Select PRESSURE and set to HI. Set time to 5 minutes. Select START/STOP to begin.

3. When pressure cooking is complete, quick release the pressure by turning the pressure release valve to the VENT position. Carefully remove lid when the unit has finished releasing pressure.

4. Remove rack and green beans. Drain the water from the pot and return to base.

5. Add the stock, milk, condensed soup, and soy sauce and stir. Add the green beans and 1 cup of fried onions. Season with salt and pepper. Stir well. Top with the remaining 1 cup of onion strings. Close crisping lid.

6. Select BAKE/ROAST, set temperature to 375°F, and set time to 30 minutes. Select START/STOP to begin.

7. When cooking is complete, open lid. Let cool for 5 minutes before serving.

*Per serving: Calories: 342; Total Fat: 20g; Saturated Fat: 12g; Cholesterol: 2mg; Sodium: 679mg; Carbohydrates: 31g; Fiber: 5g; Protein: 4g*

# Pull Apart Cheesy Garlic Bread

## by Caroline Schliep

**SERVES 6**

***Chef says:*** *Garlic bread is one of my weaknesses. I mean, when you add cheese to anything, it's happiness overload for your taste buds. Each piece of this doughy goodness is slathered with garlic-herb butter and, of course, tossed with lots of cheese. It's super simple to throw together and is perfect for a crowd because there is enough for everyone to enjoy. It is a great side option for any pasta dish like the Creamy Tuscan Chicken Pasta (page 234) or Spicy Shrimp Pasta with Vodka Sauce (page 207).*

**NUT-FREE, VEGETARIAN, UNDER 30 MINUTES**

**PREP TIME:** 10 minutes
**TOTAL COOK TIME:**
25 minutes

**BAKE/ROAST:** 25 minutes

**ACCESSORIES:** Ninja Multi-Purpose Pan, Reversible Rack

**VARIATION TIP:** Pile on your favorite toppings like pepperoni slices, sautéed onions, peppers, or olives.

- ½ pound store-bought pizza dough
- 3 tablespoons unsalted butter, melted
- 4 garlic cloves, minced
- ¼ cup shredded Parmesan cheese
- ¼ cup shredded mozzarella cheese
- ¼ cup minced parsley
- ½ teaspoon kosher salt
- ½ teaspoon garlic powder
- Cooking spray
- Marinara sauce, for serving

1. Cut the pizza dough into 1-inch cubes. Roll each cube into a ball. Place the dough balls in a large bowl. Add the butter, garlic, Parmesan cheese, mozzarella cheese, parsley, salt, and garlic powder. Toss, ensuring everything is evenly coated and mixed. Set aside.

2. Close crisping lid. Select BAKE/ROAST, set temperature to 325ºF, and set time to 30 minutes. Select START/STOP to begin. Let preheat for 5 minutes.

3. Coat the Ninja Multi-Purpose Pan with cooking spray. Place the dough balls in the pan and place pan on Reversible Rack, making sure it is in the lower position.

4. Once unit has preheated, open lid and insert the rack in pot. Close lid and cook for 25 minutes.

5. Once cooking is complete, open lid and let the bread cool slightly. Serve with marinara sauce for dipping.

*Per serving: Calories: 182; Total Fat: 10g; Saturated Fat: 5g; Cholesterol: 22mg; Sodium: 514mg; Carbohydrates: 20g; Fiber: 2g; Protein: 6g*

# 5

# Soups & Stews

# Creamy Pumpkin Soup by Craig White

SERVES 8

**Chef says:** *When I first decided to become a chef, I quit my job in radio advertising and took a month off. Blowing through my savings, I needed to make meals that would last me all week. Stews and soups were an easy pick as I could make a giant crock and live off it for days at a time. I made a pumpkin soup with a can of pumpkin I had in my pantry from who knows when. After it was done, I realized it wasn't creamy enough. I had run out of cream, so I threw in some cream cheese instead to thicken it. I'm glad I did. I gave some to my mother and sister and to this day they still talk about "that creamy pumpkin soup." Garnish this soup with toasted pumpkin seeds, maple syrup, and dried cranberries.*

GLUTEN-FREE, NUT-FREE, VEGETARIAN, UNDER 30 MINUTES

**PREP TIME:** 10 minutes
**TOTAL COOK TIME:** 23 minutes

**SEAR/SAUTÉ:** 3 minutes
**APPROX. PRESSURE BUILD:** 10 minutes
**PRESSURE COOK:** 15 minutes
**PRESSURE RELEASE:** Quick

**ACCESSORIES:** Immersion Blender

**VARIATION TIP:** Substitute unsweetened full-fat coconut milk for the heavy cream and add some fresh chiles in with the onions for a spicy tropical twist. Then add freshly squeezed lime juice.

¼ **cup unsalted butter**
½ **small onion, diced**
1 **celery stalk, diced**
1 **carrot, diced**
2 **garlic cloves, minced**
1 **(15-ounce) can pumpkin purée**
1½ **teaspoons poultry spice blend**
3 **cups chicken stock**
1 **(8-ounce) package cream cheese**
1 **cup heavy (whipping) cream**
¼ **cup maple syrup**
**Sea salt**
**Freshly ground black pepper**

1. Select SEAR/SAUTÉ and set to HI. Select START/STOP to begin. Let preheat for 5 minutes.

2. Add the butter. Once melted, add the onions, celery, carrot, and garlic. Cook, stirring occasionally, for 3 minutes

3. Add the pumpkin, poultry spice, and chicken stock. Assemble pressure lid, making sure the pressure release valve is in the SEAL position.

4. Select PRESSURE and set to HI. Set time to 15 minutes. Select START/STOP to begin.

5. When pressure cooking is complete, quick release the pressure by turning the pressure release valve to the VENT position. Carefully remove lid when the unit has finished releasing pressure.

6. Whisk in the cream cheese, heavy cream, and maple syrup. Season with salt and pepper. Using an immersion blender, purée the soup until smooth.

*Per serving: Calories: 334; Total Fat: 28g; Saturated Fat: 18g; Cholesterol: 90mg; Sodium: 266mg; Carbohydrates: 17g; Fiber: 2g; Protein: 6g*

# Goulash (Hungarian Beef Soup) by Meg Jordan

**SERVES 6**

*Chef says:* Having a Hungarian grandfather, I grew up eating many traditional dishes, but they can often be a challenge to make during the week. Enter the Ninja® Foodi™ Pressure Cooker. This recipe yields a delicious goulash in under an hour, and it's great for the fall and winter months in New England.

NUT-FREE, 360 MEAL

**PREP TIME:** 15 minutes
**TOTAL COOK TIME:**
55 minutes

**SEAR/SAUTÉ:** 18 minutes
**APPROX. PRESSURE BUILD:**
7 minutes
**PRESSURE COOK:**
30 minutes
**PRESSURE RELEASE:** Quick

INGREDIENT INFO:
In Hungary, paprika is traditionally made by hanging the red peppers on string outside on porches to dry.

½ cup all-purpose flour

1 tablespoon kosher salt

½ teaspoon freshly ground black pepper

2 pounds beef stew meat

2 tablespoons canola oil

1 medium red bell pepper, seeded and chopped

4 garlic cloves, minced

1 large yellow onion, diced

2 tablespoons smoked paprika

1½ pounds small Yukon Gold potatoes, halved

2 cups beef broth

2 tablespoons tomato paste

¼ cup sour cream

Fresh parsley, for garnish

1. Select SEAR/SAUTÉ and set to HI. Select START/STOP to begin. Let preheat for 5 minutes.

2. Mix together the flour, salt, and pepper in a small bowl. Dip the pieces of beef into the flour mixture, shaking off any extra flour.

3. Add the oil and let heat for 1 minute. Place the beef in the pot and brown it on all sides, about 10 minutes.

4. Add the bell pepper, garlic, onion, and smoked paprika. Sauté for about 8 minutes or until the onion is translucent.

5. Add the potatoes, beef broth, and tomato paste and stir. Assemble pressure lid, making sure the pressure release valve is in the SEAL position.

6. Select PRESSURE and set to LO. Set time to 30 minutes. Select START/STOP to begin.

7. When pressure cooking is complete, quick release the pressure by moving the pressure release valve to the VENT position. Carefully remove lid when unit has finished releasing pressure.

8. Add the sour cream and mix thoroughly. Garnish with parsley, if desired, and serve immediately.

*Per serving: Calories: 413; Total Fat: 13g; Saturated Fat: 4g; Cholesterol: 98mg; Sodium: 432mg; Carbohydrates: 64g; Fiber: 5g; Protein: 37g*

# Mushroom and Wild Rice Soup

**SERVES 6**

*Perfectly cozy and comforting, this soup can be enjoyed year-round. One of the reasons I love it so much is because it is packed with fresh veggies and hearty rice. I created this recipe to be dairy-free so instead of a heavy cream base, I use a clear broth that's packed with flavor. To make this a bit creamier, omit one cup of broth and stir in a cup of cream before serving. You can also stir in one bunch of kale to sneak in even more veggies.*

**DAIRY-FREE, GLUTEN-FREE, NUT-FREE, 360 MEAL, UNDER 30 MINUTES**

**PREP TIME:** 10 minutes
**TOTAL COOK TIME:** 30 minutes

**APPROX. PRESSURE BUILD:** 10 minutes
**PRESSURE COOK:** 30 minutes
**PRESSURE RELEASE:** Quick

**VARIATION TIP:** Turn this into a hearty chicken soup by adding chicken in step 1.

5 medium carrots, chopped
5 celery stalks, chopped
1 onion, chopped
3 garlic cloves, minced
1 cup wild rice
8 ounces fresh mushrooms, sliced
6 cups vegetable broth
1 teaspoon kosher salt
1 teaspoon poultry seasoning
½ teaspoon dried thyme

1. Place all the ingredients in the pot. Assemble pressure lid, making sure the pressure release valve is in the SEAL position.

2. Select PRESSURE and set to HI. Set time to 30 minutes. Select START/STOP to begin.

3. When pressure cooking is complete, quick release the pressure by turning the pressure release valve to the VENT position. Carefully remove lid when unit has finished releasing pressure.

4. Serve.

*Per serving: Calories: 175; Total Fat: 2g; Saturated Fat: 0g; Cholesterol: 0mg; Sodium: 723mg; Carbohydrates: 30g; Fiber: 4g; Protein: 11g*

# Loaded Potato Soup

SERVES 6

*This combines all the flavors of a loaded baked potato in a comforting bowl of soup. I build flavor in every step of this recipe. Smoky bacon is incorporated in the broth and crumbled on top. The dairy creates a rich, velvety base. And a bubbling cheese finish puts this dish over the top.*

**GLUTEN-FREE, NUT-FREE, UNDER 30 MINUTES, FAMILY FAVORITE**

**PREP TIME:** 15 minutes
**TOTAL COOK TIME:** 30 minutes

**SEAR/SAUTÉ:** 5 minutes
**APPROX. PRESSURE BUILD:** 10 minutes
**PRESSURE COOK:** 10 minutes
**PRESSURE RELEASE:** Quick
**BROIL:** 5 minutes

5 slices bacon, chopped

1 onion, chopped

3 garlic cloves, minced

4 pounds Russet potatoes, peeled and chopped

4 cups chicken broth

1 cup whole milk

½ teaspoon sea salt

½ teaspoon freshly ground black pepper

1½ cups shredded Cheddar cheese

Sour cream, for serving (optional)

Chopped fresh chives, for serving (optional)

1. Select SEAR/SAUTÉ and set to HI. Select START/STOP to begin. Let preheat for 5 minutes.

2. Add the bacon, onion, and garlic. Cook, stirring occasionally, for 5 minutes. Set aside some of the bacon for garnish.

3. Add the potatoes and chicken broth. Assemble pressure lid, making sure the pressure release valve is in the SEAL position.

4. Select PRESSURE and set to HI. Set time to 10 minutes, then select START/STOP to begin.

5. When pressure cooking is complete, quick release the pressure by moving the pressure release valve to the VENT position. Carefully remove lid when unit has finished releasing pressure.

6. Add the milk and mash the ingredients until the soup reaches your desired consistency. Season with the salt and black pepper. Sprinkle the cheese evenly over the top of the soup. Close crisping lid.

7. Select BROIL and set time to 5 minutes. Select START/STOP to begin.

8. When cooking is complete, top with the reserved crispy bacon and serve with sour cream and chives (if using).

*Per serving: Calories: 468; Total Fat: 19g; Saturated Fat: 9g; Cholesterol: 51mg; Sodium: 1041mg; Carbohydrates: 53g; Fiber: 8g; Protein: 23g*

# Italian Sausage, Potato, and Kale Soup by Caroline Schliep

**SERVES 8**

**Chef says:** *One of my favorite recipes, this hearty and incredibly delicious soup is comfort for the soul, especially when I'm feeling a little under the weather. It is filled with leafy kale, spicy Italian sausage, creamy potatoes, and aromatic spices. The kick from the crushed red pepper flakes will open your nasal passages right up and have you feeling better in no time!*

GLUTEN-FREE, NUT-FREE, 360 MEAL, UNDER 30 MINUTES

PREP TIME: 10 minutes
TOTAL COOK TIME: 18 minutes

SEAR/SAUTÉ: 5 minutes
APPROX. PRESSURE BUILD: 10 minutes
PRESSURE COOK: 10 minutes
PRESSURE RELEASE: Quick

SUBSTITUTION TIP: To make this soup dairy-free, substitute full-fat coconut milk for heavy cream.

1 tablespoon extra-virgin olive oil

1½ pounds hot Italian sausage, ground

1 pound sweet Italian sausage, ground

1 large yellow onion, diced

2 tablespoons minced garlic

4 large Russet potatoes, cut in ½-inch thick quarters

5 cups chicken stock

2 tablespoons Italian seasoning

2 teaspoons crushed red pepper flakes

Salt

Freshly ground black pepper

6 cups kale, chopped

½ cup heavy (whipping) cream

1. Select SEAR/SAUTÉ. Set temperature to MD:HI. Select START/STOP to begin. Let preheat for 5 minutes.

2. Add the olive oil and hot and sweet Italian sausage. Cook, breaking up the sausage with a spatula, until the meat is cooked all the way through, about 5 minutes.

3. Add the onion, garlic, potatoes, chicken stock, Italian seasoning, and crushed red pepper flakes. Season with salt and pepper. Stir to combine. Assemble pressure lid, making sure the pressure release valve is in the SEAL position.

4. Select PRESSURE and set to HI. Set time to 10 minutes. Select START/STOP to begin.

5. When pressure cooking is complete, quick release the pressure by turning the pressure release valve to the VENT position. Carefully remove lid when the unit has finished releasing pressure.

6. Stir in the kale and heavy cream. Serve.

*Per serving: Calories: 689; Total Fat: 45g; Saturated Fat: 15g; Cholesterol: 130mg; Sodium: 1185mg; Carbohydrates: 38g; Fiber: 5g; Protein: 33g*

# Butternut Squash, Apple, Bacon and Orzo Soup by Meg Jordan

**SERVES 8**

*Chef says:* Butternut squash, apple, and bacon are my fall trifecta for soup ingredients. I love the saltiness of the bacon, the tartness of the apple, and the sweetness of the butternut squash all together. This is great served with a nice toasted baguette on a chilly fall day.

DAIRY-FREE, NUT-FREE

**PREP TIME:** 10 minutes
**TOTAL COOK TIME:**
28 minutes
**SEAR/SAUTÉ:** 28 minutes

**HACK IT:** Cutting a whole butternut squash can be time consuming. Buy precut butternut squash at the grocery store to save on prep time for an easy weeknight meal.

4 slices uncooked bacon, cut into ½-inch pieces

12 ounces butternut squash, peeled and cubed

1 green apple, cut into small cubes

Kosher salt

Freshly ground black pepper

1 tablespoon minced fresh oregano

2 quarts (64 ounces) chicken stock

1 cup orzo

1. Select SEAR/SAUTÉ and set temperature to HI. Select START/STOP to begin. Let preheat for 5 minutes.

2. Place the bacon in the pot and cook, stirring frequently, about 5 minutes, or until fat is rendered and the bacon starts to brown. Using a slotted spoon, transfer the bacon to a paper towel-lined plate to drain, leaving the rendered bacon fat in the pot.

3. Add the butternut squash, apple, salt, and pepper and sauté until partially soft, about 5 minutes. Stir in the oregano.

4. Add the bacon back into the pot along with the chicken stock. Bring to a boil for about 10 minutes, then add the orzo. Cook for about 8 minutes, until the orzo is tender. Serve.

*Per serving: Calories: 247; Total Fat: 7g; Saturated Fat: 2g; Cholesterol: 17mg; Sodium: 563mg; Carbohydrates: 33g; Fiber: 3g; Protein: 12g*

# Braised Pork and Black Bean Stew by Craig White

**SERVES 8**

***Chef says:*** *I grew up eating a lot of hot dogs and beans, and while I still have an affinity for a nice "tube steak," I find myself eating fewer processed foods. This stew is an ode to my nostalgic love affair with pork and beans. The better the quality of pork, the better the stew will be. If you can get your hands on some nice fatty pork belly, by all means use that instead of the pork shoulder.*

**NUT-FREE, UNDER 30 MINUTES**

**PREP TIME:** 15 minutes
**TOTAL COOK TIME:** 30 minutes

**SEAR/SAUTÉ:** 10 minutes
**APPROX. PRESSURE BUILD:** 10 minutes
**PRESSURE COOK:** 15 minutes
**PRESSURE RELEASE:** Quick

**SUBSTITUTION TIP:** Don't have pork? Chicken or turkey would be great in this stew.

2 pounds boneless pork shoulder, cut into 1-inch pieces

¼ cup all-purpose flour

¼ cup unsalted butter

½ small onion, diced

1 carrot, diced

1 celery stalk, diced

2 garlic cloves, minced

1 tablespoon tomato paste

1 tablespoon cumin

1 tablespoon smoked paprika

4 cups chicken stock

1 (10-ounce) can diced tomatoes with chiles

1 (15-ounce) can black beans, rinsed and drained

1 (15-ounce) can hominy, rinsed and drained

Sea salt

Freshly ground black pepper

1. In a large bowl, coat the pork pieces with the flour.

2. Select SEAR/SAUTÉ and set to HI. Select START/STOP to begin. Let preheat for 5 minutes.

3. Add the butter. Once melted, add the pork and sear for 5 minutes, turning the pieces so they begin to brown on all sides.

4. Add the onion, carrot, celery, garlic, tomato paste, cumin, and paprika and cook, stirring occasionally, for 3 minutes.

5. Add the chicken stock and tomatoes. Assemble pressure lid, making sure the pressure release valve is in the SEAL position.

6. Select PRESSURE and set to HI. Set time to 15 minutes. Select START/STOP to begin.

7. When pressure cooking is complete, quick release the pressure by turning the pressure release valve to the VENT position. Carefully remove lid when the unit has finished releasing pressure.

CONTINUED ▶

# Braised Pork and Black Bean Stew

8. Select SEAR/SAUTÉ and set to HI. Select START/STOP to begin.

9. Whisk in the beans and hominy. Season with salt and pepper and cook for 2 minutes. Serve.

**Per serving:** *Calories: 342; Total Fat: 12g; Saturated Fat: 6g; Cholesterol: 64mg; Sodium: 638mg; Carbohydrates: 27g; Fiber: 6g; Protein: 29g*

# Fish Chowder and Biscuits by Sam Ferguson

*Chef says:* *Fish is a common ingredient that many people have in their freezer, but they have no idea how to quickly use it. With this recipe, you don't have to do any advance prep with the fish—just throw it in the pot frozen and let the Foodi™ do the work for you.*

**NUT-FREE, 360 MEAL, UNDER 30 MINUTES**

**PREP TIME:** 15 minutes
**TOTAL COOK TIME:**
30 minutes

**SEAR/SAUTÉ:** 15 minutes
**APPROX. PRESSURE BUILD:**
10 minutes
**PRESSURE COOK:** 5 minutes
**PRESSURE RELEASE:** Quick
**BAKE/ROAST:** 12 minutes

**ACCESSORIES:**
Reversible Rack

**VARIATION TIP:** You can substitute any frozen fish for the haddock in step 3. As an alternative, to make this dish pescatarian, remove the bacon in step 1 and add 2 cups of fresh corn kernels.

5 strips bacon, sliced
1 white onion, chopped
3 celery stalks, chopped
4 cups chicken stock
2 Russet potatoes, rinsed and cut in 1-inch pieces
4 (6-ounce) frozen haddock fillets

Kosher salt
½ cup clam juice
⅓ cup all-purpose flour
2 (14-ounce) cans evaporated milk
1 (14-ounce) tube refrigerated biscuit dough

1. Select SEAR/SAUTÉ and set to HI. Select START/STOP to begin. Let preheat for 5 minutes.

2. Add the bacon and cook, stirring frequently, for 5 minutes. Add the onion and celery and cook for an additional 5 minutes, stirring occasionally.

3. Add the chicken stock, potatoes, and haddock filets. Season with salt. Assemble pressure lid, making sure the pressure release valve is in the SEAL position.

4. Select PRESSURE and set to HI. Set time to 5 minutes. Select START/STOP to begin.

5. Whisk together the clam juice and flour in a small bowl, ensuring there are no flour clumps in the mixture.

6. When pressure cooking is complete, quick release the pressure by moving the pressure release valve to the VENT position. Carefully remove lid when unit has finished releasing pressure.

7. Select SEAR/SAUTÉ and set to MED. Select START/STOP to begin. Add the clam juice mixture, stirring well to combine. Add the evaporated milk and continue to stir frequently

CONTINUED ▶

# Fish Chowder and Biscuits  continued

for 3 to 5 minutes, until chowder has thickened to your desired texture.

8. Place the Reversible Rack in the pot in the higher position. Place the biscuits on the rack; it may be necessary to tear the last biscuit or two into smaller pieces in order to fit them all on the rack. Close crisping lid.

9. Select BAKE/ROAST, set temperature to 350°F, and set time to 12 minutes. Select START/STOP to begin.

10. After 10 minutes, check the biscuits for doneness. If desired, cook for up to an additional 2 minutes.

11. When cooking is complete, open lid and remove rack from pot. Serve the chowder and top each portion with biscuits.

*Per serving: Calories: 518; Total Fat: 22g; Saturated Fat: 9g; Cholesterol: 140mg; Sodium: 1189mg; Carbohydrates: 49g; Fiber: 2g; Protein: 33g*

# Coconut and Shrimp Bisque by Chelven Randolph

**SERVES 4**

***Chef says:*** *I grew up eating a lot of shrimp and other seafood. Shrimp was always in our freezer. Once my mother made a lobster bisque for us, and I was so enamored with it that I've spent most of my cooking career attempting to replicate it. This is my take on that delicious bisque, with Thai flavors and shrimp instead of lobster. You can add some crushed pepper flakes or jalapeño if you like spice.*

DAIRY-FREE, GLUTEN-FREE, NUT-FREE, UNDER 30 MINUTES

**PREP TIME:** 10 minutes
**TOTAL COOK TIME:** 15 minutes
**SEAR/SAUTÉ:** 12 minutes

**HACK IT:** The base of this dish can be made in advance to save time if needed. Simply prepare the dish as written but omit the shrimp. Cool the base down and refrigerate in an airtight container until ready to serve. When you are ready to serve, place the bisque base in the cooking pot and heat on MD:LO for 5 minutes. Once heated, add the shrimp and continuously stir until the shrimp is cooked through. For added color and brightness, top with fresh chopped cilantro.

¼ **cup red curry paste**

2 **tablespoons water**

1 **tablespoon extra-virgin olive oil**

1 **bunch scallions, sliced**

1 **pound medium (21-30 count) shrimp, peeled and deveined**

1 **cup frozen peas**

1 **red bell pepper, diced**

1 **(14-ounce) can full-fat coconut milk**

**Kosher salt**

1. In a small bowl, whisk together the red curry paste and water. Set aside.

2. Select SEAR/SAUTÉ and set to MED. Select START/STOP to begin. Let preheat for 3 minutes.

3. Add the oil and scallions. Cook for 2 minutes.

4. Add the shrimp, peas, and bell pepper. Stir well to combine. Stir in the red curry paste. Cook for 5 minutes, until the peas are tender.

5. Stir in coconut milk and cook for an additional 5 minutes until shrimp is cooked through and the bisque is thoroughly heated.

6. Season with salt and serve immediately.

*Per serving: Calories: 460; Total Fat: 32g; Saturated Fat: 23g; Cholesterol: 223mg; Sodium: 902mg; Carbohydrates: 16g; Fiber: 5g; Protein: 29g*

# Roasted Tomato and Seafood Stew by Chelven Randolph

*Chef says:* The town I grew up in was predominantly Italian. When I first had cioppino, the dish that inspired this stew, I was blown away by the amount of different seafood my friend's mom stuffed into it. And the beauty of it was somehow none of it was over-cooked. The key is to slowly cook the seafood in the base. I love it served with toasted French bread or sourdough. If you have any leftover pasta kicking around, it also makes a great sauce.

**DAIRY-FREE, GLUTEN-FREE, NUT-FREE**

**PREP TIME:** 10 minutes
**TOTAL COOK TIME:**
46 minutes
**SEAR/SAUTÉ:** 43 minutes

**VARIATION TIP:** Fennel can be difficult to find, and some people do not like the flavor, which is slightly like black licorice. If you cannot readily find any, you can substitute 1 teaspoon of dry fennel seed that you toast with the onions and garlic. Also try mixing up the seafood you use. Mussels, littleneck clams, crab, scallops, squid, and other white fish work just as well! Simply simmer in the stew as you would the other seafood used here.

2 tablespoons extra-virgin olive oil

1 yellow onion, diced

1 fennel bulb, tops removed and bulb diced

3 garlic cloves, minced

1 cup dry white wine

2 (14.5-ounce) cans fire-roasted tomatoes

2 cups chicken stock

1 pound medium (21-30 count) shrimp, peeled and deveined

1 pound raw white fish (cod or haddock), cubed

Salt

Freshly ground black pepper

Fresh basil, torn, for garnish

1. Select SEAR/SAUTÉ and set to MED. Select START/STOP to begin. Let preheat for 3 minutes.

2. Add the olive oil, onions, fennel, and garlic. Cook for about 3 minutes, until translucent.

3. Add the white wine and deglaze, scraping any stuck bits from the bottom of the pot using a silicone spatula. Add the roasted tomatoes and chicken stock. Simmer for 25 to 30 minutes. Add the shrimp and white fish.

4. Select SEAR/SAUTÉ and set to MD:LO. Select START/STOP to begin.

5. Simmer for 10 minutes, stirring frequently, until the shrimp and fish are cooked through. Season with salt and pepper.

6. Ladle into bowl and serve topped with torn basil.

*Per serving: Calories: 301; Total Fat: 8g; Saturated Fat: 1g; Cholesterol: 99mg; Sodium: 808mg; Carbohydrates: 21g; Fiber: 4g; Protein: 26g*

# Chicken Enchilada Soup by Caroline Schliep

***Chef says:*** *Laden with tender chicken, fire-roasted tomatoes, creamy black beans, and crisp corn, this soup is overflowing with Mexican flavor. And with an endless amount of topping options, this soup allows for so many different flavors and textures. It will surely have you licking the bowl and asking for seconds.*

**DAIRY-FREE, GLUTEN-FREE, NUT-FREE, UNDER 30 MINUTES**

**PREP TIME:** 5 minutes
**TOTAL COOK TIME:** 30 minutes

**SEAR/SAUTÉ:** 2 minutes
**APPROX. PRESSURE BUILD:** 10 minutes
**PRESSURE COOK:** 9 minutes
**PRESSURE RELEASE:** 10 minutes, then Quick

**HACK IT:** For easier and quicker shredding, place the cooked chicken breasts in a stand mixer fitted with a paddle attachment and mix on medium speed.

1 tablespoon extra-virgin olive oil

1 small red onion, diced

2 (10-ounce) cans fire-roasted tomatoes with chiles

1 (15-ounce) can corn

1 (15-ounce) can black beans, rinsed and drained

1 (10-ounce) can red enchilada sauce

1 (10-ounce) can tomato paste

3 tablespoons taco seasoning

2 tablespoons freshly squeezed lime juice

2 (8-ounce) boneless, skinless chicken breasts

Salt

Freshly ground black pepper

1. Select SEAR/SAUTÉ and set temperature to MD:HI. Select START/STOP to begin. Let preheat for 5 minutes.

2. Place the olive oil and onion in the pot. Cook until the onions are translucent, about 2 minutes.

3. Add the tomatoes, corn, beans, enchilada sauce, tomato paste, taco seasoning, lime juice, and chicken. Season with salt and pepper and stir. Assemble pressure lid, making sure the pressure release valve is in the SEAL position.

4. Select PRESSURE and set to HI. Set time to 9 minutes. Select START/STOP to begin.

5. When pressure cooking is complete, allow pressure to naturally release for 10 minutes. After 10 minutes, quick release remaining pressure by moving the pressure release valve to the VENT position. Carefully remove lid when unit has finished releasing pressure.

6. Transfer the chicken breasts to a cutting board. Using two forks, shred the chicken. Return the chicken back to the pot and stir. Serve in a bowl with toppings of choice, such as shredded cheese, crushed tortilla chips, sliced avocado, sour cream, cilantro, and lime wedges, if desired.

Per serving: *Calories: 257; Total Fat: 4g; Saturated Fat: 0g; Cholesterol: 33mg; Sodium: 819mg; Carbohydrates: 37g; Fiber: 7g; Protein: 20g*

# Chicken Noodle Soup

**SERVES 8**

*When I am under the weather, there is only one thing that makes me feel better—soup and a grilled cheese sandwich. This chicken noodle soup is based on the recipe my grandma used to make when I was little. But unlike that recipe, this one is ready in less than 30 minutes, thanks to the Ninja® Foodi™ Pressure Cooker.*

NUT-FREE, UNDER
30 MINUTES, FAMILY
FAVORITE

**PREP TIME:** 10 minutes
**TOTAL COOK TIME:**
19 minutes

**SEAR/SAUTÉ:** 11 minutes
**APPROX. PRESSURE BUILD:**
10 minutes
**PRESSURE COOK:** 8 minutes
**PRESSURE RELEASE:** Quick

**VARIATION TIP:** Omit
the chicken in this recipe
and swap chicken broth
for vegetable broth for a
vegetarian vegetable soup.

2 tablespoons
  unsalted butter

1 large onion, chopped

2 carrots, chopped

2 celery stalks, chopped

2 pounds boneless
  chicken breast

4 cups chicken broth

4 cups water

1 tablespoon chopped
  fresh parsley

1 teaspoon dried thyme

1 teaspoon dried oregano

½ teaspoon sea salt

½ teaspoon freshly
  ground black pepper

5 ounces egg noodles

1.  Select SEAR/SAUTÉ and set to HI. Select START/STOP to begin. Let preheat for 5 minutes.

2.  Add the butter. Once melted, add the onion, carrots, and celery. Cook, stirring occasionally, for 5 minutes.

3.  Add the chicken, chicken broth, water, parsley, thyme, oregano, salt, and pepper. Assemble pressure lid, making sure the pressure release valve is in the SEAL position.

4.  Select PRESSURE and set to HI. Set time to 8 minutes. Select START/STOP to begin.

5.  When pressure cooking is complete, quick release the pressure by moving the pressure release valve to the VENT position. Carefully remove lid when unit has finished releasing pressure.

6.  Remove the chicken from the soup and shred it with two forks. Set aside.

7.  Add the egg noodles. Select SEAR/SAUTÉ and set to MED. Select START/STOP to begin.

8.  Cook for 6 minutes, uncovered, or until the noodles are tender. Stir the shredded chicken back into the pot. Serve.

*Per serving: Calories: 237; Total Fat: 5g; Saturated Fat: 2g; Cholesterol: 87mg; Sodium: 413mg; Carbohydrates: 17g; Fiber: 2g; Protein: 30g*

# Chicken Potpie Soup by Chelven Randolph

***Chef says:*** *Chicken potpie has always been my favorite comfort-style meal. I first made this dish years ago when I needed to create a soup but could not get potpie off my brain. It's a perfect dish for cold winter nights.*

NUT-FREE, 360 MEAL

**PREP TIME:** 15 minutes
**TOTAL COOK TIME:** 1 hour

**APPROX. PRESSURE BUILD:** 10 minutes
**PRESSURE COOK:** 15 minutes
**PRESSURE RELEASE:** Quick
**SEAR/SAUTÉ:** 20 minutes
**BAKE/ROAST:** 15 minutes

**VARIATION TIP:** Make this dish vegetarian-friendly by swapping in mushrooms and vegetable stock instead of chicken and chicken stock.

Per serving: *Calories: 731; Total Fat: 26g; Saturated Fat: 17g; Cholesterol: 169mg; Sodium: 1167mg; Carbohydrates: 56g; Fiber: 5g; Protein: 45g*

4 (8-ounce) chicken breasts

2 cups chicken stock

2 tablespoons unsalted butter

1 yellow onion, diced

16 ounces frozen mixed vegetables

1 cup heavy (whipping) cream

1 (10.5-ounce) can condensed cream of chicken soup

2 tablespoons cornstarch

2 tablespoons water

Salt

Freshly ground black pepper

1 (16.3-ounce) tube refrigerated biscuit dough

1. Place the chicken and stock in the pot. Assemble pressure lid, making sure the pressure release valve is in the SEAL position.

2. Select PRESSURE and set to HI. Set time to 15 minutes. Select START/STOP to begin.

3. Once pressure cooking is complete, quick release the pressure by turning the pressure release valve to the VENT position. Carefully remove lid when the unit has finished releasing pressure.

4. Using a silicone-tipped utensil, shred the chicken.

5. Select SEAR/SAUTÉ and set to MED. Add the butter, onion, mixed vegetables, cream, and condensed soup and stir. Select START/STOP to begin. Simmer for 10 minutes.

6. In a small bowl, whisk together the cornstarch and water. Slowly whisk the cornstarch mixture into the soup. Set temperature to LO and simmer for 10 minutes more. Season with salt and pepper.

7. Carefully arrange the biscuits on top of the simmering soup. Close crisping lid.

8. Select BAKE/ROAST, set temperature to 325ºF, and set time to 15 minutes. Select START/STOP to begin.

9. When cooking is complete, remove the biscuits. To serve, place a biscuit in a bowl and ladle soup over it.

# Tex-Mex Chicken Tortilla Soup

*This Mexican-inspired soup is a must-add to your Tex-Mex Tuesday rotation, packed with bold spices, hearty beans, and crunchy corn. Like a traditional tortilla soup, this version is served topped with crispy fried tortilla strips, but you can always sub in crumbled tortilla chips. You can also add fresh avocado, sour cream, and pico de gallo.*

**GLUTEN-FREE, NUT-FREE, UNDER 30 MINUTES**

**PREP TIME:** 10 minutes
**TOTAL COOK TIME:**
20 minutes

**SEAR/SAUTÉ:** 10 minutes
**APPROX. PRESSURE BUILD:**
10 minutes
**PRESSURE COOK:**
10 minutes
**PRESSURE RELEASE:**
10 minutes, then Quick

*Per serving: Calories: 186;
Total Fat: 4g; Saturated Fat: 0g;
Cholesterol: 33mg; Sodium: 783mg;
Carbohydrates: 23g; Fiber: 6g;
Protein: 19g*

- 1 tablespoon extra-virgin olive oil
- 1 onion, chopped
- 1 pound boneless, skinless chicken breasts
- 6 cups chicken broth
- 1 (12-ounce) jar salsa
- 4 ounces tomato paste
- 1 tablespoon chili powder
- 2 teaspoons cumin
- ½ teaspoon sea salt
- ½ teaspoon freshly ground black pepper
- 1 pinch of cayenne pepper
- 1 (15-ounce) can black beans, rinsed and drained
- 2 cups frozen corn
- Tortilla strips, for garnish

1. Select SEAR/SAUTÉ and set to temperature to HI. Select START/STOP to begin. Let preheat for 5 minutes.

2. Place the olive oil and onions into the pot and cook, stirring occasionally, for 5 minutes.

3. Add the chicken breast, chicken broth, salsa, tomato paste, chili powder, cumin, salt, pepper, and cayenne pepper. Assemble pressure lid, making sure the pressure release valve is in the SEAL position.

4. Select PRESSURE and set to HI. Set time to 10 minutes. Select START/STOP to begin.

5. When pressure cooking is complete, allow pressure to naturally release for 10 minutes. After 10 minutes, quick release remaining pressure by moving the pressure release valve to the VENT position. Carefully remove lid when unit has finished releasing pressure.

6. Transfer the chicken breasts to a cutting board and shred with two forks. Set aside.

7. Add the black beans and corn. Select SEAR/SAUTÉ and set to MD. Select START/STOP to begin. Cook until heated through, about 5 minutes.

8. Add shredded chicken back to the pot. Garnish with tortilla strips, serve, and enjoy!

# Chicken Tomatillo Stew by Kelly Gray

*Chef says:* *My college years were spent in Southern California soaking up sunshine, salsa dancing, and enjoying local cuisine every chance I had to step away from the books. Something I find so special about the region is its Mexican influence. Mexican culture revolves around music, community, family, and amazing food, all things that are near and dear to my heart. This recipe, my version of chili verde, was developed soon after I transitioned back to the East Coast and was in the mood for some authentic Mexican food. Roasted tomatillos, poblano peppers, onions, and garlic combine with chicken thighs for a savory stew that brings my taste buds back to Southern California. The stew can be enjoyed on its own, as a base for tacos, or as a nacho topping. Garnish with sour cream, a sprig of cilantro, and a wedge of lime.*

**DAIRY-FREE, GLUTEN-FREE, NUT-FREE**

**PREP TIME:** 15 minutes
**TOTAL COOK TIME:** 46 minutes

**AIR CRISP:** 20 minutes
**SEAR/SAUTÉ:** 16 minutes
**APPROX. PRESSURE BUILD:** 10 minutes
**PRESSURE COOK:** 10 minutes
**PRESSURE RELEASE:** Quick

**ACCESSORIES:** Cook & Crisp Basket

**VARIATION TIP:** Like it spicy? Add the seeds from the jalapeño peppers!

3 medium onions, quartered

3 garlic cloves, whole

2 poblano peppers, seeded and quartered

½ pound tomatillos

2 small jalapeño peppers, seeded and quartered (optional)

2 tablespoons canola oil, divided

Kosher salt

Freshly ground black pepper

2½ pounds boneless, skinless chicken thighs (6 to 8 pieces)

1 cup chicken stock

1 teaspoon cumin

1 tablespoon oregano

1 tablespoon all-purpose flour

1 cup water

1. Place Cook & Crisp Basket in pot and close crisping lid. Select AIR CRISP and set to HIGH. Set time to 25 minutes. Select START/STOP to begin. Let preheat for 5 minutes.

2. Place the onions, garlic, poblano peppers, tomatillos, jalapeños, 1 tablespoon of canola oil, salt, and pepper in a medium-sized bowl and mix until vegetables are evenly coated.

3. Once unit has preheated, open lid and place the vegetables in the basket. Close lid and cook for 20 minutes.

4. After 10 minutes, open lid, then lift basket and shake the vegetables or toss them with silicone-tipped tongs. Lower basket back into pot and close lid to continue cooking.

5. When cooking is complete, remove basket and vegetables and set aside.

6. Select SEAR/SAUTÉ and set to HI. Select START/STOP to begin. Let preheat for 5 minutes.

7. Season the chicken thighs with salt and pepper.

8. After 5 minutes, add the remaining 1 tablespoon of oil and chicken. Sear the chicken, about 3 minutes on each side.

9. Add the chicken stock, cumin, and oregano. Scrape the pot with a rubber or wooden spoon to release any pieces that are sticking to the bottom. Assemble pressure lid, making sure the pressure release valve is in the SEAL position.

10. Select PRESSURE and set to HI. Set time to 10 minutes. Select START/STOP to begin.

11. Remove the vegetables from the basket and roughly chop.

12. In a small bowl, add the flour and water and stir.

13. When pressure cooking is complete, quick release the pressure by turning the pressure release valve to the VENT position. Carefully remove lid when unit has finished releasing pressure.

14. Remove the chicken and shred it using two forks.

15. Select SEAR/SAUTÉ and set to MED. Select START/STOP to begin. Return the chicken and vegetables and stir with a rubber or wooden spoon, being sure to scrape the bottom of the pot. Slowly stir in the flour mixture. Bring to a simmer and cook for 10 minutes, or until the broth becomes clear and has thickened.

16. When cooking is complete, serve as is or garnish with sour cream, lime, cilantro, and a flour tortilla for dipping.

*Per serving: Calories: 487; Total Fat: 20g; Saturated Fat: 3g; Cholesterol: 239mg; Sodium: 382mg; Carbohydrates: 19g; Fiber: 4g; Protein: 59g*

# Jamaican Jerk Chicken Stew by Sam Ferguson

**SERVES 6**

***Chef says:*** *This dish is packed with flavor and relatively light fare—you'll feel full and satisfied without that sluggish sensation that often accompanies overindulgence. For even more island punch, I like to add several shakes of hot sauce to the stew in step 7.*

DAIRY-FREE, GLUTEN-FREE, NUT-FREE, UNDER 30 MINUTES

PREP TIME: 15 minutes
TOTAL COOK TIME: 28 minutes

SEAR/SAUTÉ: 10 minutes
APPROX. PRESSURE BUILD: 10 minutes
PRESSURE COOK: 18 minutes
PRESSURE RELEASE: 10 minutes, then Quick

VARIATION TIP: Want to try this dish with something other than chicken? Substitute cubed pork or beef in step 2.

- 2 tablespoons canola oil
- 6 boneless, skinless chicken thighs, cut in 2-inch pieces
- 2 tablespoons Jamaican jerk spice
- 1 white onion, peeled and chopped
- 2 red bell peppers, chopped
- ½ head green cabbage, core removed and cut into 2-inch pieces
- 1½ cups wild rice blend, rinsed
- 4 cups chicken stock
- ½ cup prepared Jamaican jerk sauce
- Kosher salt

1. Select SEAR/SAUTÉ and set to HI. Select START/STOP to begin. Let preheat for 5 minutes.

2. Add the oil, chicken, and jerk spice and stir. Cook for 5 minutes, stirring occasionally.

3. Add the onions, bell pepper, and cabbage and stir. Cook for 5 minutes, stirring occasionally.

4. Add the wild rice and stock, stirring well to combine. Assemble pressure lid, making sure the pressure release valve is in the SEAL position.

5. Select PRESSURE and set to HI. Set time to 18 minutes. Select START/STOP to begin.

6. When pressure cooking is complete, allow pressure to naturally release for 10 minutes. After 10 minutes, quick release any remaining pressure by moving the pressure release valve to the VENT position. Carefully remove lid when unit has finished releasing pressure.

7. Add the jerk sauce to pot, stirring well to combine. Let the stew sit for 5 minutes, allowing it to thicken. Season with salt and serve.

*Per serving: Calories: 404; Total Fat: 10g; Saturated Fat: 1g; Cholesterol: 95mg; Sodium: 373mg; Carbohydrates: 53g; Fiber: 3g; Protein: 29g*

# Chicken Chili

**SERVES 8**

*This chili is a great alternative to a traditional beef chili. A true one pot wonder, it is my go-to on a chilly evening when I am looking for a quick homemade meal with little effort. The jalapeño and green peppers add just the right amount of spice, while the cannellini beans add creaminess. This is a different chili option because the broth is light, but if you want a thicker broth, stir in sour cream with the beans.*

**DAIRY-FREE, NUT-FREE, UNDER 30 MINUTES**

**PREP TIME:** 10 minutes
**TOTAL COOK TIME:**
30 minutes

**SEAR/SAUTÉ:** 5 minutes
**APPROX. PRESSURE BUILD:**
10 minutes
**PRESSURE COOK:**
15 minutes
**PRESSURE RELEASE:** Quick

1 tablespoon extra-virgin olive oil
1 yellow onion, chopped
4 garlic cloves, minced
2 pounds boneless chicken breast, cut in half crosswise
4 cups chicken broth
1 green bell pepper, seeded and chopped
2 jalapeños, seeded and chopped
1½ tablespoons ground cumin
1 tablespoon coriander
1 teaspoon dried oregano
1 teaspoon sea salt
1 teaspoon freshly ground black pepper
2 (15.5-ounce) cans cannellini beans, rinsed and drained
Shredded Monterey Jack cheese, for garnish
Chopped cilantro, for garnish
Lime wedge, for garnish

1. Select SEAR/SAUTÉ and set to HI. Select START/STOP to begin. Let preheat for 5 minutes.

2. Add the oil and onions and cook, stirring occasionally, for 3 minutes. Add the garlic and cook for 2 minutes.

3. Add the chicken breast, chicken broth, green bell pepper, jalapeño, cumin, coriander, oregano, salt, and black pepper. Assemble pressure lid, making sure the pressure release valve is in the SEAL position.

4. Select PRESSURE and set to HI. Set time to 15 minutes. Select START/STOP to begin.

5. When pressure cooking is complete, quick release the pressure by turning the pressure release valve to the VENT position. Carefully remove lid when unit has finished releasing pressure.

6. Remove the chicken from the soup and shred it using two forks. Set aside.

CONTINUED ▶

# Chicken Chili continued

7. Add the cannellini beans. Select SEAR/SAUTÉ and set to MED. Select START/STOP to begin. Cook until heated through, about 5 minutes.

8. Add shredded chicken back to the pot. Serve, garnished with the cheese, cilantro, and lime wedge (if using).

Per serving: *Calories: 279; Total Fat: 9g; Saturated Fat: 0g; Cholesterol: 23mg; Sodium: 523mg; Carbohydrates: 18g; Fiber: 6g; Protein: 32g*

# Pho Tom

**by CJ Volkmann, Ninja® Foodi™ Family Member**

**SERVES 6**

***CJ says:*** *This recipe will show you how to make an easy and fast pho broth and turn it into a wonderful bowl of pho tom—pho with shrimp. A good pho broth takes hours to simmer on a stove—but I do it in less than an hour in my Ninja Foodi.*

DAIRY-FREE, FAMILY
FAVORITE, NUT-FREE

PREP TIME: 10 minutes
TOTAL COOK TIME:
36 minutes

SEAR/SAUTÉ: 6 minutes
APPROX. PRESSURE BUILD:
10 minutes
PRESSURE COOK:
30 minutes
PRESSURE RELEASE: Quick

*Per serving: Calories: 242;*
*Total Fat: 7g; Saturated Fat: 2g;*
*Cholesterol: 168mg; Sodium: 2419mg;*
*Carbohydrates: 25g; Fiber: 2g;*
*Protein: 22g*

**Find CJ on Facebook &
YouTube: Cooking with CJ**

2 tablespoons canola oil

1 onion, peeled and halved

1 (2-inch) piece fresh
  ginger, peeled

2 tablespoons
  brown sugar

2 tablespoons kosher salt

1½ tablespoons Chinese
  five-spice powder

¼ cup fish sauce

4 cups beef bone broth

8 cups water

1 (14-ounce) package rice
  noodles, cooked according
  to the package directions

1 pound (16 to 20) peeled
  cooked shrimp

Bean sprouts, for
  topping (optional)

Lime wedges, for
  serving (optional)

Fresh basil, for
  topping (optional)

Sriracha, for
  topping (optional)

1.  Select SEAR/SAUTÉ and set temperature to HI. Select START/STOP to begin. Allow to preheat for 5 minutes.

2.  Add oil to the pot and allow to heat for 1 minute. Add the onion and ginger and sear on all sides, about 6 minutes. Select START/STOP to end the function.

3.  Add the sugar, salt, five-spice powder, fish sauce, bone broth, and water. Stir for 1 minute to combine.

4.  Assemble the pressure lid, making sure the pressure release valve is in the SEAL position.

5.  Select PRESSURE and set to HI. Set the time to 30 minutes. Select START/STOP to begin.

6.  When pressure cooking is complete, quick release the pressure by turning the pressure release valve to the VENT position. Carefully remove the lid when the unit has finished releasing pressure.

7.  Add the desired amount of noodles to a bowl and top with 5 or 6 shrimp and some sliced onion. Ladle the pho broth to cover the noodles, shrimp, and onion. Top as desired.

# Lasagna Soup

*This soup is one of my all-time favorites because it reminds me of my family. Growing up, my uncle was always making meatballs and sauce or lasagna, and all the cousins would get together for a big pasta dinner. It is a tradition we still keep whenever we are back in our hometown, and it is a special time that I always hold close to my heart. This soup is packed with the hearty lasagna flavors I love and remind me of family—served up in a bowl. Most importantly it is topped with ooey gooey bubbling cheese.*

**NUT-FREE, UNDER 30 MINUTES, FAMILY FAVORITE**

**PREP TIME:** 10 minutes
**TOTAL COOK TIME:** 16 minutes

**SEAR/SAUTÉ:** 10 minutes
**APPROX. PRESSURE BUILD:** 10 minutes
**PRESSURE COOK:** 6 minutes
**PRESSURE RELEASE:** Quick
**BROIL:** 5 minutes

1 tablespoon extra-virgin olive oil
16 ounces Italian sausage
1 small onion, diced
4 garlic cloves, minced
1 (24-ounce) jar marinara sauce
2 cups water
1 cup vegetable broth
1 teaspoon dried basil
1 teaspoon dried oregano
½ teaspoon dried thyme

Freshly ground black pepper
8 ounces lasagna noodles, broken up
1 cup ricotta cheese
½ cup grated Parmesan cheese
1 teaspoon dried parsley
½ cup heavy (whipping) cream
1 cup shredded mozzarella cheese

1. Select SEAR/SAUTÉ and set to HI. Select START/STOP to begin. Let preheat for 5 minutes.

2. Add the oil and sausage and cook for about 5 minutes. Using a wooden spoon, break apart the sausage and stir.

3. Add the onions and cook, stirring occasionally, for 3 minutes. Add the garlic and cook for 2 minutes, or until the meat is no longer pink.

4. Add the marinara sauce, water, vegetable broth, basil, oregano, thyme, pepper, and lasagna noodles. Assemble pressure lid, making sure the pressure release valve is in the SEAL position.

5. Select PRESSURE and set to HI. Set time to 6 minutes. Select START/STOP to begin.

6. In a medium bowl, combine the ricotta cheese, Parmesan cheese, and parsley. Cover and refrigerate.

7. When pressure cooking is complete, quick release the pressure by turning the pressure release valve to the VENT position. Carefully remove lid when unit has finished releasing pressure.

8. Stir in the heavy cream. Add the cheese mixture and stir. Top the soup with the mozzarella. Close crisping lid.

9. Select BROIL and set time to 5 minutes. Select START/ STOP to begin.

10. When cooking is complete, serve immediately.

**Per serving:** *Calories: 398; Total Fat: 22g; Saturated Fat: 10g; Cholesterol: 70mg; Sodium: 892mg; Carbohydrates: 29g; Fiber: 2g; Protein: 23g*

# Chickpea, Spinach, and Sweet Potato Stew

**SERVES 6**

*Pressure cookers make a stew that's as hearty, flavorful, and tender as if you had cooked it for hours on the stove. This vegan stew is great with any hardy root vegetable, taking it from raw to melt-in-your-mouth tender in minutes. Use this recipe as a base for other vegetarian and vegan stews: just swap out the sweet potato for other root veggies and the chickpeas for whatever lentils or beans you have in the pantry.*

**DAIRY-FREE, GLUTEN-FREE, NUT-FREE, VEGAN, UNDER 30 MINUTES**

**PREP TIME:** 15 minutes
**TOTAL COOK TIME:** 23 minutes

**SEAR/SAUTÉ:** 5 minutes
**APPROX. PRESSURE BUILD:** 8 minutes
**PRESSURE COOK:** 8 minutes
**PRESSURE RELEASE:** Quick

**SUBSTITUTION TIP:** You can also make this recipe using the slow cooker function. Instead of using PRESSURE, select SLOW COOK and set to LO for 6 to 7 hours. Stir in the spinach before serving.

1 tablespoon extra-virgin olive oil
1 yellow onion, diced
4 garlic cloves, minced
4 sweet potatoes, peeled and diced
4 cups vegetable broth
1 (15-ounce) can fire-roasted diced tomatoes, undrained
2 (15-ounce) cans chickpeas, drained
1½ teaspoons ground cumin
1 teaspoon ground coriander
½ teaspoon paprika
½ teaspoon sea salt
½ teaspoon freshly ground black pepper
4 cups baby spinach

1. Select SEAR/SAUTÉ and set to MD:HI. Select START/STOP to begin. Allow the pot to preheat for 5 minutes.

2. Combine the oil, onion, and garlic in the pot. Cook, stirring occasionally, for 5 minutes.

3. Add the sweet potatoes, vegetable broth, tomatoes, chickpeas, cumin, coriander, paprika, salt, and black pepper to the pot. Assemble the pressure lid, making sure the pressure release valve is in the SEAL position.

4. Select PRESSURE and set to HI. Set the time to 8 minutes, then select START/STOP to begin.

5. When pressure cooking is complete, quick release the pressure by moving the pressure release valve to the VENT position. Carefully remove the lid when the unit has finished releasing pressure.

6. Add the spinach to the pot and stir until wilted. Serve.

*Per serving: Calories: 220; Total Fat: 4g; Saturated Fat: 0g; Cholesterol: 0mg; Sodium: 593mg; Carbohydrates: 42g; Fiber: 8g; Protein: 7g*

# 6
# Meatless

# Quinoa Stuffed Butternut Squash by Caroline Schliep

*Chef says:* This meal is something I came up with while in culinary school during my vegetarian cuisine class. It's an uber simple dish with an amazing array of colors and flavors, including a flawless combination of fresh citrus, wilted kale, creamy chick-peas, and tri-colored quinoa all nestled in a perfectly cooked butternut squash. It is a delicious and effortless workweek lunch that will leave you forgetting you ever wanted meat in the first place.

**DAIRY-FREE, GLUTEN-FREE, VEGAN, UNDER 30 MINUTES**

**PREP TIME:** 10 minutes
**TOTAL COOK TIME:** 13 minutes

**SEAR/SAUTÉ:** 2 minutes
**APPROX. PRESSURE BUILD:** 10 minutes
**PRESSURE COOK:** 10 minutes
**PRESSURE RELEASE:** 10 minutes, then Quick

**ACCESSORIES:** Reversible Rack

**SUBSTITUTION TIP:** Don't have dried cranberries? Use raisins or your favorite dried fruit.

- 2 tablespoons extra-virgin olive oil
- 1 tablespoon minced garlic
- 1 small shallot, minced
- Kosher salt
- Freshly ground black pepper
- ½ cup dried cranberries
- 1 cup tri-colored quinoa
- 2¾ cups water, divided
- 2 cups roughly chopped kale
- 1 small butternut squash, top trimmed, halved lengthwise
- 1 tablespoon freshly squeezed orange juice
- Zest of 1 orange
- 1 (2-ounce) jar pine nuts
- 1 (15-ounce) can chickpeas, rinsed and drained

1. Select SEAR/SAUTÉ and set to HI. Select START/STOP to begin. Let preheat for 5 minutes.

2. Add the olive oil, garlic, shallot, salt, and pepper. Cook until garlic and shallot have softened and turned golden brown, about 2 minutes.

3. Stir in the cranberries, quinoa, and 1¼ cups of water. Assemble pressure lid, making sure the pressure release valve is in the SEAL position.

4. Select PRESSURE and set to HI. Set time to 2 minutes. Select START/STOP to begin.

5. When pressure cooking is complete, allow pressure to naturally release for 10 minutes. After 10 minutes, quick release remaining pressure by turning the pressure release valve to the VENT position. Carefully remove lid when the unit has finished releasing pressure.

6. Place the quinoa in a large bowl. Stir in the kale. Cover the bowl with aluminum foil and set aside.

CONTINUED ▶

# Quinoa Stuffed Butternut Squash continued

7. Pour the remaining 1½ cups of water into the pot. Place the butternut squash cut-side up on the Reversible Rack, then lower it into the pot. Assemble pressure lid, making sure the pressure release valve is in the SEAL position.

8. Select PRESSURE and set to HI. Set the time to 8 minutes. Select START/STOP to begin.

9. Mix the orange juice, orange zest, pine nuts, and chickpeas into the quinoa mixture.

10. When pressure cooking is complete, quick release the pressure by turning the pressure release valve to the VENT position. Carefully remove lid when unit has finished releasing pressure.

11. Carefully remove rack from pot. Using a spoon slightly hollow out the squash. Spoon the quinoa mixture into the squash. Cut in half and serve.

Per serving: *Calories: 563; Total Fat: 21g; Saturated Fat: 2g; Cholesterol: 0mg; Sodium: 66mg; Carbohydrates: 83g; Fiber: 13g; Protein: 16g*

# Roasted Cauliflower Salad

**SERVES 6**

*When you think of salad you probably think of cool and crisp veggies. Why not change it up with a little heat and crispiness? The cauliflower and chickpeas get nice and toasty in the Cook & Crisp Basket and complement tender baby greens. Top it all off with a little feta cheese and a simple mustard dressing, and you have a salad fit for any meal.*

**GLUTEN-FREE, NUT-FREE, VEGETARIAN, UNDER 30 MINUTES, FAMILY FAVORITE**

**PREP TIME:** 10 minutes
**TOTAL COOK TIME:** 15 minutes

**AIR CRISP:** 15 minutes

**ACCESSORIES:** Cook & Crisp Basket

1 head cauliflower, cut into florets

1 (14-ounce) can chickpeas, rinsed and drained

3 tablespoons, plus ¼ cup extra-virgin olive oil

1 tablespoon chili powder

2 teaspoons paprika

3 garlic cloves, minced

4 cups mixed baby greens

1 cucumber, sliced

3 tablespoons chopped fresh parsley

Juice of 1 lemon

2 tablespoons honey

2 tablespoons Dijon mustard

2 tablespoons apple cider vinegar

⅓ cup crumbled feta cheese

Sea salt

Freshly ground black pepper

1. Insert Cook & Crisp Basket in pot. Close crisping lid. Select AIR CRISP, set temperature to 390ºF, and set the time to 5 minutes. Select START/STOP to begin preheating.

2. In a large bowl combine the cauliflower florets, chickpeas, 3 tablespoons of olive oil, chili powder, paprika, and garlic.

3. Once unit has preheated, open lid and add the cauliflower and chickpeas to the basket. Close lid.

4. Select AIR CRISP, set temperature to 390ºF, and set time to 15 minutes. Select START/STOP to begin.

5. In another large bowl, combine the mixed greens, cucumber, and parsley.

6. In a small bowl, whisk together the lemon juice, honey, mustard, and vinegar.

7. When cooking is complete, carefully remove basket with cauliflower and chickpeas. Add them to the bowl of greens and toss well to combine. Top with feta cheese and dressing, season with salt and pepper, and serve.

*Per serving: Calories: 291; Total Fat: 20g; Saturated Fat: 4g; Cholesterol: 7mg; Sodium: 226mg; Carbohydrates: 36g; Fiber: 6g; Protein: 7g*

# Mushroom Poutine by Chelven Randolph

SERVES 4

**Chef says:** *Poutine is a French-Canadian dish that tops roasted or fried potatoes with a brown gravy and cheese curds. When I worked at a French bistro, we served it with a chicken stock-based gravy and would sometimes add meat like ground pork. For this recipe I substituted mushrooms to provide a great meat-like texture in a vegetarian dish.*

**NUT-FREE, VEGETARIAN**

**PREP TIME:** 10 minutes
**TOTAL COOK TIME:**
46 minutes

**SEAR/SAUTÉ:** 23 minutes
**AIR CRISP:** 23 minutes

**ACCESSORIES:** Cook & Crisp Basket

**SUBSTITUTION TIP:** Classic poutine is served with cheese curds. You may be able to find them in the specialty section of your grocery store. If not, fontina cheese is a great substitute.

**Per serving:** *Calories: 550; Total Fat: 32g; Saturated Fat: 17g; Cholesterol: 75mg; Sodium: 941mg; Carbohydrates: 42g; Fiber: 3g; Protein: 20g*

**2 tablespoons unsalted butter**

**1 small yellow onion, diced**

**1 garlic clove, minced**

**8 ounces cremini mushrooms, sliced**

**¼ cup red wine**

**3 cups vegetable stock**

**¼ cup all-purpose flour**

**Kosher salt**

**Freshly ground black pepper**

**1 pound frozen French fries**

**8 ounces Cheddar cheese, cubed**

1. Select SEAR/SAUTÉ and set to MED. Select START/STOP to begin. Let preheat for 3 minutes.

2. Add the butter, onion, and garlic. Cook, stirring occasionally, for 5 minutes. Add the mushrooms and sauté for 5 minutes. Add the wine and let it simmer and reduce for 3 minutes.

3. In large bowl, slowly whisk together the stock and flour. Whisk this mixture into the vegetables in the pot. Cook the gravy for 10 minutes. Season with salt and pepper. Transfer the gravy to a medium bowl and set aside. Clean out the pot and return to unit.

4. Insert Cook & Crisp Basket and add the French fries. Close crisping lid.

5. Select AIR CRISP, set temperature to 360°F, and set time to 18 minutes. Select START/STOP to begin.

6. Every 5 minutes, open lid and remove and shake basket to ensure even cooking.

7. Once cooking is complete, remove fries from basket and place in the pot. Add the cheese and stir. Cover with the gravy. Close crisping lid.

8. Select AIR CRISP, set temperature to 375°F, and set time 5 minutes. Select START/STOP to begin.

9. When cooking is complete, serve immediately.

# Whole Roasted Cabbage with White Wine Cream Sauce by Caroline Schliep

**SERVES 8**

**Chef says:** *I've hated cabbage for as long as I can remember—sauerkraut being the culprit for it all. But when fresh cabbage is roasted to utter perfection, drowned in a creamy white wine sauce, and topped with fresh herbs, it is truly delectable. This whole roasted cabbage is an eye-catching dish that is sure to amaze any guest, make the perfect holiday meal, or serve as a quick meatless Monday dinner option.*

**GLUTEN-FREE, NUT-FREE, VEGETARIAN, UNDER 30 MINUTES**

**PREP TIME:** 5 minutes
**TOTAL COOK TIME:** 32 minutes

**APPROX. PRESSURE BUILD:** 10 minutes
**PRESSURE COOK:** 15 minutes
**PRESSURE RELEASE:** Quick
**AIR CRISP:** 12 minutes
**SEAR/SAUTÉ:** 8 minutes

**SUBSTITUTION TIP:** Want to make this vegan? Just swap the heavy cream for full-fat coconut milk.

1 head green cabbage

½ cup, plus 1 tablespoon water

1 tablespoon extra-virgin olive oil

Kosher salt

Freshly ground black pepper

2 cups white wine

¼ cup minced red onion

1 cup heavy (whipping) cream

¼ cup minced fresh dill

¼ cup minced fresh parsley

2 tablespoons whole-grain mustard

1 tablespoon cornstarch

1. Place the cabbage and ½ cup of water, stem-side down, in the pot.

2. With a knife cut an X into the top of the cabbage cutting all the way through to the bottom through the core. Assemble pressure lid, making sure the pressure release valve is in the SEAL position.

3. Select PRESSURE and set temperature to HI. Set time to 15 minutes. Select START/STOP to begin.

4. When pressure cooking is complete, quick release the pressure by turning the pressure release valve to the VENT position. Carefully remove lid when unit has finished releasing pressure.

5. Brush the cabbage with the olive oil and season with salt and pepper. Close crisping lid.

6. Select AIR CRISP, set temperature to 390°F, and set time to 12 minutes. Select START/STOP to begin.

7. Once cooking is complete, open lid, lift out the cabbage, wrap with foil, and set aside. Leave any remaining water in the pot.

8. Select SEAR/SAUTÉ. Set temperature to HI. Select START/STOP to begin.

9. Add the white wine and onion and stir, scraping any brown bits off the bottom of the pot. Stir in the cream, dill, parsley, and mustard. Let simmer for 5 minutes.

10. In a small bowl, whisk together the cornstarch and the remaining 1 tablespoon of water until smooth. Stir it into the mixture in the pot. Cook until the sauce has thickened and coats the back of a spoon, about 2 minutes.

11. Pour half of the sauce over the cabbage. Cut the cabbage into 8 pieces and serve with remaining sauce.

*Per serving: Calories: 206; Total Fat: 14g; Saturated Fat: 8g; Cholesterol: 41mg; Sodium: 129mg; Carbohydrates: 10g; Fiber: 3g; Protein: 3g*

# Quick Indian-Style Curry

by Katie Spurlock, Ninja® Foodi™ Family Member

**SERVES 8**

***Katie says:*** *Typical Indian food is deliciously slow cooked—pungent and full of spices and exotic flavors. Get those same flavors faster in your own kitchen! Serve with naan or rice, or your favorite Indian appetizer.*

DAIRY-FREE, FAMILY
FAVORITE, GLUTEN-FREE,
NUT-FREE, VEGAN

PREP TIME: 15 minutes
TOTAL COOK TIME:
35 minutes

SEAR/SAUTÉ: 5 minutes
PRESSURE COOK:
15 minutes
APPROX. PRESSURE BUILD:
10 minutes
PRESSURE RELEASE:
10 minutes, then Quick

INGREDIENT TIP: Paneer
is available at specialty
grocers, such as Whole
Foods, or Indian groceries. It
originated as a simple farm
cheese made from milk. You
can find garam masala in the
same places and in many
grocery stores.

1 tablespoon vegetable oil

1 small onion, diced

1 small bell pepper, diced

1 large potato, cut
into 1-inch cubes

1 teaspoon ground turmeric

1 teaspoon cumin seeds

1 teaspoon ground cumin

1 teaspoon garam
masala (optional)

1 teaspoon curry powder

1 (15-ounce) jar curry
sauce, plus 1 jar water

1 (14-ounce) can
diced tomatoes

1 cup dried red lentils

8 ounces paneer,
cubed (optional)

1 cup fresh cilantro, roughly
chopped (optional)

Salt

Freshly ground black pepper

1. Select SEAR/SAUTÉ and set temperature to HI. Select START/STOP to begin and allow to preheat for 5 minutes.

2. Add the oil to the pot and allow to heat for 1 minute. Add the onion and bell pepper and sauté for 3 to 4 minutes.

3. Add the potato, turmeric, cumin seeds, cumin, garam masala, and curry powder. Stir and cook for 5 minutes.

4. Stir in the curry sauce, water, tomatoes, and lentils.

5. Assemble the pressure lid, making sure the pressure release valve is in the SEAL position.

6. Select PRESSURE and set to HI. Set the time to 15 minutes. Select START/STOP to begin.

7. When pressure cooking is complete, allow the pressure to naturally release for 10 minutes. After 10 minutes, quick release any remaining pressure by moving the pressure release valve to the VENT position. Carefully remove the lid when the unit has finished releasing pressure.

8. Stir in the paneer (if using) and cilantro. Taste and season with salt and pepper, as needed.

*Per serving: Calories: 217; Total Fat: 6g; Saturated Fat: 0g; Cholesterol: 0mg; Sodium: 27mg; Carbohydrates: 33g; Fiber: 10g; Protein: 8g*

# Whole Roasted Broccoli and White Beans with Harissa, Tahini, and Lemon by Craig White

**SERVES 4**

***Chef says:*** *My buddy Dave and I were always finding new ways to put broccoli on the menu. He used to leave roasted broccoli, cheese, and sriracha sandwiches on my station when he knew I was "hangry" and needed a quick bite. We always found ourselves roasting broccoli as it intensifies the flavor and brings out a nuttiness you don't get when it's raw or steamed. The Middle Eastern condiments harissa and tahini really bring the flavor in this vegetarian option.*

**GLUTEN-FREE, VEGETARIAN, UNDER 30 MINUTES**

**PREP TIME:** 10 minutes
**TOTAL COOK TIME:** 30 minutes

**APPROX. PRESSURE BUILD:** 10 minutes
**STEAM:** 8 minutes
**PRESSURE RELEASE:** Quick
**SEAR/SAUTÉ:** 7 minutes
**AIR CRISP:** 15 minutes

**ACCESSORIES:**
Reversible Rack

**INGREDIENT INFO:** I worked an event with famed chef Yotam Ottolenghi. His use of vegetables and spices really inspired me not to overlook vegetables, that they themselves can be a truly satisfying, nourishing, and interesting meal. Since that day I have tried my best to give vegetables the respect that they deserve.

2 cups water

2 small heads broccoli, cut in half

2 tablespoons unsalted butter

½ white onion, minced

2 garlic cloves, minced

1 (15.5-ounce) can cannellini beans, rinsed and drained

1 (10-ounce) can fire-roasted tomatoes and peppers

1 tablespoon spicy harissa

Sea salt

Freshly ground black pepper

¼ cup tahini

¼ cup walnuts, toasted and chopped

Zest of 1 lemon

Juice of 1 lemon

1. Place Reversible Rack in pot, making sure it is in the lowest position. Pour the water into the pot and place the broccoli on the rack. Assemble the pressure lid, making sure the pressure release valve is in the SEAL position.

2. Select STEAM. Set time to 8 minutes. Select START/STOP to begin.

3. When steaming is complete, quick release the pressure by turning the pressure release valve to the VENT position. Carefully remove lid when unit has finished releasing pressure.

4. Remove rack and broccoli and set aside. Drain the remaining water from the pot and reinsert it in base.

5. Select SEAR/SAUTÉ and set to HI. Select START/STOP to begin. Let preheat for 5 minutes.

CONTINUED ▶

# Whole Roasted Broccoli and White Beans with Harissa, Tahini, and Lemon continued

6. Add the butter to pot. Once melted, add the onions and garlic and cook for 3 minutes. Add the beans, tomatoes, harissa, and season with salt and pepper. Cook for 4 minutes.

7. Reinsert rack and broccoli. Close crisping lid.

8. Select AIR CRISP, set temperature to 390°F, and set time to 15 minutes. Select START/STOP to begin.

9. After 10 minutes, open lid and flip the broccoli. Close lid and continue cooking.

10. When cooking is complete, remove rack with broccoli from pot. Place the beans in serving dishes and top with the broccoli. Drizzle tahini over the broccoli and sprinkle with walnuts. Garnish with the lemon zest and juice and serve.

*Per serving: Calories: 426; Total Fat: 25g; Saturated Fat: 6g; Cholesterol: 15mg; Sodium: 435mg; Carbohydrates: 39g; Fiber: 13g; Protein: 15g*

# Tempeh Hash by Chelven Randolph

SERVES 6

***Chef says:*** *This dish is one I created for a vegan brunch I once catered. I wanted something that was still in the style of my Southern roots while incorporating seasonal ingredients and contemporary techniques. This hash came out so well that I serve it at home. If you are not able to find tempeh, you can use pressed tofu instead by searing it the same way you would the tempeh.*

**DAIRY-FREE, NUT-FREE, VEGAN, UNDER 30 MINUTES**

**PREP TIME:** 20 minutes
**TOTAL COOK TIME:**
20 minutes

**APPROX. PRESSURE BUILD:**
10 minutes
**PRESSURE COOK:** 2 minutes
**PRESSURE RELEASE:** Quick
**SEAR/SAUTÉ:** 5 minutes
**AIR CRISP:** 10 minutes

**ACCESSORIES:** Cook & Crisp Basket

**INGREDIENT INFO:** Tempeh is a dense, cake-like plant-based option made from cooked and slightly fermented soybeans. Tempeh is high in protein and is widely used in place of meat for vegans, vegetarians, and those looking to eat less meat.

2 pounds Red Bliss potatoes, diced
½ cup water
2 tablespoons coconut oil
8 ounces tempeh, diced
1 yellow onion, diced
3 garlic cloves, minced
3 Roma tomatoes, diced

Kosher salt
Freshly ground black pepper
2 tablespoons soy sauce
1 tablespoon maple syrup
2 cups baby kale
1 ripe avocado, diced

1. Place the potatoes in the Cook & Crisp Basket. Add the water to the pot and insert basket into unit. Assemble pressure lid, making sure the pressure release valve is in the SEAL position.

2. Select PRESSURE and set to HI. Set time to 2 minutes. Select START/STOP to begin.

3. Once pressure cooking is complete, quick release the pressure by turning the pressure release valve to the VENT position. Carefully remove lid when unit has finished releasing pressure.

4. Remove basket. Drain any remaining water from the pot and reinsert it into base.

5. Select SEAR/SAUTÉ and set to MD:HI. Select START/STOP to begin. Let preheat for 3 minutes.

6. Add the coconut oil and tempeh. Crisp the tempeh for 5 minutes, stirring occasionally.

7. Transfer the tempeh to a plate and add the onion, garlic, and tomatoes. Season with salt and pepper. Stir to incorporate, then add the potatoes.

8. Press START/STOP to pause. Stir in the tempeh, soy sauce, and maple syrup. Fold in the kale. Close crisping lid.

CONTINUED ▶

# Tempeh Hash continued

9. Select AIR CRISP, set temperature to 375ºF, and set time to 10 minutes. Select START/STOP to begin.

10. When cooking is complete, top with diced avocados and serve.

**Per serving:** *Calories: 311; Total Fat: 13g; Saturated Fat: 4g; Cholesterol: 0mg; Sodium: 356mg; Carbohydrates: 40g; Fiber: 7g; Protein: 13g*

# Spicy Kimchi and Tofu Fried Rice by Craig White

SERVES 6

***Chef says:*** *Fried rice would be on my "Last Meal" menu if I had to write one. This recipe is a mashup of some of the best versions I've ever had. The Thai basil fried rice at Kowloon in Saugus, Massachusetts, is the one I always crave. If you're not enjoying a Mai Tai while you're cooking this, you're doing it wrong.*

DAIRY-FREE, NUT-FREE, VEGAN, UNDER 30 MINUTES

PREP TIME: 10 minutes
TOTAL COOK TIME:
30 minutes

APPROX. PRESSURE BUILD:
10 minutes
PRESSURE COOK: 2 minutes
PRESSURE RELEASE:
10 minutes, then Quick
SEAR/SAUTÉ: 12 minutes

HACK IT: Cooling the rice overnight after cooking makes for rice that doesn't clump up and stick. While you're cooling the rice, why not freeze that tofu? Freezing tofu gives it extra bite and chew. Marinate it if you really want to chef it up. Thaw the tofu before using.

1 cup Texmati brown rice
1¼ cups water
2 tablespoons canola oil
2 garlic cloves, minced
1 tablespoon minced
 fresh ginger
8 ounces extra-firm tofu,
 cut into ½-inch squares
½ cup frozen peas
 and carrots

1 large egg, beaten
½ cup kimchi, chopped
2 scallions, sliced thin
¼ cup basil,
 coarsely chopped
1 tablespoon soy sauce
Kosher salt
Freshly ground black pepper

1. Rinse the rice under cold running water in a fine-mesh strainer.

2. Place the rice and water in the pot. Assemble pressure lid, making sure the pressure release valve is in the SEAL position.

3. Select PRESSURE and set to HI. Set time to 2 minutes. Select START/STOP to begin.

4. When pressure cooking is complete, allow pressure to naturally release for 10 minutes. After 10 minutes, quick release remaining pressure by moving the pressure release valve to the VENT position. Carefully remove lid when unit has finished releasing pressure.

5. Evenly layer the rice on a sheet pan and refrigerate until cool, preferably overnight.

6. Select SEAR/SAUTÉ and set to HI. Select START/STOP to begin. Add the canola oil and let heat for 5 minutes.

7. Add the garlic and ginger and cook for 1 minute. Add the tofu, rice, and peas and carrots, and cook for 5 minutes, stirring occasionally.

CONTINUED ▶

# Spicy Kimchi and Tofu Fried Rice continued

8. Move the rice to one side and add the egg to empty side of pot. Cook 30 seconds, stirring occasionally to scramble it. Add the kimchi, scallions, basil, and soy sauce, and stir. Cook for 5 minutes, stirring frequently.

9. Season with salt, pepper, and more soy sauce, if needed. Serve.

Per serving: *Calories: 229; Total Fat: 9g; Saturated Fat: 1g; Cholesterol: 31mg; Sodium: 928mg; Carbohydrates: 30g; Fiber: 2g; Protein: 8g*

# Veggie Loaded Pasta by Sam Ferguson

SERVES 8

**Chef says:** *There used to be a dish similar to this on the kids' menu at one of the restaurants I worked at, and over time it ended up on the regular menu because it is just so satisfying. It can be a meal, a dish to share, or a lunch on the go. Whichever way you choose to serve it, enjoy!*

**NUT-FREE, VEGETARIAN, UNDER 30 MINUTES**

**PREP TIME:** 15 minutes
**TOTAL COOK TIME:** 2 minutes

**APPROX. PRESSURE BUILD:** 7 minutes
**PRESSURE COOK:** 2 minutes
**PRESSURE RELEASE:** 10 minutes, then Quick

**VARIATION TIP:** This recipe also creates a perfect cold pasta salad. After straining, toss pasta gently with 1 tablespoon of oil to prevent sticking and clumping, then place pasta in refrigerator for an hour to cool. Once cool, toss pasta with avocado sauce and serve cold.

1 (16-ounce) box dry pasta, such as rigatoni or penne

4 cups water

2 tablespoons extra-virgin olive oil, divided

2 teaspoons kosher salt, divided

3 avocados

Juice of 2 limes

2 tablespoons minced cilantro

1 red onion, chopped

1 cup cherry tomatoes, halved

4 heaping cups spinach, half an 11-ounce container

¼ cup shredded Parmesan cheese, divided

Freshly ground black pepper, for serving

1. Place the pasta, water, 1 tablespoon of olive oil, and 1 teaspoon of salt in the pot. Stir to incorporate. Assemble pressure lid, making sure the pressure release valve is in the SEAL position.

2. Select PRESSURE and set to LO. Set time to 2 minutes. Select START/STOP to begin.

3. While pasta is cooking, place the avocados in a medium-sized mixing bowl and mash well with a wooden spatula until a thick paste forms. Add all remaining ingredients to the bowl and mix well to combine.

4. When pressure cooking is complete, allow pressure to naturally release for 10 minutes. After 10 minutes, quick release remaining pressure by moving the pressure release valve to the VENT position. Carefully remove lid when unit has finished releasing pressure.

5. If necessary, strain pasta to remove any residual water and return pasta to pot. Add avocado mixture to pot and stir.

6. Garnish pasta with Parmesan cheese and black pepper, as desired, then serve.

*Per serving: Calories: 372; Total Fat: 16g; Saturated Fat: 3g; Cholesterol: 3mg; Sodium: 149mg; Carbohydrates: 49g; Fiber: 12g; Protein: 11g*

# Cauliflower Enchiladas by Meg Jordan

***Chef says:*** *Mexican is my favorite cuisine—I could eat it every day. Air-crisped cauliflower stands up to the tortillas and sauce to provide a flavorful vegetarian Mexican entrée that non-meat eaters can enjoy.*

**NUT-FREE, VEGETARIAN, UNDER 30 MINUTES, FAMILY FAVORITE**

**PREP TIME:** 15 minutes
**TOTAL COOK TIME:** 25 minutes

**AIR CRISP:** 15 minutes
**BROIL:** 10 minutes

**ACCESSORIES:** Cook & Crisp Basket

**SUBSTITUTION TIP:** Use a nut-based cheese instead of the shredded dairy cheese in this recipe to make it vegan friendly.

- 2 tablespoons canola oil
- 1 large head cauliflower, cut into 1-inch florets
- 2 teaspoons ground cumin
- 1 teaspoon ground chili pepper
- 2 teaspoons kosher salt
- ½ teaspoon freshly ground black pepper
- 1 (14.5-ounce) can diced tomatoes, drained
- 5 (6-inch) flour tortillas
- 1 (10-ounce) can red enchilada sauce
- 1½ cups shredded Mexican blend cheese
- ½ cup chopped cilantro, for garnish

1. In a medium bowl, toss together the oil, cauliflower, cumin, chili pepper, salt, and black pepper. Place the cauliflower in the Cook & Crisp Basket and place the basket in pot. Close crisping lid.

2. Select AIR CRISP, set temperature to 390°F, and set time to 15 minutes. Select START/STOP to begin.

3. After 8 minutes, open lid, then lift the basket and shake the cauliflower. Lower basket back into pot and close lid. Continue cooking, until the cauliflower reaches your desired crispiness.

4. When cooking is complete, remove basket from pot. Place the cauliflower in a bowl and mix with the tomatoes.

5. Lay the tortillas on a work surface. Divide the cauliflower-tomato mixture between the tortillas and roll them up. Place the filled tortillas seam-side down in the pot. Pour the enchilada sauce on top.

6. Close crisping lid. Select BROIL and set time to 10 minutes. Select START/STOP to begin.

7. After 5 minutes, open lid and add the cheese on top. Close lid and continue cooking until cheese is golden brown.

8. When cooking is complete, add cilantro and serve.

*Per serving: Calories: 315; Total Fat: 19g; Saturated Fat: 8g; Cholesterol: 30mg; Sodium: 822mg; Carbohydrates: 28g; Fiber: 8g; Protein: 13g*

# Caprese Pasta Salad

**SERVES 8**

*This pasta salad will be a lifesaver for your next cookout. Whether you are celebrating Memorial Day, the Fourth of July, or just enjoying the warm summer weather, no one wants to spend hours cooking in the hot kitchen. With this recipe, you cook the pasta to a perfect al dente without ever needing to turn on the stove to boil water. Once the pasta is cooked, fold in the veggies and toss with dressing. Voila!*

**NUT-FREE, VEGETARIAN, UNDER 30 MINUTES**

**PREP TIME:** 10 minutes
**TOTAL COOK TIME:**
3 minutes

**APPROX. PRESSURE BUILD:**
10 minutes
**PRESSURE COOK:** 3 minutes
**PRESSURE RELEASE:**
10 minutes, then Quick

**VARIATION TIP:** Use this base recipe to make a variety of pasta salads. Try adding diced cucumbers, chickpeas, feta cheese, and arugula for a Mediterranean twist.

1 (16-ounce) box elbow pasta
4 cups water
1 tablespoon sea salt
2 tablespoons extra-virgin olive oil
½ cup red bell pepper, diced
1 cup cherry tomatoes, sliced
¼ cup black olives, sliced
½ pound (8 ounces) fresh mozzarella, diced
½ cup chopped fresh basil
½ cup Italian dressing

1. Place the pasta, water, and salt in the pot. Assemble pressure lid, making sure the pressure release valve is in the SEAL position.

2. Select PRESSURE and set to HI. Set time to 3 minutes. Select START/STOP to begin.

3. When pressure cooking is complete, allow pressure to naturally release for 10 minutes. After 10 minutes, quick release remaining pressure by moving the pressure release valve to the VENT position. Carefully remove lid when unit has finished releasing pressure.

4. Drain the pasta in a colander. Place the pasta in a large bowl and toss with the olive oil. Set aside to cool for 20 minutes.

5. Stir in the bell pepper, cherry tomatoes, olives, mozzarella, and basil. Gently fold in the Italian seasoning.

6. Serve immediately or cover and refrigerate for later.

**Per serving:** *Calories: 377; Total Fat: 15g; Saturated Fat: 5g; Cholesterol: 30mg; Sodium: 694mg; Carbohydrates: 45g; Fiber: 3g; Protein: 14g*

# Pasta Primavera

*One pot meals are a big craze and it's easy to see why: Fewer dishes to clean up means you have more time to spend doing the things you love. Start out by crisping some flavorful fresh vegetables and let them rest while you pressure cook the pasta. Bring it all back together in the pot, and you'll have a veggie-filled meal that the whole family will love.*

**NUT-FREE, VEGETARIAN, UNDER 30 MINUTES, FAMILY FAVORITE**

**PREP TIME:** 10 minutes
**TOTAL COOK TIME:** 18 minutes

**AIR CRISP:** 15 minutes
**APPROX. PRESSURE BUILD:** 10 minutes
**PRESSURE COOK:** 3 minutes
**PRESSURE RELEASE:** 10 minutes, then Quick

**ACCESSORIES:** Cook & Crisp Basket

**VARIATION TIP:** You can add any vegetables that you want to your primavera. Try peas or asparagus if you have them on hand.

- ½ **red onion, sliced**
- 1 **carrot, thinly sliced**
- 1 **head broccoli, cut into florets**
- 1 **red bell pepper, thinly sliced**
- 1 **yellow squash, halved lengthwise and sliced into half moons**
- 1 **zucchini, halved lengthwise and sliced into half moons**
- ¼ **cup extra-virgin olive oil**
- ½ **teaspoon dried basil**
- ½ **teaspoon dried oregano**
- ½ **teaspoon dried parsley**
- ¼ **teaspoon dried rosemary**
- ¼ **teaspoon crushed red pepper flakes**
- 1 **(16-ounce) box penne pasta**
- 4 **cups water**
- 2 **tablespoons freshly squeezed lemon juice**
- ½ **cup grated Parmesan cheese, divided**

1. Place Cook & Crisp Basket in pot. Close crisping lid. Select AIR CRISP, set temperature to 390°F, and set time to 5 minutes. Select START/STOP to begin preheating.

2. In a large bowl, combine the red onion, carrot, broccoli, bell pepper, yellow squash, zucchini, olive oil, basil, oregano, parsley, rosemary, and red pepper flakes, and toss to combine.

3. Once unit has preheated, add the vegetable mixture to the basket. Close lid.

4. Select AIR CRISP, set temperature to 390°F, and set time to 15 minutes. Select START/STOP to begin.

5. When cooking is complete, remove the vegetables and basket, and set aside.

6. Add the pasta and water. Assemble pressure lid, making sure the pressure release valve is in the SEAL position.

7. Select PRESSURE and set to HI. Set time to 3 minutes. Select START/STOP to begin.

CONTINUED ▶

# Pasta Primavera continued

8. When pressure cooking is complete, allow pressure to naturally release for 10 minutes. After 10 minutes, quick release remaining pressure by moving the pressure release valve to the VENT position. Carefully remove lid when unit has finished releasing pressure.

9. Add vegetables to pasta. Add the lemon juice and ¼ cup of Parmesan cheese and stir. Serve and top with remaining cheese.

*Per serving: Calories: 388; Total Fat: 12g; Saturated Fat: 2g; Cholesterol: 7mg; Sodium: 127mg; Carbohydrates: 60g; Fiber: 6g; Protein: 15g*

# Veggie Potpie

**by Ginnie Leeming, Ninja® Foodi™ Family Member**

**SERVES 6**

***Ginnie says:*** *My veggie potpie recipe was inspired by the countless frozen potpies I ate as a child, but using fresh ingredients instead—it's so much better! The recipe features tender vegetables in a rich, creamy sauce topped with a flaky crust. This crave-worthy recipe was a hit on my blog, and although potpie might seem like a labor-intensive dish, it couldn't be easier to make in the Ninja Foodi. Once you've mastered this basic recipe, try substituting your favorite vegetables and herbs.*

**FAMILY FAVORITE, NUT-FREE, VEGETARIAN**

**PREP TIME:** 10 minutes
**TOTAL COOK TIME:**
22 minutes

**SEAR/SAUTÉ:** 7 minutes
**PRESSURE COOK:** 5 minutes
**APPROX. PRESSURE BUILD:**
10 minutes
**PRESSURE RELEASE:** Quick
**BROIL:** 10 minutes

**Find Ginnie
at Hellolittlehome.com**

- 4 tablespoons unsalted butter
- ½ large onion, diced
- 1½ cups diced carrot (about 2 large carrots)
- 1½ cups diced celery (about 3 celery stalks)
- 2 garlic cloves, minced
- 3 cups red potatoes, diced
- 1 cup vegetable broth
- ½ cup frozen peas
- ½ cup frozen corn
- 1 tablespoon chopped fresh Italian parsley
- 2 teaspoons fresh thyme leaves
- ¼ cup all-purpose flour
- ½ cup heavy (whipping) cream
- Salt
- Freshly ground black pepper
- 1 prepared piecrust

1. Select SEAR/SAUTÉ and set temperature to MD:HI. Set the time to 5 minutes to preheat. Select START/STOP to begin.

2. Add the butter to the pot to melt. Add the onion, carrot, and celery to the melted butter. Sauté for about 3 minutes until softened.

3. Stir in the garlic and cook, stirring constantly, for about 30 seconds until fragrant. Select START/STOP to end the function.

4. Add the potatoes and vegetable broth to pot and stir to combine.

5. Assemble the pressure lid, making sure the pressure release valve is in the SEAL position.

6. Select PRESSURE and set to HI. Set the time to 5 minutes. Select START/STOP to begin.

CONTINUED ▶

# Veggie Potpie continued

7. When pressure cooking is complete, quick release the pressure by turning the pressure release valve to the VENT position. Carefully remove the lid when the unit has finished releasing pressure.

8. Add the peas, corn, parsley, and thyme to the pot. Season with salt and pepper. Sprinkle the flour over the top and stir to mix well. Stir in the heavy cream.

9. Select SEAR/SAUTÉ and set temperature to MD:HI. Select START/STOP to begin. Cook for 2 to 3 minutes, stirring constantly, until the sauce thickens and is hot. Select START/STOP to end the function.

10. Place the piecrust over the vegetable mixture. Fold over the edges of the crust to fit the pot. Make a small slit in the center of the crust for steam to release. Close the crisping lid.

11. Select BROIL. Set the time to 10 minutes. Select START/STOP to begin.

12. After the cooking is complete, carefully transfer the inner pot to a heat-proof surface. Let the potpie sit for 10 minutes before serving.

*Per serving: Calories: 361; Total Fat: 22g; Saturated Fat: 11g; Cholesterol: 47mg; Sodium: 339mg; Carbohydrates: 36g; Fiber: 4g; Protein: 6g*

# Tomato Galette by Kelly Gray

*Chef says: Tomatoes come in all shapes, colors, and sizes, and this simple appetizer is made to showcase all of them. A savory tomato-leek mixture nestled in a flaky pie crust topped with a blend of cheeses is a great appetizer or a light lunch on a hot summer day.*

**NUT FREE, VEGETARIAN**

**PREP TIME:** 15 minutes
**TOTAL COOK TIME:**
40 minutes

**BAKE/ROAST:** 40 minutes

**ACCESSORIES:** Ninja Multi-Purpose Pan, Reversible Rack

**VARIATION TIP:** Tomatoes out of season? Substitute tomatoes with mushrooms and onions for an equally delicious galette in the winter months. Just be sure to sauté the mushrooms and onions first to add some caramelized flavor and eliminate excess water.

- **½ pound mixed tomatoes, cut into ¼-inch slices**
- **3 inches of leek, thinly sliced**
- **2 garlic cloves, diced**
- **Kosher salt**
- **1 store-bought refrigerated pie crust**
- **2 tablespoons bread crumbs**
- **4 tablespoons shredded Parmesan cheese, divided**
- **4 tablespoons shredded mozzarella, divided**
- **1 egg, beaten**
- **Freshly ground black pepper**

1. Place the tomatoes, leeks, and garlic into large bowl. Sprinkle with salt and set aside for at least 5 minutes to draw out the juices from the vegetables.

2. Strain the excess juice off the tomato mixture and pat down the vegetables with paper towels.

3. Unroll the pie crust and place it in the Ninja Multi-Purpose Pan or a 1½-quart round ceramic baking dish and form it to the bottom of the pan. Lay the extra dough loosely on the sides of the pan.

4. Sprinkle the bread crumbs in a thin layer on the pie crust bottom, then scatter 3 tablespoons each of Parmesan and mozzarella cheese on top. Place the tomato mixture in a heap in the middle of the dough and top with the remaining 1 tablespoon each of Parmesan and mozzarella cheese.

5. Fold the edges of the crust over the tomatoes and brush with the egg.

6. Close crisping lid. Select BAKE/ROAST, set temperature to 350ºF, and set time to 45 minutes. Select START/STOP to begin. Let preheat for 5 minutes.

7. Place pan on the Reversible Rack, making sure the rack is in the lower position. Cover galette loosely with aluminum foil (do not seal the pan).

CONTINUED ▶

# Tomato Galette continued

8. Once unit has preheated, open lid and carefully place the rack with pan in the pot. Close crisping lid.

9. After 20 minutes, open lid and remove the foil. Close lid and continue cooking.

10. When cooking is complete, remove rack with pan and set aside to let cool. Cut into slices, season with pepper, and serve.

Per serving: *Calories: 288; Total Fat: 15g; Saturated Fat: 4g; Cholesterol: 52mg; Sodium: 409mg; Carbohydrates: 31g; Fiber: 2g; Protein: 9g*

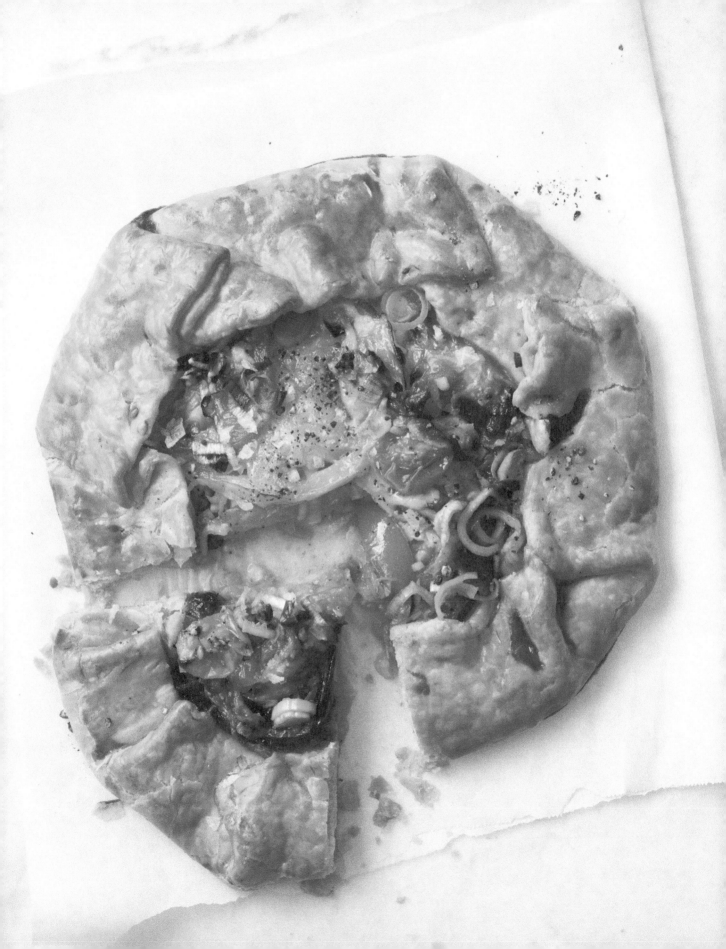

# Veggie Lover's Pizza

by Lauren Cardona, Ninja® Foodi™ Family Member

**MAKES 1 PIZZA**

**Lauren says:** *Now you can involve the entire family in the fun of creating their own pizzas! Making pizzas in the Ninja® Foodi™ Pressure Cooker proved to be a great way to bring everyone together for a fun day of cooking. I hope your family enjoys the time spent together—and the pizza!—as much as we did. Use any toppings you like, if you don't like what I've included here.*

FAMILY FAVORITE, NUT-FREE, UNDER 30 MINUTES, VEGETARIAN

PREP TIME: 10 minutes
TOTAL COOK TIME:
8 minutes

BAKE/ROAST: 8 minutes

ACCESSORIES: Cook & Crisp Basket

VARIATION TIP: Take this pizza over the top and add a slice of bacon (cut into small pieces) to it!

Find Lauren at
TheTastyTravelers.com
/ Facebook: The
Tasty Travelers & The
Ninja Community

1 (7-ounce) store-bought pizza dough, rolled into an 8-inch circle

¼ cup traditional pizza sauce

1 teaspoon minced garlic

⅔ cup shredded mozzarella cheese

¼ cup chopped green bell pepper

¼ cup sliced mushrooms

Crushed red pepper flakes, for garnish

1. Select BAKE/ROAST, set the temperature to 400°F, and set time to 5 minutes to preheat. Select START/STOP to begin.

2. Place the rolled dough in the Ninja Cook & Crisp Basket. Spread the pizza sauce over the crust, leaving about a 1-inch border uncovered. Sprinkle on the garlic, top with the mozzarella cheese, and evenly distribute the green bell pepper and mushrooms over the pizza.

3. Place the Cook & Crisp Basket into the pot and close the crisping lid.

4. Select BAKE/ROAST, set the temperature to 400°F, and set the time to 8 minutes. Select START/STOP to begin.

5. When cooking is complete, carefully open the lid and remove the pizza. Serve, garnished with red pepper flakes, if using.

*Per serving: Calories: 636; Total Fat: 20g; Saturated Fat: 9g; Cholesterol: 38mg; Sodium: 1150mg; Carbohydrates: 95g; Fiber: 9g; Protein: 33g*

# Garlic Bread Pizza

**SERVES 6**

*This simple recipe is perfect when you need to throw together a quick snack. Packed with flavor, this garlic bread pizza is made from just three simple ingredients. Crisp toast, bold garlic, and ooey gooey cheese complete this quick and easy snack or side.*

NUT-FREE, VEGETARIAN,
UNDER 30 MINUTES,
FAMILY FAVORITE,
5 INGREDIENT

**PREP TIME:** 2 minutes
**TOTAL COOK TIME:**
10 minutes

**AIR CRISP:** 5 minutes

**ACCESSORIES:** Cook &
Crisp Basket

**VARIATION TIP:** Let
everyone customize
their own mini pizza by
adding toppings like
fresh vegetables.

**6 slices frozen garlic
bread or Texas Toast**

**¾ cup tomato-basil sauce or
your favorite tomato sauce**

**6 slices mozzarella cheese**

1. Insert Cook & Crisp Basket in pot. Close crisping lid. Select AIR CRISP, set temperature to 390ºF, and set time to 5 minutes. Select START/STOP to begin preheating.

2. Once unit has preheated, place three of the garlic bread slices in the basket, and top with half the sauce and 3 slices of cheese. Close crisping lid.

3. Select AIR CRISP, set temperature to 375ºF, and set time to 5 minutes. Select START/STOP to begin.

4. When cooking is complete, remove the pizzas from the basket. Repeat steps 2 and 3 with the remaining slices of garlic bread, sauce, and cheese.

**Per serving:** *Calories: 192; Total Fat: 7g; Saturated Fat: 4g; Cholesterol: 22mg; Sodium: 548mg; Carbohydrates: 21g; Fiber: 2g; Protein: 10g*

# 7

# Seafood

# Fish Finger Sandwich

SERVES 4

*A comfort food favorite in Great Britain, the fish finger sandwich can be made every which way, from traditional with tartar sauce (like this recipe) to the more daring chili sauce topping. While many of the classic recipes use deep-fried fish, you can pull together light, crispy, and flavorful fish sticks with a few simple ingredients and prepare them guilt-free using the Cook & Crisp Basket.*

**DAIRY-FREE, NUT-FREE, UNDER 30 MINUTES**

**PREP TIME:** 5 minutes
**TOTAL COOK TIME:** 15 minutes

**AIR CRISP:** 15 minutes

**ACCESSORIES:** Cook & Crisp Basket

**VARIATION TIP:** Top your sandwiches with fresh lettuce and a tomato slice if you'd like.

2 eggs

8 ounces ale

1 cup cornstarch

1 cup all-purpose flour

½ tablespoon chili powder

1 tablespoon ground cumin

1 teaspoon sea salt

1 teaspoon freshly ground black pepper

4 (5- to 6-ounce) cod fillets, cut into 16 half-inch strips

Cooking spray

Tartar sauce, for garnish

8 slices sandwich bread

1. Insert Cook & Crisp Basket in pot. Close crisping lid. Select AIR CRISP, set temperature to 375ºF, and set time to 5 minutes. Select START/STOP to begin preheating.

2. In a shallow bowl, whisk together the eggs and beer. In a medium bowl, whisk together the cornstarch, flour, chili powder, cumin, salt, and pepper.

3. Dip each strip of cod fillet in the egg mixture, then dredge in the flour mixture, coating on all sides.

4. Once unit has preheated, spray the basket with the cooking spray. Place the fish strips in the basket and coat them with cooking spray. Close crisping lid.

5. Select AIR CRISP, set temperature to 375ºF, and set time to 15 minutes. Select START/STOP to begin.

6. When cooking is complete, check the fish for your desired crispiness. Remove the fish from the basket.

7. Spread tartar sauce on four slices of bread. Place four fish strips on each slice and top the sandwiches with the four remaining slices. Serve.

*Per serving: Calories: 565; Total Fat: 13g; Saturated Fat: 2g; Cholesterol: 163mg; Sodium: 1216mg; Carbohydrates: 74g; Fiber: 2g; Protein: 36g*

# Garlic Shrimp and Veggies

SERVES 4

*Use the Sauté and Pressure functions of the Foodi to create tender, garlicky shrimp and steamed broccoli for a quick and easy meal. The shrimp cook so quickly that all you need to do is build pressure and they will be done. Serve alongside your favorite rice dish or a simple pasta to complete your plate.*

**DAIRY-FREE, GLUTEN-FREE, NUT-FREE, UNDER 30 MINUTES**

**PREP TIME:** 5 minutes
**TOTAL COOK TIME:** 5 minutes

**SEAR/SAUTÉ:** 5 minutes
**APPROX. PRESSURE BUILD:** 10 minutes
**PRESSURE COOK:** 0 minutes
**PRESSURE RELEASE:** Quick

**SUBSTITUTION TIP:** Swap out the broccoli for another vegetable or mix of veggies of your choice, like bell peppers or snow peas.

2 tablespoons unsalted butter

1 shallot, minced

3 garlic cloves, minced

¼ cup white wine

½ cup chicken stock

Juice of ½ lemon

½ teaspoon sea salt

½ teaspoon freshly ground black pepper

1½ pounds frozen shrimp, thawed

1 large head broccoli, cut into florets

1. Add the butter. Select SEAR/SAUTÉ and set to MED. Select START/STOP to begin.

2. Once the butter is melted, add the shallots and cook for 3 minutes. Add the garlic and cook for 1 minute.

3. Deglaze the pot by adding the wine and using a wooden spoon to scrape the bits of garlic and shallot off the bottom of the pot. Stir in the chicken stock, lemon juice, salt, pepper, and shrimp.

4. Place the broccoli florets on top of the shrimp mixture. Assemble pressure lid, making sure the pressure release valve is in the SEAL position.

5. Select PRESSURE and set to HI. Set time to 0 minutes. Select START/STOP to begin.

6. When pressure cooking is complete, quick release the pressure by moving the pressure release valve to the VENT position. Carefully remove lid when the unit has finished releasing pressure. Serve immediately.

*Per serving: Calories: 281; Total Fat: 8g; Saturated Fat: 5g; Cholesterol: 312mg; Sodium: 692mg; Carbohydrates: 9g; Fiber: 3g; Protein: 39g*

# Low Country Boil by Chelven Randolph

*Chef says:* *My father is from a small town outside of Charleston, South Carolina, where a dish called Frogmore Stew is wildly popular. It uses ocean water as the base to stew freshly caught shrimp, clams, and crawfish with potatoes, corn, and sausage. This is my take on that dish adapted as a beginner version for those who love a complete meal made in a single pot. And if you can find crawfish (think tiny lobsters; you can sometimes find them at Asian specialty markets), they really bring the dish home!*

DAIRY-FREE, GLUTEN-FREE, NUT-FREE, 360 MEAL, UNDER 30 MINUTES, 5 INGREDIENT

PREP TIME: 10 minutes
TOTAL COOK TIME:
10 minutes

APPROX. PRESSURE BUILD:
10 minutes
PRESSURE COOK: 5 minutes
PRESSURE RELEASE: Quick
SEAR/SAUTÉ: 5 minutes

VARIATION TIP: Try this dish with red or green curry paste for a cool twist. Whisk in 2 to 3 tablespoons in place of the Creole seasoning and enjoy.

2 pounds Red Bliss potatoes, diced

3 ears corn, cut crosswise into thirds

1 (14-ounce) package smoked sausage or kielbasa, sliced into 1-inch pieces

4 cups water

2½ tablespoons Creole seasoning

1 pound medium (21–30 count) shrimp, peeled and deveined

1. Place the potatoes, corn, sausage, water, and Creole seasoning into the pot and stir. Assemble pressure lid, making sure the pressure release valve is in the SEAL position.

2. Select PRESSURE and set to HI. Set time to 5 minutes. Select START/STOP to begin.

3. When pressure cooking is complete, quick release the pressure by turning the pressure release valve to the VENT position. Carefully remove lid when unit has finished releasing pressure.

4. Stir in the shrimp.

5. Select SEAR/SAUTÉ and set to MD:LO. Simmer for about 5 minutes, until the shrimp is cooked through.

6. When cooking is complete, serve immediately.

*Per serving: Calories: 445; Total Fat: 20g; Saturated Fat: 6g; Cholesterol: 188mg; Sodium: 1251mg; Carbohydrates: 40g; Fiber: 6g; Protein: 28g*

# New England Lobster Rolls by Craig White

SERVES 4

**Chef says:** *Nothing says summer in New England like lobster. I have seen live lobsters for sale in gas stations and in a claw machine in a local dive bar. Lobster rolls are often overpriced, but you can make your own for a fraction of the cost.*

NUT-FREE, UNDER
30 MINUTES, FAMILY
FAVORITE

PREP TIME: 10 minutes
TOTAL COOK TIME:
20 minutes

AIR CRISP: 14 minutes

ACCESSORIES: Cook &
Crisp Basket

INGREDIENT INFO: Lobster
was so overabundant
centuries ago that it was
looked at as a poor man's
food. The amount served
to prisoners and slaves
had to be limited as it was
viewed as cruel and unusual
punishment. Now a symbol
of luxury, it's on many death
row meal requests.

4 (4-ounce) lobster tails
¼ cup mayonnaise
1 celery stalk, minced
Zest of 1 lemon
Juice of 1 lemon
¼ teaspoon celery seed

Kosher salt
Freshly ground black pepper
4 split-top hot dog buns
4 tablespoons
   unsalted butter, at
   room temperature
4 leaves butter lettuce

1. Insert Cook & Crisp Basket into the pot and close the crisping lid. Select AIR CRISP, set temperature to 375ºF, and set time to 15 minutes. Select START/STOP to begin. Let preheat for 5 minutes.

2. Once unit has preheated, open lid and add the lobster tails to the basket. Close the lid and cook for 10 minutes.

3. In a medium bowl, mix together the mayonnaise, celery, lemon zest and juice, and celery seed, and add salt and pepper.

4. Fill a large bowl with a tray of ice cubes and enough water to cover the ice.

5. When cooking is complete, open lid. Transfer the lobster into the ice bath for 5 minutes. Close lid to keep unit warm.

6. Spread butter on the hot dog buns. Open lid and place the buns in the basket. Close crisping lid.

7. Select AIR CRISP, set temperature to 375ºF, and set time to 4 minutes. Select START/STOP to begin.

8. Remove the lobster meat from the shells and roughly chop. Place in the bowl with the mayonnaise mixture and stir.

9. When cooking is complete, open lid and remove the buns. Place lettuce in each bun, then fill with the lobster salad.

*Per serving: Calories: 408; Total Fat: 24g; Saturated Fat: 9g; Cholesterol: 199mg; Sodium: 798mg; Carbohydrates: 22g; Fiber: 1g; Protein: 26g*

# Cod with Ginger and Scallion Sauce

*Elevate mellow cod fillets with a zingy taste of ginger in this quick, simple recipe. Serve with a green vegetable like broccoli or bok choy—or place it atop some steamed rice noodles. The options are endless to build a complete meal.*

**DAIRY-FREE, NUT-FREE, UNDER 30 MINUTES**

**PREP TIME:** 5 minutes
**TOTAL COOK TIME:** 10 minutes

**SEAR/SAUTÉ:** 10 minutes

2 tablespoons rice vinegar
2 tablespoons soy sauce
1 tablespoon chicken stock
1 tablespoon grated fresh ginger

4 skinless cod fillets (about 1½ pounds)
Sea salt
Freshly ground black pepper
Greens of 6 scallions, thinly sliced

1. In a small bowl, mix together the rice vinegar, soy sauce, chicken stock, and ginger.

2. Season the cod fillets on both sides with salt and pepper. Place them in the pot and cover with the vinegar mixture.

3. Select SEAR/SAUTÉ and set to MED. Bring the liquid to a low boil.

4. Once boiling, turn the heat to LO and cover with the pressure lid. Cook for 8 minutes.

5. Remove lid and add the scallion greens to the top of the fish. Cover with the pressure lid and cook for 2 minutes more. Serve.

*Per serving: Calories: 149; Total Fat: 2g; Saturated Fat: 0g; Cholesterol: 60mg; Sodium: 642mg; Carbohydrates: 2g; Fiber: 0g; Protein: 30g*

# Tuscan Cod by Kelly Gray

***Chef says:*** *This dish was inspired by the one my dad makes at our friend's summer house in Cape Cod. It sticks out in my mind because it was the first seafood dish that I willingly tried and enjoyed as a child. I must admit that I was an incredibly picky eater at that age. Fresh cod topped with zesty bread crumbs cooked above a Mediterranean-inspired potato medley is an easy and delicious way to mix up a weeknight meal.*

---

**NUT-FREE, 360 MEAL**

---

**PREP TIME:** 20 minutes
**TOTAL COOK TIME:**
32 minutes

---

**SEAR/SAUTÉ:** 20 minutes
**BAKE/ROAST:** 12 minutes

---

**ACCESSORIES:**
Reversible Rack

---

**VARIATION TIP:** Don't have poultry seasoning? Substitute with a blend of any or all the following dried spices: rosemary, sage, marjoram, tarragon, and a pinch of nutmeg.

- 2 tablespoons canola oil, divided
- 1½ pounds baby red potatoes, cut into ½-inch pieces
- 2½ teaspoons kosher salt, divided
- 1 teaspoon freshly ground black pepper, divided
- 1 cup panko bread crumbs
- 6 tablespoons unsalted butter, divided
- 2 teaspoons poultry seasoning
- Juice of 1 lemon
- 1 medium onion, thinly sliced
- 1½ cups cherry tomatoes, halved
- 4 garlic cloves, quartered lengthwise
- ⅓ cup Kalamata olives, roughly chopped
- 4 (6-ounce) fresh cod fillets
- 1 teaspoon fresh mint, finely chopped
- 1 lemon, cut into wedges

1. Select SEAR/SAUTÉ and set to HI. Select START/STOP to begin. Let preheat for 5 minutes.

2. Add 1 tablespoon of oil and the potatoes. Season with 1½ teaspoons of salt and ½ teaspoon of pepper. Sauté for about 15 minutes, stirring occasionally, until the potatoes are golden brown.

3. While potatoes are cooking, combine the bread crumbs, 4 tablespoons of butter, poultry seasoning, the remaining 1 teaspoon of salt and ½ teaspoon of pepper, and lemon juice in a medium bowl. Stir well.

4. Once the potatoes are browned, carefully remove them from the pot and set aside. Add the remaining 1 tablespoon of oil, then the onion. Sauté for 2 to 3 minutes, until the onions are lightly browned. Add the tomatoes, garlic, and olives and cook for about 2 minutes more, stirring

CONTINUED ▶

# Tuscan Cod continued

occasionally. Return the potatoes to the pot, stir. Select START/STOP to pause cooking. Close crisping lid to retain heat.

5. Coat the cod on both sides with the remaining 2 tablespoons of butter. Evenly distribute the bread-crumb mixture on top of the cod, pressing the crumbs down firmly.

6. Open lid and place the Reversible Rack in the pot over the potato mixture, making sure it is the higher position. Place the cod fillets on the rack, bread-side up. Close crisping lid.

7. Select BAKE/ROAST, set temperature to 375°F, and set time to 12 minutes. Select START/STOP to begin.

8. When cooking is complete, leave the cod in the pot with the crisping lid closed for 5 minutes to rest before serving. After resting, the internal temperature of the cod should be at least 145°F and the bread crumbs should be golden brown. Serve with potato mixture and garnish with chopped mint and lemon wedges.

Per serving: Calories: 583; Total Fat: 28g; Saturated Fat: 12g; Cholesterol: 128mg; Sodium: 815mg; Carbohydrates: 48g; Fiber: 7g; Protein: 37g

# Mustard and Apricot-Glazed Salmon with Smashed Potatoes by Meg Jordan

SERVES 4

**Chef says:** *Smashed potatoes are something I love to see on restaurant menus, but they are often cooked in animal fat or fried, making them not so healthy. This version cuts down on the fat and still provides a crispy and delicious end result. Paired with the sweet and spicy combination on the salmon, you have an elevated meal that is easy to make during the week.*

DAIRY-FREE, NUT-FREE, 360 MEAL, UNDER 30 MINUTES

PREP TIME: 10 minutes
TOTAL COOK TIME: 25 minutes

APPROX. PRESSURE BUILD: 10 minutes
PRESSURE COOK: 5 minutes
PRESSURE RELEASE: Quick
AIR CRISP: 15 minutes
BROIL: 5 minutes

ACCESSORIES: Reversible Rack, Cook & Crisp Basket

20 ounces baby potatoes, whole
1½ cups water
4 (6-ounce) frozen skinless salmon fillets
¼ cup apricot preserves

2 teaspoons Dijon mustard
2 tablespoons extra-virgin olive oil
½ teaspoon kosher salt
½ teaspoon freshly ground black pepper

1. Place the potatoes and water in the pot. Put Reversible Rack in pot, making sure it is in the higher position. Place salmon on the rack. Assemble pressure lid, making sure the pressure release valve is in the SEAL position.

2. Select PRESSURE and set to HI. Set time to 5 minutes. Select START/STOP to begin.

3. Mix together the apricot preserves and mustard in a small bowl.

4. When pressure cooking is complete, quick release the pressure by turning the pressure release valve to the VENT position. Carefully remove lid when unit has finished releasing pressure.

5. Carefully remove rack with salmon. Remove potatoes from pot and drain. Place the potatoes on a cutting board and, using the back of a knife, carefully press down to flatten each. Drizzle the flattened potatoes with the olive oil and season with salt and pepper.

6. Place Cook & Crisp Basket in the pot. Place the potatoes into the basket and close crisping lid.

7. Select AIR CRISP, set temperature to 390°F, and set time to 15 minutes. Select START/STOP to begin.

CONTINUED ▶

# Mustard and Apricot-Glazed Salmon with Smashed Potatoes continued

8. After 8 minutes, open lid, and using silicone-tipped tongs, gently flip the potatoes. Lower basket back into pot and close lid to resume cooking.

9. When cooking is complete, remove basket from pot. Return the rack with the salmon to the pot, making sure the rack is in the higher position. Gently brush the salmon with the apricot and mustard mixture.

10. Close crisping lid. Select BROIL and set time to 5 minutes. Select START/STOP to begin.

11. When cooking is complete, remove salmon and serve immediately with the potatoes.

*Per serving: Calories: 359; Total Fat: 11g; Saturated Fat: 2g; Cholesterol: 68mg; Sodium: 711mg; Carbohydrates: 36g; Fiber: 4g; Protein: 31g*

# Salmon with Balsamic-Glazed Brussels Sprouts

by Carly Schwartzbach, Ninja® Foodi™ Family Member

**SERVES 2**

*Kenzie says:* I love this recipe from Carly because it shows how easy it is to create a heathy and delicious meal with the Ninja® Foodi™ Pressure Cooker! Easily whip up delicious salmon and balsamic-glazed Brussels sprouts for a perfect weeknight meal.

DAIRY-FREE, GLUTEN-FREE, NUT-FREE, 5 INGREDIENT

PREP TIME: 10 minutes
TOTAL COOK TIME: 57 minutes

APPROX. PRESSURE BUILD: 10 minutes
PRESSURE COOK: 30 minutes
PRESSURE RELEASE: 10 minutes, then Quick
AIR CRISP: 27 minutes

ACCESSORIES: Cook & Crisp Basket

Find Carly
@everything_but_the_bagel

2 cups brown rice
2½ cups water
2 (4- to 6-ounce) salmon fillets
4 tablespoons everything bagel seasoning, divided
1 pound Brussels sprouts, ends trimmed, cut in half
1 tablespoon olive oil
2 tablespoons balsamic glaze

1. Place the rice and water in the cooking pot. Assemble the pressure lid, making sure the pressure release valve is in the SEAL position.

2. Select PRESSURE and set to HI. Set the time to 30 minutes. Select START/STOP to begin.

3. Meanwhile, season both sides of the salmon fillets with the everything bagel seasoning, using one tablespoon per fillet. Set aside.

4. When pressure cooking is complete, allow the pressure to release naturally for 10 minutes. After 10 minutes, quick release any remaining pressure by moving the pressure release valve to the VENT position. Carefully remove the lid when the unit has finished releasing pressure.

5. Season both sides of each salmon fillet with one table-spoon of the everything bagel seasoning.

6. In a medium bowl, combine the Brussels sprouts and olive oil. Toss to coat, and then sprinkle with one tablespoon of the everything bagel seasoning. Toss again to ensure Brussels sprouts are coated.

7. Place the Cook & Crisp Basket into the cooking pot. Close the crisping lid. Select AIR CRISP, set the temperature to 390°F, and set the time to 16 minutes. Select START/STOP to begin. Allow to preheat for 5 minutes, then add the

CONTINUED ▶

# Salmon with Balsamic-Glazed Brussels Sprouts continued

sprouts to the Cook & Crisp Basket. Close the crisping lid to begin cooking.

8. After 8 minutes, open the crisping lid, lift the basket, and shake the sprouts. Lower the basket back into the pot and close the lid to resume cooking another 8 minutes or until the Brussels sprouts reach your desired crispiness.

9. Once timer is complete, transfer the sprouts to a bowl and toss with remaining tablespoon of seasoning and the balsamic glaze.

10. Close the crisping lid. Select AIR CRISP, set the temperature to 390°F, and set the time to 11 minutes. Select START/STOP to begin. Allow to preheat for 5 minutes, then add the salmon fillets to the Cook & Crisp basket. Close the lid to begin cooking.

11. Once timer is complete, remove fillets from basket and serve alongside sprouts and rice.

Per serving: *Calories: 1028; Total Fat: 30g; Saturated Fat: 6g; Cholesterol: 62mg; Sodium: 1440mg; Carbohydrates: 154g; Fiber: 7g; Protein: 55g*

# Blackened Tilapia with Cilantro-Lime Rice and Avocado Salsa by Caroline Schliep

**SERVES 4**

***Chef says:*** *If you are a fellow seafood lover and connoisseur like me and are craving something fresh and light yet still satisfying, this recipe is the one for you. The tilapia is delicate in flavor yet super flaky and moist. Plus, the simple and clean flavors from the avocado salsa really complement the spice from the blackening seasoning perfectly. This is a great dish for summer or a quick weeknight pescatarian meal.*

DAIRY-FREE, GLUTEN-FREE, NUT-FREE, 360 MEAL, UNDER 30 MINUTES

PREP TIME: 10 minutes
TOTAL COOK TIME: 12 minutes

APPROX. PRESSURE BUILD: 10 minutes
PRESSURE COOK: 2 minutes
PRESSURE RELEASE: 10 minutes, then Quick
BROIL: 10 minutes

ACCESSORIES: Reversible Rack

VARIATION TIP: Switch it up and serve with mango salsa instead of avocado salsa.

2 cups white rice, rinsed
2 cups water
¼ cup blackening seasoning
4 (4-ounce) tilapia fillets
2 tablespoons freshly squeezed lime juice, divided
1 bunch cilantro, minced
1 tablespoon extra-virgin olive oil
2 avocados, diced
1 large red onion, diced
2 Roma tomatoes, diced
Kosher salt
Freshly ground black pepper

1. Place the rice and water in the pot and stir. Assemble pressure lid, making sure the pressure release valve is in the SEAL position.

2. Select PRESSURE and set to HI. Set time to 2 minutes. Select START/STOP to begin.

3. Place the blackening seasoning on a plate. Dredge the tilapia fillets in the seasoning.

4. When pressure cooking is complete, allow pressure to naturally release for 10 minutes. After 10 minutes, quick release remaining pressure by turning the pressure release valve to the VENT position. Carefully remove lid when unit has finished releasing pressure.

5. Transfer the rice to a large bowl and stir in 1 tablespoon of lime juice and half the cilantro. Cover the bowl with aluminum foil and set aside.

6. Place the Reversible Rack in the pot and arrange tilapia fillets on top. Close crisping lid.

7. Select BROIL and set time to 10 minutes. Select START/STOP to begin.

CONTINUED ▶

# Blackened Tilapia with Cilantro-Lime Rice and Avocado Salsa continued

8. In a medium bowl, stir together the remaining cilantro, remaining 1 tablespoon of lime juice, olive oil, avocado, onion, tomato, and season with salt and pepper.

9. When cooking is complete, open lid and lift the rack out of the pot. Serve the fish over the rice and top with avocado salsa.

*Per serving: Calories: 637; Total Fat: 19g; Saturated Fat: 3g; Cholesterol: 55mg; Sodium: 108mg; Carbohydrates: 89g; Fiber: 9g; Protein: 30g*

# Drunken Saffron Mussels

**by Gretchen Guttman, Ninja® Foodi™ Family Member**

**SERVES 4**

***Gretchen says:*** *This decadent recipe for fresh mussels is bursting with spices. The contrast between the acidity and velvety-rich consistency of the drunken cream sauce makes this dish a must-have for any at-home meal all year (or whenever you can find fresh mussels).*

**FAMILY FAVORITE, NUT-FREE, PESCATARIAN**

**PREP TIME:** 15 minutes
**TOTAL COOK TIME:**
25 minutes

**SEAR/SAUTÉ:** 6 minutes
**STEAM:** 20 minutes

**PREPARATION TIP:** Toast the whole bread loaf, before slicing, in a 350°F oven for 10 minutes.

- 2 tablespoons vegetable oil
- 2 shallots, sliced
- 3 garlic cloves, minced
- 1 cup cherry tomatoes, halved
- 2 pounds fresh mussels, washed with cold water, strained, scrubbed, and debearded, as needed
- 2 cups white wine (chardonnay or sauvignon blanc)
- 2 cups heavy cream
- 1½ teaspoons cayenne pepper
- 1½ teaspoons freshly ground black pepper
- ½ teaspoon saffron threads
- 1 loaf sourdough bread, cut into slices, for serving

1. Select SEAR/SAUTÉ and set the temperature to HI. Select START/STOP to begin and allow to preheat for 5 minutes.
2. Add oil to the pot and allow to heat for 1 minute. Add the shallots, garlic, and cherry tomatoes. Stir to ensure the ingredients are coated and sauté for 5 minutes.
3. Add the mussels, wine, heavy cream, cayenne, black pepper, and saffron threads to the pot.
4. Assemble the pressure lid, making sure the pressure release valve is in the VENT position.
5. Select STEAM and set the temperature to HI. Set the time to 20 minutes. Select START/STOP to begin.
6. When cooking is complete, carefully remove the lid.
7. Transfer the mussels and broth to bowls or eat straight from the pot. Discard any mussels that have not opened.
8. Serve with the bread and enjoy!

*Per serving: Calories: 882; Total Fat: 54g; Saturated Fat:29 g; Cholesterol: 179mg; Sodium: 769mg; Carbohydrates: 61g; Fiber: 3g; Protein: 20g*

# Coconut Shrimp with Pineapple Rice by Meg Jordan

SERVES 4

***Chef says:*** *When I traveled to the Caribbean a few years ago for vacation, I ate coconut shrimp almost every day. Not so healthy when it's deep fried in oil! This version utilizes the Air Crisp function to provide delicious, crispy shrimp without all the fat. I'm also a huge fan of adding fruit to rice, which helps bring brightness to this dish.*

**DAIRY-FREE, NUT-FREE, 360 MEAL, UNDER 30 MINUTES, FAMILY FAVORITE**

**PREP TIME:** 15 minutes
**TOTAL COOK TIME:** 45 minutes

**SEAR/SAUTÉ:** 9 minutes
**APPROX. PRESSURE BUILD:** 10 minutes
**PRESSURE COOK:** 2 minutes
**PRESSURE RELEASE:** 10 minutes, then Quick
**AIR CRISP:** 10 minutes

**ACCESSORIES:** Cook & Crisp Basket

**VARIATION TIP:** If you're not a fan of coconut, omit it from the breading and use only the panko bread crumbs.

2 tablespoons canola oil

1 (20-ounce) can diced pineapple

1 yellow onion, diced

1 cup long-grain white rice

1½ cups chicken stock

½ cup freshly squeezed lime juice

¾ cup all-purpose flour

1 tablespoon kosher salt

½ teaspoon freshly ground black pepper

2 large eggs

½ cup coconut flakes

½ cup plain panko bread crumbs

10 ounces, deveined shrimp, tails removed

Cooking spray

1. Select SEAR/SAUTÉ and set temperature to HI. Select START/STOP to begin. Let preheat for 5 minutes.

2. Add the oil and heat for 1 minute. Add the pineapple and onion. Cook, stirring frequently, for about 8 minutes, or until the onion is translucent.

3. Add the rice, chicken stock, and lime juice. Assemble pressure lid, making sure the pressure release valve is in the SEAL position.

4. Select PRESSURE and set to HI. Set time to 2 minutes. Select START/STOP to begin.

5. When pressure cooking is complete, allow press to naturally release for 10 minutes. After 10 minutes, quick release remaining pressure by turning the pressure release valve to the VENT position. Carefully remove lid when unit has finished releasing pressure.

6. Transfer the rice mixture to a bowl and cover to keep warm. Clean the cooking pot and return to the unit.

7. Create a batter station with three medium bowls. In the first bowl, mix together the flour, salt and pepper. In the

second bowl, whisk the eggs. In the third bowl, combine the coconut flakes and bread crumbs. Dip each shrimp into the flour mixture. Next dip it in the egg. Finally, coat in the coconut mixture, shaking off excess as needed. Once all the shrimp are battered, spray them with cooking spray.

8. Place Cook & Crisp Basket into pot. Place the shrimp in basket and close crisping lid.

9. Select AIR CRISP, set temperature to 390ºF, and set time to 10 minutes. Select START/STOP to begin.

10. After 5 minutes, open lid, then lift basket and shake the shrimp. Lower basket back into the pot and close the lid to continue cooking until the shrimp reach your desired crispiness.

11. When cooking is complete, serve the shrimp on top of the rice.

Per serving: *Calories: 601; Total Fat: 15g; Saturated Fat: 5g; Cholesterol: 232mg; Sodium: 784mg; Carbohydrates: 88g; Fiber: 5g; Protein: 28g*

# Spicy Shrimp Pasta with Vodka Sauce by Caroline Schliep

**SERVES 6**

***Chef says:*** *This pasta dish is a simple and foolproof recipe that comes out delicious every time. Add your ingredients to the cooking pot and let the Ninja® Foodi™ Pressure Cooker do the rest. I particularly like making this meal during a busy work week because it comes together well under 30 minutes. And if you are forgetful like me, you don't even have to worry about thawing the shrimp.*

NUT-FREE, UNDER 30 MINUTES

PREP TIME: 5 minutes
TOTAL COOK TIME:
11 minutes

SEAR/SAUTÉ: 3 minutes
APPROX. PRESSURE BUILD:
10 minutes
PRESSURE COOK: 6 minutes
PRESSURE RELEASE: Quick
AIR CRISP: 5 minutes

SUBSTITUTION TIP: If you have a shellfish allergy or are just looking to switch things up, try swapping the shrimp for chicken or Italian sausage.

- 2 tablespoons extra-virgin olive oil
- 2 tablespoons minced garlic
- 1 teaspoon crushed red pepper flakes
- 1 small red onion, diced
- Kosher salt
- Freshly ground black pepper
- ¾ cup vodka
- 2¾ cups vegetable stock
- 1 (28-ounce) can crushed tomatoes
- 1 (16-ounce) box penne pasta
- 1 pound frozen shrimp, peeled and deveined
- 1 (8-ounce) package cream cheese, cubed
- 4 cups shredded mozzarella cheese

1. Select SEAR/SAUTÉ and set to MD:HI. Select START/STOP to begin. Let preheat for 5 minutes.

2. Add the olive oil, garlic, and crushed red pepper flakes. Cook until garlic is golden brown, about 1 minute. Add the onions and season with salt and pepper and cook until translucent, about 2 minutes.

3. Stir in the vodka, vegetable stock, crushed tomatoes, penne pasta, and frozen shrimp. Assemble pressure lid, making sure the pressure release valve is in the SEAL position.

4. Select PRESSURE and set temperature to HI. Set time to 6 minutes. Select START/STOP to begin.

5. When pressure cooking is complete, quick release the pressure by turning the pressure release valve to the VENT position. Carefully remove lid when unit has finished releasing pressure.

6. Stir in the cream cheese until it has melted. Layer the mozzarella on top of the pasta. Close crisping lid.

CONTINUED ▶

# Spicy Shrimp Pasta with Vodka Sauce continued

7. Select AIR CRISP, set temperature to 400ºF, and set time to 5 minutes. Select START/STOP to begin.

8. When cooking is complete, open lid and serve.

Per serving: *Calories: 789; Total Fat: 35g; Saturated Fat: 18g; Cholesterol: 162mg; Sodium: 1302mg; Carbohydrates: 63g; Fiber: 6g; Protein: 47g*

# Crab Cake Casserole by Sam Ferguson

**SERVES 8**

***Chef says:*** *I know so many people who love eating crab cakes but are completely intimidated by the idea of making them at home. They must be pan-seared just right in order to be delicious; otherwise the texture just isn't there. The Foodi™ Pressure Cooker takes away that stress by perfectly crisping the top of this casserole. Plus, with the Foodi, you won't just get two skimpy crab cakes—you get an entire casserole.*

NUT-FREE, UNDER
30 MINUTES

PREP TIME: 10 minutes
TOTAL COOK TIME:
17 minutes

SEAR/SAUTÉ: 5 minutes
APPROX. PRESSURE BUILD:
10 minutes
PRESSURE COOK: 2 minutes
PRESSURE RELEASE:
10 minutes, then Quick
BAKE/ROAST: 10 minutes

VARIATION TIP: It is easy to transform this recipe from a crunchy casserole into a game-day dip. Just add 1 cup of room-temperature cream cheese to the pot in step 6 and stir well until incorporated.

2 tablespoons canola oil
1 large onion, chopped
2 celery stalks, chopped
1 red bell pepper, chopped
1½ cups basmati rice, rinsed
2 cups chicken stock
¼ cup mayonnaise

¼ cup Dijon mustard
3 (8-ounce) cans
lump crab meat
1 cup shredded Cheddar
cheese, divided
1 (5-ounce) sleeve butter
crackers, crumbled

1.  Select SEAR/SAUTÉ and set to HI. Select START/STOP to begin. Let preheat for 5 minutes.

2.  Add the oil. Once hot, add the onion, celery, and bell pepper and stir. Cook for 5 minutes, stirring occasionally.

3.  Stir in the rice and chicken stock. Assemble pressure lid, making sure the pressure release valve is in the SEAL position.

4.  Select PRESSURE and set to HI. Set time to 2 minutes. Select START/STOP to begin.

5.  When pressure cooking is complete, allow pressure to naturally release for 10 minutes. After 10 minutes, quick release any remaining pressure by moving the pressure release valve to the VENT position. Carefully remove lid when unit has finished releasing pressure.

6.  Stir in the mayonnaise, mustard, crab, and ½ cup of Cheddar cheese. Top evenly with the crackers, then top with remaining ½ cup of cheese. Close crisping lid.

7.  Select BAKE/ROAST, set temperature to 350°F, and set time to 10 minutes. Select START/STOP to begin.

8.  When cooking is complete, open lid and serve immediately.

*Per serving: Calories: 448; Total Fat: 25g; Saturated Fat: 5g; Cholesterol: 67mg; Sodium: 819mg; Carbohydrates: 46g; Fiber: 1g; Protein: 22g*

# Shrimp and Chorizo Potpie by Craig White

**Chef says:** *Shrimp and sausage are a classic culinary pairing. You see this combination in dishes like gumbo, paella, and jambalaya. The roux created by the butter and flour thickens the liquids in the pot to create a sauce. If you like heat, feel free to hit it with a few dashes of your favorite hot sauce. Adding the pie crust makes it hearty comfort food at its finest.*

NUT-FREE, UNDER
30 MINUTES, 360 MEAL

PREP TIME: 10 minutes
TOTAL COOK TIME:
23 minutes

SEAR/SAUTÉ: 8 minutes
BROIL: 10 minutes

SUBSTITUTION TIP: If you don't have all the vegetables listed, you can substitute similar vegetables that you have on hand, like frozen peas and corn.

- ¼ cup unsalted butter
- ½ large onion, diced
- 1 celery stalk, diced
- 1 carrot, peeled and diced
- 8 ounces chorizo, fully cooked, cut into ½-inch wheels
- ¼ cup all-purpose flour
- 16 ounces frozen tail-off shrimp, cleaned and deveined
- ¾ cup chicken stock
- 1 tablespoon Cajun spice mix
- ½ cup heavy (whipping) cream
- Sea salt
- Freshly ground black pepper
- 1 refrigerated store-bought pie crust, at room temperature

1. Select SEAR/SAUTÉ and set to MD:HI. Select START/STOP to begin. Let preheat for 5 minutes.

2. Add the butter. Once melted, add the onion, celery, carrot, and sausage, and cook until softened, about 3 minutes. Stir in the flour and cook 2 minutes, stirring occasionally.

3. Add the shrimp, stock, Cajun spice mix, and cream and season with salt and pepper. Stir until sauce thickens and bubbles, about 3 minutes.

4. Lay the pie crust evenly on top of the filling, folding over the edges if necessary. Make a small cut in center of pie crust so that steam can escape during baking. Close crisping lid.

5. Select BROIL and set time to 10 minutes. Select START/STOP to begin.

6. When cooking is complete, open lid and remove pot from unit. Let rest 10 to 15 minutes before serving.

Per serving: Calories: 528; Total Fat: 37g; Saturated Fat: 17g; Cholesterol: 227mg; Sodium: 776mg; Carbohydrates: 19g; Fiber: 1g; Protein: 28g

# Salmon with Almonds, Cranberries, and Rice by Sam Ferguson

**SERVES 4**

*Chef says:* *This style of recipe highlights the transformative power of the Ninja® Foodi™ Pressure Cooker—you can cook rice at the same time as salmon, and then develop a flavorful, crispy crust on the top of the fish without drying out your rice. These kinds of recipes are a great way to utilize the frozen proteins hiding in your freezer.*

**DAIRY-FREE, 360 MEAL, UNDER 30 MINUTES**

**PREP TIME:** 10 minutes
**TOTAL COOK TIME:**
10 minutes

**APPROX. PRESSURE BUILD:**
10 minutes
**PRESSURE COOK:** 2 minutes
**PRESSURE RELEASE:**
10 minutes, then Quick
**BROIL:** 8 minutes

**ACCESSORIES:**
Reversible Rack

**SUBSTITUTION TIP:**
Don't have sunflower seeds? Any nut or seed would work great as a substitute—pecans, walnuts, pistachios, etc.

1½ cups long-grain white rice, rinsed

1½ cups water

⅓ cup dry cranberries

⅓ cup slivered almonds

Kosher salt

4 (4-ounce) frozen salmon fillets

⅓ cup dry roasted sunflower seeds

¼ cup Dijon mustard

⅓ cup panko bread crumbs

1 tablespoon honey

1 tablespoon minced parsley

1. Place the rice, water, cranberries, and almonds in the pot. Season with salt and stir. Place Reversible Rack in pot in the higher broil position. Place a circle of aluminum foil on top of the rack, then place the salmon fillets on the foil. Assemble pressure lid, making sure the pressure release valve is in the SEAL position.

2. Select PRESSURE and set to HI. Set time to 2 minutes. Select START/STOP to begin.

3. Add the sunflower seeds, mustard, bread crumbs, honey, and parsley to a small bowl and mix well.

4. When pressure cooking is complete, allow pressure to naturally release for 10 minutes. After 10 minutes, quick release remaining pressure by moving the pressure release valve to the VENT position. Carefully remove lid when unit has finished releasing pressure.

5. Using a spoon, spread a thick, even layer of the sunflower mixture across the top of each fillet. Close crisping lid.

6. Select BROIL and set time to 8 minutes. Select START/STOP to begin. When cooking is complete, open lid and remove the rack and salmon. Use a silicone-coated spatula to fluff the rice. Serve the salmon fillets over the rice.

*Per serving: Calories: 505; Total Fat: 10g; Saturated Fat: 1g; Cholesterol: 0mg; Sodium: 536mg; Carbohydrates: 75g; Fiber: 4g; Protein: 28g*

# 8
# Poultry

# Garlic-Herb Roasted Chicken

**SERVES 4**

*Nothing beats an easy-to-prepare roast chicken that is versatile enough for a week-night dinner or weekend dinner party. With the Ninja® Foodi™ Pressure Cooker, a roast chicken is foolproof and delicious. In fact, in the Ninja Test Kitchen we have cooked thousands of chickens to ensure that your chickens come out perfect every time. This version is basted with butter and herbs and roasted to golden, brown perfection.*

**DAIRY-FREE, GLUTEN-FREE, NUT-FREE**

**PREP TIME:** 10 minutes
**TOTAL COOK TIME:**
40 minutes

**APPROX. PRESSURE BUILD:**
10 minutes
**PRESSURE COOK:**
15 minutes
**PRESSURE RELEASE:** Quick
**AIR CRISP:** 20 minutes

**ACCESSORIES:** Cook & Crisp Basket

1 (4½- to 5-pound) whole chicken
1 head garlic
2 fresh whole sprigs rosemary
2 fresh whole sprigs parsley
1 lemon, halved
¼ cup hot water
¼ cup white wine
Juice of 2 lemons
¼ cup unsalted butter, melted

3 tablespoons extra-virgin olive oil
5 garlic cloves, minced
2 teaspoons minced fresh parsley
2 teaspoons minced fresh rosemary
½ teaspoon sea salt
¼ teaspoon freshly ground black pepper

1. Discard the neck from inside the chicken cavity and remove any excess fat and leftover feathers. Rinse the chicken inside and out under running cold water. Stuff the garlic head into the chicken cavity along with the rosemary and parsley sprigs and lemon halves. Tie the legs together with cooking twine.

2. Add the water, wine, and lemon juice. Place the chicken into the Cook & Crisp Basket and insert the basket in the pot. Assemble pressure lid, making sure the pressure release valve is in the SEAL position.

3. Select PRESSURE and set to HI. Set time to 15 minutes. Select START/STOP to begin.

4. When pressure cooking is complete, quick release the pressure by moving the pressure release valve to the VENT position. Carefully remove lid when the unit has finished releasing pressure.

5. In a small bowl, combine the butter, olive oil, minced garlic, minced parsley, minced rosemary, salt, and pepper. Brush the mixture over the chicken. Close crisping lid.

6. Select AIR CRISP, set temperature to 400ºF, and set time to 20 minutes. Select START/STOP to begin. (If you prefer a crispier chicken, add 5 to 10 minutes to the time.)

7. Cooking is complete when the internal temperature of the chicken reaches 165ºF on a meat thermometer inserted into the thickest part of the meat (it should not touch the bone). Carefully remove the chicken from the basket using 2 large serving forks.

8. Let the chicken rest for 10 minutes before carving and serving.

**Per serving:** *Calories: 693; Total Fat: 50g; Saturated Fat: 11g; Cholesterol: 50mg; Sodium: 323mg; Carbohydrates: 12g; Fiber: 1g; Protein: 48g*

# Cashew Chicken by Craig White

SERVES 4

***Chef says:*** *When I was a green line cook, I would meet up with friends and head to Chinatown for some late-night food. Sure, we ate plenty of odd foods like jellyfish salad or duck tongues, but there were always dishes like this on the table, which we washed down with "cold tea" at 2:00 a.m.*

DAIRY-FREE, UNDER 30 MINUTES

PREP TIME: 10 minutes, plus 4 hours to marinate
TOTAL COOK TIME: 13 minutes

SEAR/SAUTÉ: 8 minutes

VARIATION TIP: Why is your tongue tingling? That's the Sichuan peppercorns working their magic! For those who don't like spicy food, you can easily omit the chiles and peppercorns.

1 pound chicken breast, cut into ½-inch pieces

4 tablespoons stir-fry sauce, divided

3 tablespoons canola oil

12 arbol chiles

1 teaspoon Sichuan peppercorns

2 teaspoons grated fresh ginger

2 garlic cloves, minced

¾ cup cashews

6 scallions, cut into 1-inch pieces

2 teaspoons dark soy sauce

½ teaspoon sesame oil

1. Place the chicken in a zip-top bag and add 2 tablespoons of stir-fry sauce. Let marinate for 4 hours, or overnight.

2. Select SEAR/SAUTÉ and set to HI. Select START/STOP to begin. Let preheat for 5 minutes.

3. Add the oil, chiles, peppercorns, ginger, and garlic and cook for 1 minute.

4. Add half the chicken and cook for 2 minutes, stirring occasionally. Transfer the chicken to a plate and set aside. Add the remaining chicken and cook for 2 minutes, stirring occasionally. Return the first batch of chicken to the pot and add the cashews. Cook for 2 minutes, stirring occasionally.

5. Add the scallions, soy sauce, sesame oil, and remaining 2 tablespoons of stir-fry sauce to pot and cook for 1 minute, stirring frequently.

6. When cooking is complete, serve immediately over steamed rice, if desired.

*Per serving: Calories: 431; Total Fat: 26g; Saturated Fat: 3g; Cholesterol: 73mg; Sodium: 809mg; Carbohydrates: 19g; Fiber: 1g; Protein: 29g*

# Chicken and Broccoli Stir-Fry by Meg Jordan

**SERVES 4**

**Chef says:** *Chinese food is a guilty pleasure of mine, but I've been searching for a way to make this classic dish healthier. This recipe uses only teriyaki sauce to cut down on the salt, and ground ginger gives it an extra kick—all in less than 30 minutes.*

---

DAIRY-FREE, NUT-FREE,
UNDER 30 MINUTES,
FAMILY FAVORITE,
360 MEAL

---

PREP TIME: 5 minutes
TOTAL COOK TIME:
20 minutes

---

APPROX. PRESSURE BUILD:
10 minutes
PRESSURE COOK: 2 minutes
PRESSURE RELEASE:
10 minutes, then Quick
SEAR/SAUTÉ: 15 minutes

---

VARIATION TIP: Make this
ready for Meatless Mondays
by using tofu instead
of chicken.

---

1 cup long-grain white rice

1 cup chicken stock

2 tablespoons canola oil

3 boneless, skinless
chicken breasts, cut
into 1-inch cubes

1 medium head broccoli,
cut into 1-inch florets

2 teaspoons kosher salt

½ teaspoon freshly
ground black pepper

1 tablespoon ground ginger

¼ cup teriyaki sauce

Sesame seeds, for garnish

1. Place the rice and chicken stock into the pot. Assemble pressure lid, making sure the pressure release valve is in the SEAL position.

2. Select PRESSURE and set to HI. Set time to 2 minutes. Select START/STOP to begin.

3. When pressure cooking is complete, allow pressure to naturally release for 10 minutes. After 10 minutes, quick release remaining pressure by turning the pressure release valve to the VENT position. Carefully remove lid when unit has finished releasing pressure.

4. Transfer the rice to a bowl and cover to keep warm. Clean the cooking pot and return to unit.

5. Select SEAR/SAUTÉ and set to HI. Select START/STOP to begin. Let preheat for 5 minutes.

6. Add the oil and heat for 1 minute. Add the chicken and cook, stirring frequently, for about 6 minutes.

7. Stir in the broccoli, salt, pepper, and ginger. Cook for 5 minutes, stirring frequently. Stir in the teriyaki sauce and cook, stirring frequently, until the chicken has reached internal temperature of 165°F on a food thermometer.

8. Serve the chicken and broccoli mixture over the rice. Garnish with sesame seeds if desired.

---

*Per serving: Calories: 425; Total Fat: 10g; Saturated Fat: 1g; Cholesterol: 67mg; Sodium: 1176mg; Carbohydrates: 49g; Fiber: 3g; Protein: 35g*

# Chicken Burrito Bowl

**SERVES 4**

*One of my guilty pleasure go-to meals when eating takeout is a burrito bowl. There are so many flavors and textures coming together—and you get a little bit of everything with protein, grains, and veggies. I love that I can recreate this favorite of mine at home using the Ninja® Foodi™ Pressure Cooker. Everything goes right into the pot with no fuss, and cleanup is a breeze.*

GLUTEN-FREE, NUT-FREE,
UNDER 30 MINUTES,
FAMILY FAVORITE

PREP TIME: 5 minutes
TOTAL COOK TIME:
10 minutes

APPROX. PRESSURE BUILD:
10 minutes
PRESSURE COOK:
10 minutes
PRESSURE RELEASE: Quick

HACK IT: Add a little crunch to your burrito bowl by crumbling some of your favorite tortilla chips on top of each serving.

- 1 pound boneless, skinless chicken breasts, cut into 1-inch chunks
- 1 tablespoon chili powder
- 1½ teaspoons cumin
- 1 teaspoon sea salt
- 1 teaspoon freshly ground black pepper
- ½ teaspoon paprika
- ¼ teaspoon garlic powder
- ¼ teaspoon onion powder
- ¼ teaspoon cayenne pepper
- ¼ teaspoon dried oregano
- 1 cup chicken stock
- ¼ cup water
- 1¼ cups of your favorite salsa
- 1 (15-ounce) can corn kernels, drained
- 1 (15-ounce) can black beans, rinsed and drained
- 1 cup rice
- ¾ cup shredded Cheddar cheese

1. Add the chicken, chili powder, cumin, salt, black pepper, paprika, garlic powder, onion powder, cayenne pepper, oregano, chicken stock, water, salsa, corn, and beans and stir well.

2. Add the rice to the top of the ingredients in the pot. Assemble pressure lid, making sure the pressure release valve is in the SEAL position.

3. Select PRESSURE and set to HI. Set time to 10 minutes. Select START/STOP to begin.

4. When pressure cooking is complete, quick release the pressure by moving the pressure release valve to the VENT position. Carefully remove lid when the unit has finished releasing pressure.

5. Add the cheese and stir. Serve immediately.

*Per serving: Calories: 570; Total Fat: 11g; Saturated Fat: 5g; Cholesterol: 87mg; Sodium: 1344mg; Carbohydrates: 77g; Fiber: 11g; Protein: 45g*

# Garlic-Herb Chicken and Rice

**SERVES 4**

*I love cooking with chicken thighs because they are so versatile. Pressure cooking them and then crisping up the skin gives them an unbelievable combination of textures: moist and flavorful on the inside, and nice and crispy on the outside. Serve them alongside a rice pilaf, which cooks in the bottom of the pot at the same time.*

NUT-FREE, UNDER
30 MINUTES, FAMILY
FAVORITE

PREP TIME: 5 minutes
TOTAL COOK TIME:
14 minutes

APPROX. PRESSURE BUILD:
10 minutes
PRESSURE COOK: 4 minutes
PRESSURE RELEASE: Quick
BROIL: 10 minutes

ACCESSORIES:
Reversible Rack

VARIATION TIP: If you have
some room left on your
rack, place some vegetables
alongside your chicken
in step 2 for a complete,
360 meal. Just make sure to
season well.

1 (6-ounce) box rice pilaf

1¾ cups water

1 tablespoon unsalted butter

4 boneless, skin-on
chicken thighs

1 tablespoon extra-virgin
olive oil

1 teaspoon kosher salt

1 teaspoon garlic powder

1. Place the rice pilaf, water, and butter in the pot and stir.

2. Place Reversible Rack in pot, making sure it is in the higher position. Place the chicken thighs on the rack. Assemble pressure lid, making sure the pressure release valve is in the SEAL position.

3. Select PRESSURE and set to HI. Set time to 4 minutes. Select START/STOP to begin.

4. Stir together the olive oil, salt, and garlic powder in a small bowl.

5. When pressure cooking is complete, quick release the pressure by moving the pressure release valve to the VENT position. Carefully remove lid when unit has finished releasing pressure.

6. Brush the chicken with the olive oil mixture. Close crisping lid.

7. Select BROIL and set time to 10 minutes. Select START/STOP to begin.

8. When cooking is complete, serve the chicken with the rice.

*Per serving: Calories: 451; Total Fat: 32g; Saturated Fat: 10g; Cholesterol: 133mg; Sodium: 577mg; Carbohydrates: 18g; Fiber: 1g; Protein: 23g*

# Jerk Chicken Thighs with Sweet Potato and Banana Mash by Craig White

**SERVES 6**

*Chef says:* The first time I ate jerk chicken was about 15 years ago on a beach in Ochos Rios, Jamaica. I remember the clear blue water, steel drums playing off in the distance, ice-cold rum punch, and feeling like I didn't have a care in the world. As cliché as the memory is, that is still the best chicken I have had to this day and the benchmark for what I think jerk chicken should taste like. And the beach and the rum probably helped.

DAIRY-FREE, GLUTEN-FREE, NUT-FREE, 360 MEAL, UNDER 30 MINUTES

**PREP TIME:** 10 minutes
**TOTAL COOK TIME:** 20 minutes

**APPROX. PRESSURE BUILD:** 10 minutes
**PRESSURE COOK:** 4 minutes
**PRESSURE RELEASE:** Quick
**BROIL:** 15 minutes

**ACCESSORIES:** Reversible Rack

**SUBSTITUTION TIP:** Honey or maple syrup can easily be substituted for the agave nectar in this recipe.

- 4 boneless, skin-on chicken thighs
- ½ cup spicy jerk marinade
- 3 large sweet potatoes, peeled and cut into 1-inch cubes
- ½ cup unsweetened full-fat coconut milk
- Kosher salt
- Freshly ground black pepper
- 2 bananas, peeled and quartered
- 2 tablespoons agave nectar

1. Place the chicken thighs and jerk marinade in a container, rubbing the marinade all over the chicken. Cover the container with plastic wrap and marinate 15 minutes.

2. Place the sweet potatoes, coconut milk, salt, and pepper in the pot. Place Reversible Rack in pot, making sure it is in the higher position. Place the chicken skin-side up on the rack, leaving space between the pieces. Assemble pressure lid, making sure the pressure release valve is in the SEAL position.

3. Select PRESSURE and set to HI. Set time to 4 minutes. Select START/STOP to begin.

4. When pressure cooking is complete, quick release the pressure by turning the pressure release valve to the VENT position. Carefully remove lid when unit has finished releasing pressure.

5. Place the bananas in the spaces between chicken thighs. Close crisping lid.

6. Select BROIL and set time to 15 minutes. Select START/STOP to begin.

7. After 10 minutes, remove the bananas and set aside. Turn over the chicken thighs. Close lid and continue cooking.

CONTINUED ▶

# Jerk Chicken Thighs with Sweet Potato and Banana Mash continued

8. When cooking is complete, remove rack and chicken and let rest 5 to 10 minutes. Add the roasted bananas and agave nectar and mash them along with the sweet potatoes. Once rested, serve the chicken and sweet potato and banana mash.

*Per serving: Calories: 397; Total Fat: 22g; Saturated Fat: 9g; Cholesterol: 83mg; Sodium: 709mg; Carbohydrates: 35g; Fiber: 4g; Protein: 20g*

# Simple Chicken Parmesan

**SERVES 4**

*There are hundreds (maybe thousands) of chicken parm recipes in the world, but it remains one of the most requested. This version is easy, simple, and classic. With a crispy breadcrumb exterior and melted mozzarella cheese on top, you really can't go wrong. Use your favorite marinara recipe or sub in a jarred sauce if you are in a pinch—either way, you will be sure to step up Italian night with this quick and simple recipe.*

NUT-FREE, UNDER
30 MINUTES, FAMILY
FAVORITE

**PREP TIME:** 5 minutes
**TOTAL COOK TIME:**
20 minutes

**AIR CRISP:** 15 minutes
**BROIL:** 5 minutes

**ACCESSORIES:**
Reversible Rack

1 cup all-purpose flour
1 teaspoon sea salt
2 eggs, beaten
2 tablespoons water
1 cup seasoned bread crumbs
½ cup grated
   Parmesan cheese

4 (6-ounce) chicken cutlets
2 tablespoons
   extra-virgin olive oil
¼ cup marinara sauce
1 cup shredded
   mozzarella cheese

1. Place the flour and salt in a shallow bowl and stir. In another shallow bowl, add the eggs and water, whisking to combine. Place the bread crumbs and Parmesan cheese in a third shallow bowl.

2. Dredge each piece of chicken in the flour. Tap off any excess, then coat the chicken in the egg wash. Transfer the chicken to the breadcrumb mixture and evenly coat. Repeat until all the chicken is coated.

3. Place Reversible Rack in pot, making sure it is in the higher position. Place the chicken on the rack and brush lightly with the oil. Close crisping lid.

4. Select AIR CRISP, set temperature to 325ºF, and set time to 15 minutes. Select START/STOP to begin.

5. After 15 minutes, open lid and spread the marinara sauce on top of the chicken. Top with the mozzarella. Close crisping lid.

6. Select BROIL and set time to 5 minutes. Select START/STOP to begin.

7. When the cheese is fully melted, cooking is complete. Serve.

Per serving: *Calories: 589; Total Fat: 23g; Saturated Fat: 8g; Cholesterol: 215mg; Sodium: 1215mg; Carbohydrates: 38g; Fiber: 2g; Protein: 54g*

# Garlic Chicken and Bacon Pasta

**SERVES 4**

*Sometimes there is nothing better than cozying up with a warm bowl of pasta. This creamy pasta is reminiscent of an alfredo, but with a garlic flavor that really comes through. Add some smoky, crispy bacon, and you will have a pot full of comfort food goodness.*

NUT-FREE, UNDER 30 MINUTES, FAMILY FAVORITE

PREP TIME: 5 minutes
TOTAL COOK TIME:
10 minutes

SEAR/SAUTÉ: 7 minutes
APPROX. PRESSURE BUILD:
10 minutes
PRESSURE COOK: 3 minutes
PRESSURE RELEASE:
2 minutes, then Quick

HACK IT: Want to get a head start on this recipe in the morning or over the weekend? Cook the bacon ahead of time and store in an airtight container or resealable bag in the refrigerator for up to 4 days.

3 strips bacon, chopped

½ pound boneless, skinless chicken breast, cut into ½-pieces

1 teaspoon dried basil

1 teaspoon dried oregano

¼ teaspoon sea salt

1 tablespoon unsalted butter

3 garlic cloves, minced

1 cup chicken stock

1½ cups water

8 ounces dry penne pasta

½ cup half-and-half

½ cup grated Parmesan cheese, plus more for serving

1. Select SEAR/SAUTÉ and set to HI. Select START/STOP to begin. Let preheat for 5 minutes.

2. Add the bacon and cook, stirring frequently, for about 5 minutes or until crispy. Using a slotted spoon, transfer the bacon to a paper towel-lined plate to drain.

3. Season the chicken with the basil, oregano, and salt, coating all the pieces.

4. Add the butter, chicken, and garlic and sauté for 2 minutes, until the chicken begins to brown and the garlic is fragrant.

5. Add the chicken stock, water, and penne pasta. Assemble pressure lid, making sure the pressure release valve is in the SEAL position.

6. Select PRESSURE and set to HI. Set time to 3 minutes. Select START/STOP to begin.

7. When pressure cooking is complete, allow pressure to naturally release for 2 minutes. After 2 minutes, quick release remaining pressure by moving the pressure release valve to the VENT position. Carefully remove lid when unit has finished releasing pressure.

8. Add the half-and-half, cheese, and bacon, and stir constantly to thicken the sauce and melt the cheese. Serve immediately, with additional Parmesan cheese to garnish.

*Per serving: Calories: 458; Total Fat: 18g; Saturated Fat: 8g; Cholesterol: 81mg; Sodium: 809mg; Carbohydrates: 45g; Fiber: 2g; Protein: 30g*

# Creamy Chicken Carbonara

*Carbonara is one of those Italian classics that has made its way to America and seen a ton of variations. By swapping out the traditional guanciale for bacon, this becomes a delicious dinner that you can make with pantry and refrigerator staple ingredients. The biggest trick is to make sure you don't scramble the eggs toward the end of the recipe—but that extra bit of attention is worth it once you take your first bite.*

**NUT-FREE, UNDER 30 MINUTES, FAMILY FAVORITE**

**PREP TIME:** 5 minutes
**TOTAL COOK TIME:** 15 minutes

**SEAR/SAUTÉ:** 10 minutes
**APPROX. PRESSURE BUILD:** 10 minutes
**PRESSURE COOK:** 6 minutes
**PRESSURE RELEASE:** 5 minutes, then Quick

**SUBSTITUTION TIP:** Spaghetti is the traditional pasta choice for carbonara, but you can pick anything from fettuccine to farfalle. For shorter cuts of pasta, try pressure cooking for 3 to 4 minutes instead.

- 4 strips bacon, chopped
- 1 medium onion, diced
- 1½ pounds chicken breast, cut into ¾ inch-cubes
- 6 garlic cloves, minced
- 2 cups chicken stock
- 8 ounces dry spaghetti, with noodles broken in half
- 2 cups freshly grated Parmesan cheese, plus more for serving
- 2 eggs
- Sea salt
- Freshly ground black pepper

1. Select SEAR/SAUTÉ and set to HI. Select START/STOP to begin. Let preheat for 5 minutes.

2. Add the bacon and cook, stirring frequently, for about 6 minutes, or until crispy. Using a slotted spoon, transfer the bacon to a paper towel-lined plate to drain. Leave any bacon fat in the pot.

3. Add the onion, chicken, and garlic and sauté for 2 minutes, until the onions start to become translucent and the garlic is fragrant.

4. Add the chicken stock and spaghetti noodles. Assemble pressure lid, making sure the pressure release valve is in the SEAL position.

5. Select PRESSURE and set to HI. Set time to 6 minutes. Select START/STOP to begin.

6. When pressure cooking is complete, allow pressure to naturally release for 5 minutes. After 5 minutes, quick release remaining pressure by moving the pressure release valve to the VENT position. Carefully remove lid when unit has finished releasing pressure.

7. Add the cheese and stir to fully combine. Close the crisping lid, leaving the unit off, to keep the heat inside and allow the cheese to melt.

8. Whisk the eggs until full beaten.

9. Open lid, select SEAR/SAUTÉ, and set to LO. Select START/ STOP to begin. Add the eggs and stir gently to incorporate, taking care to ensure the eggs are not scrambling while you work toward your desired sauce consistency. If your pot gets too warm, turn unit off.

10. Add the bacon back to the pot and season with salt and pepper. Stir to combine. Serve, adding more cheese as desired.

*Per serving: Calories: 732; Total Fat: 28g; Saturated Fat: 12g; Cholesterol: 250mg; Sodium: 1518mg; Carbohydrates: 47g; Fiber: 7g; Protein: 70g*

# Bacon Ranch Chicken Bake

**SERVES 6**

*Creamy, cheesy, and comforting, this casserole is all you need on a busy weeknight. It is loaded with ranch, chicken, and bacon—just a few of my all-time favorites. Not to mention an ooey gooey cheesy top that sends this dish right over the edge.*

**GLUTEN-FREE, NUT-FREE, UNDER 30 MINUTES**

**PREP TIME:** 10 minutes
**TOTAL COOK TIME:** 30 minutes

**SEAR/SAUTÉ:** 15 minutes
**APPROX. PRESSURE BUILD:** 10 minutes
**PRESSURE COOK:** 7 minutes
**PRESSURE RELEASE:** Quick
**BROIL:** 8 minutes

**VARIATION TIP:** Sneak in some veggies by adding broccoli florets to the pot after the chicken is cooked and before pressure cooking.

*Per serving: Calories: 512; Total Fat: 27g; Saturated Fat: 12g; Cholesterol: 109mg; Sodium: 999mg; Carbohydrates: 28g; Fiber: 1g; Protein: 35g*

1 pound chicken breast, cut in 1-inch cubes

2 tablespoons extra-virgin olive oil

3 tablespoons ranch seasoning mix, divided

4 strips bacon, chopped

1 small onion, chopped

2 garlic cloves, minced

1 cup long-grain white rice

2 cups chicken broth

½ cup half-and-half

2 cups shredded Cheddar cheese, divided

2 tablespoons chopped fresh parsley

1. Select SEAR/SAUTÉ and set to HI. Select START/STOP to begin. Let preheat for 5 minutes.

2. In a large bowl, toss the chicken with the olive oil and 2 tablespoons of ranch seasoning mix.

3. Add the bacon to the pot and cook, stirring frequently, for about 6 minutes, or until crispy. Using a slotted spoon, transfer the bacon to a paper towel-lined plate to drain.

4. Add the onion and cook for about 5 minutes. Add the garlic and cook for 1 minute more. Add the chicken and stir, cooking until chicken is cooked through, about 3 minutes.

5. Add the rice, chicken broth, and remaining ranch mix. Assemble pressure lid, making sure the pressure release valve is in the SEAL position.

6. Select PRESSURE and set to HI. Set time to 7 minutes. Select START/STOP to begin.

7. When complete, quick release the pressure by turning the valve to the VENT position. Carefully remove lid when unit has finished releasing pressure.

8. Stir in half-and-half and 1 cup of Cheddar cheese. Top with the remaining 1 cup of cheese. Close crisping lid.

9. Select BROIL and set time to 8 minutes. Select START/STOP to begin. When cooking is complete, serve garnished with fresh parsley.

# Creamy Tuscan Chicken Pasta

**by Caroline Schliep**

SERVES 8

**Chef says:** *This is one of those "set it and forget it" meals that comes together effort-lessly within minutes. Instead of spending your money going out to a fancy Italian restaurant, wow your friends by making this dish right in the comfort of your own home. With the mouthwatering combination of pasta, chicken, sun-dried tomatoes, and spinach tossed in a luscious cream sauce, this is sure to be a crowd pleaser.*

NUT-FREE, UNDER
30 MINUTES

PREP TIME: 10 minutes
TOTAL COOK TIME:
6 minutes

APPROX. PRESSURE BUILD:
10 minutes
PRESSURE COOK: 6 minutes
PRESSURE RELEASE: Quick

VARIATION TIP: Make this
pasta dish meatless by
replacing the chicken with
roasted red peppers and
more spinach.

- 32 ounces (1 quart) chicken stock
- 1 (7-ounce) jar oil-packed sun-dried tomatoes, drained
- 2 teaspoons Italian seasoning
- 3 garlic cloves, minced
- 1 pound chicken breast, cubed
- 1 (16-ounce) box penne pasta
- 4 cups spinach
- 1 (8-ounce) package cream cheese, cubed
- 1 cup shredded Parmesan cheese
- Kosher salt
- Freshly ground black pepper

1. Place the chicken stock, sun-dried tomatoes, Italian sea-soning, garlic, chicken breast, and pasta and stir. Assemble pressure lid, making sure the pressure release valve is in the SEAL position.

2. Select PRESSURE and set to HI. Set time to 6 minutes. Select START/STOP to begin.

3. When pressure cooking is complete, quick release the pressure by turning the pressure release valve to the VENT position. Carefully remove lid when unit has finished releasing pressure.

4. Add the spinach and stir, allowing it to wilt with the resid-ual heat. Add the cream cheese, Parmesan cheese, salt and pepper and stir until melted. Serve.

*Per serving: Calories: 429; Total Fat: 21g; Saturated Fat: 9g; Cholesterol: 83mg; Sodium: 567mg; Carbohydrates: 32g; Fiber: 4g; Protein: 29g*

# Slow Cooked Chicken in White Wine and Garlic by Meg Jordan

**Chef says:** *In the winter months in New England, I love braising meats in my Dutch oven on the stove. However, I usually don't have all day to dedicate to checking on the food and adjusting temperatures as needed. By using the Slow Cook function on the Foodi™ Pressure Cooker, I'm able to replicate this hearty dish in less time. This dish is great served over buttered egg noodles for a full meal.*

DAIRY-FREE, GLUTEN-FREE, NUT-FREE

PREP TIME: 5 minutes
TOTAL COOK TIME: 4 hours

SLOW COOK: 4 hours

SUBSTITUTION TIP: Don't like capers? Olives can be used instead for a less briny flavor.

- 6 (4- to 6-ounce) bone-in, skin-on, chicken thighs
- 10 garlic cloves, peeled
- 6 cups chicken broth
- 1 cup dry white wine
- 2 teaspoons dried oregano
- 2 teaspoons kosher salt
- 1 teaspoon freshly ground black pepper
- ¼ cup capers, drained
- 1 tablespoon chopped fresh parsley

1. Place the chicken, garlic cloves, chicken broth, wine, oregano, salt, and pepper in the cooking pot.

2. Assemble pressure lid, making sure the pressure release valve is in the VENT position. Select SLOW COOK and set to HI. Set time to 4 hours. Select START/STOP to begin.

3. When cooking is complete, carefully remove the lid. Stir in the capers.

4. Serve garnished with fresh parsley.

*Per serving: Calories: 343; Total Fat: 36g; Saturated Fat: 8g; Cholesterol: 135mg; Sodium: 578mg; Carbohydrates: 4g; Fiber: 1g; Protein: 24g*

# Buttermilk Fried Chicken

**by Aurelia McCollom, Ninja® Foodi™ Family Member**

**SERVES 4**

*Aurelia says:* A classic favorite, this dish uses my basic chicken breading recipe and makes it healthier using the Ninja Foodi.

**FAMILY FAVORITE, NUT-FREE**

**PREP TIME:** 15 minutes, plus 4 hours soaking time
**TOTAL COOK TIME:** 30 minutes

**AIR CRISP:** 30 minutes

**ACCESSORIES:** Cook & Crisp Basket

**SUBSTITUTION TIP:** For bone-in, skin-on chicken, set the temperature to 400°F and set the time to 28 minutes, turning the chicken after 14 minutes. Check the chicken at 24 to 26 minutes for an internal temperature of 165°F on a digital food temperature.

**Find Aurelia on Facebook: Ninja Foodi & All Ninja Multi-Cooker Systems+ Recipes—since 2013!**

- 1½ pounds boneless, skinless chicken breasts
- 1 to 2 cups buttermilk
- 2 large eggs
- ¾ cup all-purpose flour
- ¾ cup potato starch
- ½ teaspoon granulated garlic, divided
- 1 teaspoon salt, divided
- 2 teaspoons freshly ground black pepper, divided
- 1 cup bread crumbs
- ½ cup panko bread crumbs
- Olive oil or cooking spray

1. In a large bowl, combine the chicken breasts and buttermilk, turning the chicken to coat. Cover the bowl with plastic wrap and refrigerate the chicken to soak at least 4 hours or overnight.

2. In a medium shallow bowl, whisk the eggs. In a second shallow bowl, stir together the flour, potato starch, ¼ teaspoon of granulated garlic, ½ teaspoon of salt, and 1 teaspoon of pepper. In a third shallow bowl, stir together the bread crumbs, panko, remaining ¼ teaspoon of granulated garlic, remaining ½ teaspoon of salt, and remaining 1 teaspoon of pepper.

3. Working one piece at a time, remove the chicken from the buttermilk, letting the excess drip into the bowl. Dredge the chicken in the flour mixture, coating well on both sides. Then dip the chicken in the eggs, coating both sides. Finally, dip the chicken in the bread crumb mixture, coating both sides and pressing the crumbs onto the chicken. Spritz both sides of the coated chicken pieces with olive oil.

4. Place the Cook & Crisp Basket into the unit.

5. Select AIR CRISP, set the temperature to 400°F, and set the time to 30 minutes. Select START/STOP to begin and allow to preheat for 5 minutes.

6. Spritz both sides of the coated chicken pieces with olive oil. Working in batches as needed, place the chicken breasts in the Cook & Crisp Basket, ensuring the chicken pieces do not touch each other.

7. After 12 minutes, turn the chicken with a spatula so you don't tear the breading. Close the crisping lid and continue to cook, checking the chicken for an internal temperature of 165ºF.

8. When cooking is complete, transfer the chicken to a wire rack to cool.

Per serving: *Calories: 574; Total Fat: 7g; Saturated Fat: 2g; Cholesterol: 193mg; Sodium: 995mg; Carbohydrates: 67g; Fiber: 3g; Protein: 51g*

# Cheesy Chicken and Broccoli Casserole by Chelven Randolph

***Chef says:*** *My mom used to make a version of this dish once or twice a year, and I always looked forward to it. I thought she invented it until one day I realized she had developed it as a play on one from a famous Southern eatery. Now I make it for my children, and they love it. Great as a pre-prepped meal to reheat in a pinch or a dish to throw together quickly.*

**NUT-FREE, FAMILY FAVORITE**

**PREP TIME:** 10 minutes
**TOTAL COOK TIME:** 30 minutes

**APPROX. PRESSURE BUILD:** 10 minutes
**PRESSURE COOK:** 20 minutes
**PRESSURE RELEASE:** Quick
**AIR CRISP:** 10 minutes

4 (8-ounce) boneless, skinless chicken breasts

2 cups chicken stock

1 cup whole milk

1 (10.5-ounce) cans condensed Cheddar cheese soup

1 teaspoon paprika

2 cups shredded Cheddar cheese

Kosher salt

Freshly ground black pepper

2 cups crushed buttered crackers

1. Place the chicken and stock in the pot. Assemble pressure lid, making sure the pressure release valve is in the SEAL position.

2. Select PRESSURE and set to HI. Set timer to 20 minutes. Select START/STOP to begin.

3. When pressure cooking is complete, quick release the pressure by turning the pressure release valve to the VENT position. Carefully remove lid when unit has finished releasing pressure.

4. Using silicone-tipped utensils, shred the chicken inside the pot.

5. Add the milk, condensed soup, paprika, and cheese. Stir to combine with the chicken. Season with salt and pepper. Top with the crushed crackers. Close crisping lid.

6. Select AIR CRISP, set temperature to 360ºF, and set time to 10 minutes. Select START/STOP to begin.

7. When cooking is complete, open lid and let cool before serving.

*Per serving: Calories: 449; Total Fat: 23g; Saturated Fat: 12g; Cholesterol: 122mg; Sodium: 925mg; Carbohydrates: 18g; Fiber: 1g; Protein: 42g*

# Frozen Chicken and Mozzarella Casserole by Sam Ferguson

**SERVES 6**

***Chef says:*** *One of my favorite games in the Ninja® Test Kitchen is to find frozen foods to use as a topping for casseroles and other TenderCrisp™ dishes. This casserole was a simple and convenient discovery—chicken, sauce, and frozen mozzarella sticks all rolled into one quick and easy meal.*

NUT-FREE, UNDER
30 MINUTES, 5 INGREDIENT

PREP TIME: 5 minutes
TOTAL COOK TIME:
35 minutes

APPROX. PRESSURE BUILD:
10 minutes
PRESSURE COOK:
20 minutes
PRESSURE RELEASE: Quick
BAKE/ROAST: 15 minutes

VARIATION TIP: Frozen prepared foods (like mozzarella sticks) are the most amazing vehicle for easy, crispy, and delicious toppings to casseroles. Do some browsing in the freezer aisle to see what looks good. I also like to use pizza rolls and jalapeño poppers as toppers to my pressure-cooked pasta meals.

2 (11-ounce) boxes frozen breaded mozzarella sticks

4 (6-ounce) frozen boneless, skinless chicken breasts

½ cup water

1 (23-ounce) jar marinara sauce

1. Remove the mozzarella sticks from freezer and let sit at room temperature for 15 to 20 minutes to assure easy chopping.

2. Place the chicken and water in the pot. Assemble pressure lid, making sure the pressure release valve is in the SEAL position.

3. Select PRESSURE and set to HI. Set time to 20 minutes. Select START/STOP to begin.

4. Chop up the mozzarella sticks.

5. When pressure cooking is complete, quick release the pressure by moving the pressure release valve to the VENT position. Carefully remove lid when unit has finished releasing pressure.

6. Using a silicone-tipped utensil, shred the chicken inside the pot. Stir in the marinara sauce. Evenly sprinkle the top of chicken with the pieces of mozzarella sticks. Close crisping lid.

7. Select BAKE/ROAST, set temperature to 390ºF, and set time to 15 minutes. Select START/STOP to begin.

8. After 10 minutes, open lid and check the mozzarella sticks for desired crispiness and doneness. If necessary, cook for up to 5 minutes more.

9. When cooking is complete, open lid and serve.

*Per serving: Calories: 410; Total Fat: 14g; Saturated Fat: 6g; Cholesterol: 84mg; Sodium: 1351mg; Carbohydrates: 32g; Fiber: 2g; Protein: 41g*

# Southwest Chicken Bake by Caroline Schliep

***Chef says:*** *This meal is a one-pot wonder. Packed with fresh Mexican flavors and topped with a layer of crispy cheese, this recipe is great for a potluck or family reunion.*

**GLUTEN-FREE, NUT-FREE, UNDER 30 MINUTES**

**PREP TIME:** 10 minutes
**TOTAL COOK TIME:** 20 minutes

**SEAR/SAUTÉ:** 5 minutes
**APPROX. PRESSURE BUILD:** 10 minutes
**PRESSURE COOK:** 7 minutes
**PRESSURE RELEASE:** Quick
**BROIL:** 8 minutes

1 tablespoon extra-virgin olive oil

2 (8-ounce) boneless, skinless chicken breasts, cut into 1-inch cubes

½ red onion, diced

½ red bell pepper, diced

1 cup white rice

1 (10-ounce) can fire-roasted tomatoes with chiles

1 (15-ounce) can black beans, rinsed and drained

1 (15-ounce) can corn, rinsed

1 (1-ounce) packet taco seasoning

2 cups chicken broth

Kosher salt

Freshly ground black pepper

2 cups shredded Cheddar cheese

1. Select SEAR/SAUTÉ and set to MD:HI. Select START/STOP to begin. Let preheat for 5 minutes.

2. Place the olive oil and chicken into the pot and cook, stirring occasionally, until the chicken is cooked through, 2 to 3 minutes. Add the onion and bell pepper and cook until softened, about 2 minutes.

3. Add the rice, tomatoes, beans, corn, taco seasoning, broth, salt, and pepper and stir. Assemble pressure lid, making sure the pressure release valve is in the SEAL position.

4. Select PRESSURE and set to HI. Set time to 7 minutes. Select START/STOP to begin.

5. When complete, quick release the pressure by turning the pressure release valve to the VENT position. Carefully remove lid when unit has finished releasing pressure.

6. Add the cheese on top of the mixture. Close crisping lid.

7. Select BROIL and set time to 8 minutes. Select START/STOP to begin.

8. When cooking is complete, serve along with your choice of toppings, such as chopped cilantro, diced avocado, diced fresh tomatoes, sour cream, and sliced scallions.

*Per serving: Calories: 333; Total Fat: 17g; Saturated Fat: 7g; Cholesterol: 72mg; Sodium: 630mg; Carbohydrates: 27g; Fiber: 6g; Protein: 25g*

# Creamy Turkey and Mushroom Ragu by Chelven Randolph

**SERVES 4**

***Chef says:*** *Tetrazzini is an American dish that I thought for years was a classic Italian dish. It is served in some Italian restaurants and comes in a variety of presentations. Some serve it with spaghetti, some top it with bread crumbs, or incorporate Swiss cheese. My version is the way we traditionally had it when serving our restaurant staff. The egg noodles cook in the sauce and really absorb the flavors. Plus, it makes for an easy cleanup.*

GLUTEN-FREE, NUT-FREE

PREP TIME: 15 minutes
TOTAL COOK TIME:
40 minutes

SEAR/SAUTÉ: 40 minutes

HACK IT: This is the perfect dish to use leftover turkey from Thanksgiving. Simply chop up 2 to 3 cups of cooked turkey in place of the ground turkey.

- 2 tablespoons unsalted butter
- 1 pound ground turkey
- 8 ounces cremini mushrooms, sliced
- 1 (10.5-ounce) can condensed cream of celery soup
- 4 cups chicken stock
- 1 (10-ounce) package egg noodles
- 16 ounces frozen peas
- 1 cup sour cream
- ¾ cup grated Parmesan cheese
- Kosher salt
- Freshly ground black pepper

1. Select SEAR/SAUTÉ and set to MED. Press START/STOP to begin. Let preheat for 3 minutes.

2. Add the butter, ground turkey, and mushrooms. Using a silicone-tipped utensil, break up the turkey as it browns, about 10 minutes.

3. Add the condensed soup and stock. Whisk well to combine. Bring to a simmer for 15 minutes.

4. Add the egg noodles and peas and stir well. Cook until the noodles are tender and cooked through, 8 to 10 minutes.

5. Select START/STOP to stop cooking. Stir in sour cream and Parmesan cheese until melted and incorporated. Season with salt and pepper. Serve immediately.

**Per serving:** *Calories: 854; Total Fat: 39g; Saturated Fat: 19g; Cholesterol: 212mg; Sodium: 1714mg; Carbohydrates: 79g; Fiber: 10g; Protein: 48g*

# Cajun Turkey Breast by Sam Ferguson

**SERVES 8**

**Chef says:** *The Ninja® Foodi™ Pressure Cooker's large capacity makes it great for cooking large cuts of meat. One of my favorite things to do on Sunday afternoon is TenderCrisp™ a turkey breast and use it for a week's worth of deli meat. Once the cooked turkey cools, I slice it as thin as possible and use it for sandwiches and salads for lunch at work.*

**DAIRY-FREE, GLUTEN-FREE, NUT-FREE, 5 INGREDIENT**

**PREP TIME:** 5 minutes
**TOTAL COOK TIME:** 35 minutes

**APPROX. PRESSURE BUILD:** 10 minutes
**PRESSURE COOK:** 20 minutes
**PRESSURE RELEASE:** Quick
**AIR CRISP:** 15 minutes

**ACCESSORIES:** Cook & Crisp Basket

**VARIATION TIP:** This recipe can be customized by changing the spice rub to anything you want. Use a prepared rub found in the spice aisle of the grocery store, or get adventurous and make your own out of any spices hanging around your spice cabinet at home.

1 (4-pound) boneless, skinless turkey breast

2 tablespoons Cajun spice seasoning

1 tablespoon kosher salt

½ cup water

1. Season turkey breast liberally, evenly, and on all sides with the Cajun spice seasoning and salt.

2. Pour the water into the pot. Place the Cook & Crisp Basket in the pot, then place the turkey into the basket. Assemble pressure lid, making sure the pressure release valve is in the SEAL position.

3. Select PRESSURE and set to HI. Set time to 20 minutes. Select START/STOP to begin.

4. When pressure cooking is complete, quick release the pressure by moving the pressure release valve to the VENT position. Carefully remove lid when unit has finished releasing pressure.

5. Close crisping lid. Select AIR CRISP, set temperature to 360ºF, and set time to 15 minutes. Select START/STOP to begin.

6. When cooking is complete, open lid and transfer the turkey breast to a cutting board. Let rest for at least 10 minutes before slicing or serving.

*Per serving: Calories: 229; Total Fat: 1g; Saturated Fat: 0g; Cholesterol: 0mg; Sodium: 230mg; Carbohydrates: 0g; Fiber: 0g; Protein: 54g*

# 9

# Beef, Pork & Lamb

# Orecchiette and Pork Ragu

*Don't let the recipe title intimidate you. It's just a fancy name for pasta and meat sauce. While a traditional ragu is braised on the stovetop for hours, this version comes together in under 30 minutes thanks to the Ninja® Foodi™ Pressure Cooker. Plus, you cook the pasta in the sauce—no need to boil water or dirty another dish. This one pot meal is the perfect, indulgent weeknight meal.*

**NUT-FREE, UNDER 30 MINUTES**

**PREP TIME:** 10 minutes
**TOTAL COOK TIME:** 25 minutes

**SEAR/SAUTÉ:** 15 minutes
**APPROX. PRESSURE BUILD:** 7 minutes
**PRESSURE COOK:** 0 minutes
**PRESSURE RELEASE:** 10 minutes, then Quick

- **3 tablespoons extra-virgin olive oil, divided**
- **1 pound pork shoulder, cut into large pieces**
- **1 small onion, diced**
- **1 carrot, diced**
- **1 celery stalk, diced**
- **1 garlic clove, minced**
- **1 (28-ounce) can crushed tomatoes**
- **1 (28-ounce) can tomato purée**
- **1 cup red wine**
- **2 cups beef stock**
- **1 (16-ounce) box orecchiette pasta**
- **1 teaspoon sea salt**
- **1 teaspoon Italian seasoning**
- **1 bunch Tuscan kale, ribs and stems removed, torn**
- **¼ cup unsalted butter, cubed**
- **½ cup grated Parmesan cheese**

1. Select SEAR/SAUTÉ and set to HI. Select START/STOP to begin. Let preheat for 5 minutes.

2. Place 2 tablespoons of oil in the pot. Once hot, add the pork pieces and sear on all sides, turning until brown, about 10 minutes in total. Transfer the pork to a large plate and set aside.

3. Add onion, carrot, and celery and cook for about 5 minutes. Add the garlic and cook for 1 minute.

4. Add the crushed tomatoes, tomato purée, red wine, beef stock, pasta, salt, and Italian seasoning. Place the pork back in the pot. Assemble pressure lid, making sure the pressure release valve is in the SEAL position.

5. Select PRESSURE and set to LO. Set time to 0 minutes. Select START/STOP to begin.

6. When pressure cooking is complete, allow pressure to naturally release for 10 minutes. After 10 minutes, quick release remaining pressure by moving the pressure release valve to the VENT position. Carefully remove lid when unit has finished releasing pressure.

7.  Pull the pork pieces apart using two forks. Add the remaining 1 tablespoon of olive oil, kale, butter, and Parmesan cheese and stir until the butter melts and the kale is wilted. Serve.

Per serving:  *Calories: 556; Total Fat: 21g; Saturated Fat: 8g; Cholesterol: 71mg; Sodium: 1277mg; Carbohydrates: 59g; Fiber: 10g; Protein: 30g*

# Bacon-Wrapped Hot Dogs

**SERVES 4**

*In my book, the only thing better than a hot dog is a hot dog wrapped in bacon. Whether it is a hot summer afternoon or the middle of winter, with the Ninja® Foodi™ you can crisp these bacon-wrapped hot dogs to perfection in just minutes and enjoy summertime flavors year-round!*

NUT-FREE, UNDER
30 MINUTES, 5 INGREDIENT

PREP TIME: 15 minutes
TOTAL COOK TIME:
15 minutes

AIR CRISP: 15 minutes

ACCESSORIES: Cook &
Crisp Basket

**VARIATION TIP:** Have fun and switch up the toppings based on your favorites. Try sautéed onions and peppers, cheese and jalapeños, or relish and barbecue sauce. The options are endless.

**4 beef hot dogs**

**4 bacon strips**

**Cooking spray**

**4 bakery hot dog buns,
split and toasted**

**½ red onion, chopped**

**1 cup sauerkraut, rinsed
and drained**

1. Place Cook & Crisp Basket in pot. Close crisping lid. Select AIR CRISP, set temperature to 360ºF, and set time to 5 minutes. Select START/STOP to begin preheating.

2. Wrap each hot dog with 1 strip of bacon, securing it with toothpicks as needed.

3. Once unit has preheated, open lid and coat the basket with cooking spray. Place the hot dogs in the basket in a single layer. Close crisping lid.

4. Select AIR CRISP, set temperature to 360ºF, and set time to 15 minutes. Select START/STOP to begin.

5. After 10 minutes, open lid and check doneness. If needed, continue cooking until it reaches your desired doneness.

6. When cooking is complete, place the hot dog in the buns with the onion and sauerkraut. Top, if desired, with condiments of your choice, such as yellow mustard, ketchup, or mayonnaise.

*Per serving: Calories: 336; Total Fat: 17g; Saturated Fat: 6g; Cholesterol: 51mg; Sodium: 1297mg; Carbohydrates: 27g; Fiber: 1g; Protein: 20g*

# Southern-Style Lettuce Wraps by Chelven Randolph

*Chef says:* When I lived in California, I lived next to Koreatown. I didn't make a lot of money, so I gorged on cheap eats whenever I was out of work. One thing I came to love was lettuce wraps. They are so simple and delicious. And they are very interchangeable. You can make so many versions by swapping out the proteins and garnish. Whether you want to go Mexican and incorporate taco toppings or even just traditional with Asian flavors, the possibilities are endless.

**DAIRY-FREE**

**PREP TIME:** 10 minutes
**TOTAL COOK TIME:**
30 minutes

**APPROX. PRESSURE BUILD:**
10 minutes
**PRESSURE COOK:**
30 minutes
**PRESSURE RELEASE:** Quick

**VARIATION TIP:** This dish also works great with chicken thighs. Substitute 3 pounds of boneless, skinless chicken thighs and pressure cook for 20 minutes.

3 pounds boneless pork shoulder, cut into 1- to 2-inch cubes

2 cups light beer

1 cup brown sugar

1 teaspoon chipotle chiles in adobo sauce

1 cup barbecue sauce

1 head iceberg lettuce, quartered and leaves separated

1 cup roasted peanuts, chopped or ground

Cilantro leaves

1. Place the pork, beer, brown sugar, chipotle, and barbecue sauce in the pot. Assemble pressure lid, making sure the pressure release valve is in the SEAL position.

2. Select PRESSURE and set to HI. Set the timer to 30 minutes. Select START/STOP to begin.

3. When pressure cooking is complete, quick release the pressure by turning the pressure release valve to the VENT position. Carefully remove lid when unit has finished releasing pressure.

4. Using a silicone-tipped utensil, shred the pork in the pot. Stir to mix the meat in with the sauce.

5. Place a small amount of pork in a piece of lettuce. Top with peanuts and cilantro to serve.

Per serving: *Calories: 811; Total Fat: 58g; Saturated Fat: 18g; Cholesterol: 160mg; Sodium: 627mg; Carbohydrates: 22g; Fiber: 3g; Protein: 45g*

# Cheesy Taco Pasta Bake

**SERVES 6**

*This pasta dish is in constant rotation at our house. It is loaded with taco flavors but is prepared with the convenience of a pasta bake. Not only does the beef stock and taco seasoning impart delicious flavor, the chiles add a nice kick while the cream cheese keeps the sauce creamy. Top it off with bubbly melted cheese for a one pot meal your whole family will love.*

**NUT-FREE, UNDER 30 MINUTES, FAMILY FAVORITE, 360 MEAL**

**PREP TIME:** 10 minutes
**TOTAL COOK TIME:** 20 minutes

**SEAR/SAUTÉ:** 7 minutes
**APPROX. PRESSURE BUILD:** 7 minutes
**PRESSURE COOK:** 0 minutes
**PRESSURE RELEASE:** 10 minutes, then Quick
**BROIL:** 5 minutes

- 1 tablespoon extra-virgin olive oil
- 1 small onion, diced
- 1 pound ground beef
- 1 packet taco seasoning
- 1 (14.5-ounce) can diced tomatoes
- 1 (4-ounce) can diced green chiles
- 1 (16-ounce) box dry elbow pasta
- 4 cups beef broth
- 2 ounces cream cheese, cut into pieces
- 3 cups shredded Mexican blend cheese, divided

Optional toppings:

Sour cream, for garnish

Red onion, for garnish

Chopped cilantro, for garnish

1. Select SEAR/SAUTÉ and set to MD:HI. Select START/STOP to begin. Let preheat for 5 minutes.

2. Place the oil, onion, and beef in the pot and cook for about 5 minutes, using a wooden spoon to break apart the beef as it cooks. Add the taco seasoning and mix until the beef is coated.

3. Add the tomatoes, green chiles, pasta, and beef broth. Assemble pressure lid, making sure the pressure release valve is in the SEAL position.

4. Select PRESSURE and set to LO. Set time to 0 minutes. Select START/STOP to begin.

5. When pressure cooking is complete, allow pressure to naturally release for 10 minutes. After 10 minutes, quick release remaining pressure by moving the pressure release valve to the VENT position. Carefully remove lid when unit has finished releasing pressure.

6. Add the cream cheese and 2 cups of cheese. Stir well to melt cheese and ensure all ingredients are combined. Cover the pasta evenly with the remaining 1 cup of cheese. Close crisping lid.

7. Select BROIL and set time to 5 minutes. Select START/STOP to begin.

8. When cooking is complete, serve immediately.

Per serving: *Calories: 633; Total Fat: 40g; Saturated Fat: 20g; Cholesterol: 119mg; Sodium: 1154mg; Carbohydrates: 36g; Fiber: 4g; Protein: 37g*

# Fresh Kielbasa and Braised Sweet and Sour Cabbage by Craig White

**SERVES 6**

***Chef says:*** *I catered an Oktoberfest-themed wedding for a couple of friends a few years back and this dish was a big hit. Although I served it with bratwurst, I love using fresh kielbasa because it reminds me of my nana. She would always get freshly made kielbasa from a small butcher shop down the street. I recommend serving it family-style with the whole sausage coil served right on top of the cabbage for extra dramatic effect.*

**GLUTEN-FREE, NUT-FREE, FAMILY FAVORITE**

**PREP TIME:** 10 minutes
**TOTAL COOK TIME:** 1 hour

**AIR CRISP:** 15 minutes
**SEAR/SAUTÉ:** 18 minutes
**APPROX. PRESSURE BUILD:** 10 minutes
**PRESSURE COOK:** 10 minutes
**PRESSURE RELEASE:** Quick

**ACCESSORIES:** Cook & Crisp Basket

**SUBSTITUTION TIP:** You can substitute other links of sausage such as bratwurst, bockwurst, or weisswurst.

1½ pounds fresh kielbasa sausage links
½ stick (¼ cup) unsalted butter
½ medium onion, thinly sliced
2 garlic cloves, minced
1 large head red cabbage, cut into ¼-inch slices
¼ cup granulated sugar
⅓ cup apple cider vinegar
½ cup water
2 teaspoons caraway seeds
Kosher salt
Freshly ground black pepper

1. Insert Cook & Crisp Basket into pot and close crisping lid. Select AIR CRISP, set temperature to 390ºF, and set time to 15 minutes. Select START/STOP to begin. Let preheat for 5 minutes.

2. Add the sausage to the basket. Close lid and cook for 10 minutes.

3. When cooking is complete, open lid and remove basket and sausage. Set aside.

4. Select SEAR/SAUTÉ and set to HI. Select START/STOP to begin.

5. Add the butter and let it heat for 5 minutes. Add the onion and garlic and cook for 3 minutes.

6. Add the cabbage, sugar, vinegar, water, and caraway seeds, and season with salt and pepper. Assemble pressure lid, making sure the pressure release valve is in the SEAL position.

7. Select PRESSURE and set to HI. Set time to 10 minutes. Select START/STOP to begin.

8. When pressure cooking is complete, quick release the pressure by moving the pressure release valve to the VENT position.

CONTINUED ▶

# Fresh Kielbasa and Braised
# Sweet and Sour Cabbage continued

9.  Select SEAR/SAUTÉ and set to HI. Set time to 10 minutes. Select START/STOP to begin.

10. After 5 minutes, open lid and add the sausage to the top of cabbage. Close lid and continue cooking.

11. When cooking is complete, open lid and serve.

Per serving: *Calories: 351; Total Fat: 19g; Saturated Fat: 8g; Cholesterol: 80mg; Sodium: 588mg; Carbohydrates: 24g; Fiber: 6g; Protein: 23g*

# Baked Bacon Macaroni and Cheese

**SERVES 6**

*I developed this recipe for my little brother Nickolas. He is one of my biggest fans and is always asking my mom to make my recipes for dinner. He has been asking for a bacon mac and cheese recipe for the Foodi™ Pressure Cooker for quite some time, and I decided it was about time I delivered. In this recipe, I start by cooking the bacon right in the pot so that as the macaroni and cheese cooks, bacony goodness is built into every layer. Plus, this version is topped with buttery bread crumbs for the ultimate baked bacon macaroni and cheese.*

NUT-FREE, UNDER
30 MINUTES, FAMILY
FAVORITE

---

**PREP TIME:** 10 minutes
**TOTAL COOK TIME:**
30 minutes

---

**SEAR/SAUTÉ:** 6 minutes
**APPROX. PRESSURE BUILD:**
7 minutes
**PRESSURE COOK:**
0 minutes
**PRESSURE RELEASE:**
10 minutes, then Quick
**AIR CRISP:** 7 minutes

4 strips bacon, chopped

5 cups water

1 (16-ounce) box elbow pasta

2 tablespoons
  unsalted butter

1 tablespoon ground mustard

1 (5-ounce) can
  evaporated milk

8 ounces Cheddar
  cheese, shredded

8 ounces Gouda, shredded

Sea salt

Freshly ground black pepper

2 cups panko or Italian
  bread crumbs

1 stick (½ cup) butter, melted

1. Select SEAR/SAUTÉ and set temperature to HI. Select START/STOP to begin. Let preheat for 5 minutes.

2. Add the bacon and cook, stirring frequently, for about 6 minutes or until crispy. Using a slotted spoon, transfer the bacon to a paper towel-lined plate to drain.

3. Add the water, pasta, 2 tablespoons of butter, and mustard. Assemble pressure lid, making sure the pressure release valve is in the SEAL position.

4. Select PRESSURE and set to LO. Set time to 0 minutes. Select START/STOP to begin.

5. When pressure cooking is complete, allow pressure to naturally release for 10 minutes. After 10 minutes, quick release remaining pressure by moving the pressure release valve to the VENT position. Carefully remove lid when unit has finished releasing pressure.

6. Add the evaporated milk, Cheddar cheese, Gouda cheese and the bacon. Season with salt and pepper. Stir well to melt the cheeses and ensure all ingredients are combined.

CONTINUED ▶

# Baked Bacon Macaroni and Cheese continued

7. In a medium bowl, stir together the bread crumbs and melted butter. Cover the pasta evenly with the mixture. Close crisping lid.

8. Select AIR CRISP, set temperature to 360°F, and set time to 7 minutes. Select START/STOP to begin.

9. When cooking is complete, serve immediately.

Per serving: *Calories: 721; Total Fat: 45g; Saturated Fat: 26g; Cholesterol: 148mg; Sodium: 1213mg; Carbohydrates: 44g; Fiber: 4g; Protein: 35g*

# Italian Pasta Potpie by Craig White

**Chef says:** *This dish is a riff of something called "timpano." Traditionally the filling is baked inside of a pasta crust. I decided to bake it like a potpie because I LOVE PIE CRUST. This recipe is hearty, comforting, and can feed an army. It reminds me of something I would serve to my staff for family meal when I was a restaurant chef, only I called it "discomfort food" because the staff would eat too much of it. I hope your family loves it.*

**NUT-FREE, FAMILY FAVORITE**

**PREP TIME:** 20 minutes
**TOTAL COOK TIME:**
55 minutes

**APPROX. PRESSURE BUILD:**
7 minutes
**PRESSURE COOK:**
0 minutes
**PRESSURE RELEASE:** Quick
**AIR CRISP:** 25 minutes
**BAKE/ROAST:** 30 minutes

**ACCESSORIES:** Cook & Crisp Basket

**SUBSTITUTION TIP:** This recipe is very substitute friendly. Try it with spaghetti or chicken meatballs or linguica. Use your favorite pasta sauce. That is the beauty of cooking—you can adapt recipes to suit the tastes and preferences of your family.

5 cups, plus 1 teaspoon water, divided

1 (16-ounce) box rigatoni pasta

4 (4-ounce) fresh Italian sausage links

1 (12-ounce) bag frozen cooked meatballs

16 ounces whole milk ricotta

1 (25.5-ounce) jar marinara sauce

2 cups shredded mozzarella cheese

1 refrigerated store-bought pie crust, room temperature

1 large egg

1. Pour 5 cups of water and the rigatoni in the pot. Assemble pressure lid, making sure the pressure release valve is in the SEAL position.

2. Select PRESSURE and set to LO. Set time to 0 minutes. Select START/STOP to begin.

3. When pressure cooking is complete, quick release the pressure by turning the pressure release valve to the VENT position. Carefully remove lid when unit has finished releasing pressure.

4. Drain the pasta and set it aside, keeping warm. Wipe out pot and return it to base. Insert Cook & Crisp Basket into pot. Close crisping lid.

5. Select AIR CRISP, set temperature to 390°F, and set time to 15 minutes. Select START/STOP to begin. Let preheat for 5 minutes.

6. Open lid and place the sausages in the basket. Close lid and cook for 10 minutes.

7. When cooking is complete, remove sausages to a cutting board. Add the meatballs to the basket. Close crisping lid.

CONTINUED ▶

# Italian Pasta Potpie  continued

8. Select AIR CRISP, set temperature to 390ºF, and set time to 10 minutes. Select START/STOP to begin.

9. Slice sausages into very thin rounds.

10. When cooking is complete, transfer the meatballs to the cutting board and slice them in half.

11. In the pot, in this order, add a layer of ricotta, marinara sauce, sausage, mozzarella cheese, pasta, marinara sauce, meatballs, mozzarella cheese, pasta, ricotta, and marinara sauce. Place the pie crust on top of the filling.

12. In a small bowl, whisk together the egg and remaining 1 teaspoon of water. Brush this on top of the pie crust. With a knife, slice a couple of small holes in the middle of crust to vent it. Close crisping lid.

13. Select BAKE/ROAST, set temperature to 350ºF, and set time to 30 minutes. Select START/STOP to begin.

14. When cooking is complete, open lid. Let sit for 10 minutes before serving.

**Per serving:** *Calories: 821; Total Fat: 41g; Saturated Fat: 18g; Cholesterol: 134mg; Sodium: 1414mg; Carbohydrates: 67g; Fiber: 5g; Protein: 40g*

# Easy Burnt Ends by Sam Ferguson

SERVES 6

**Chef says:** *In traditional barbecue, burnt ends take over 12 hours to transform into a delicious meal. The Ninja® Foodi™ Pressure Cooker is able to deliver the same tender and crispy-charred results in a fraction of the time. I love to use these burnt ends in a grilled cheese sandwich—so good!*

DAIRY-FREE, NUT-FREE,
5 INGREDIENT

---

PREP TIME: 5 minutes
TOTAL COOK TIME: 1 hour,
50 minutes

---

APPROX. PRESSURE BUILD:
10 minutes
PRESSURE COOK: 1 hour,
30 minutes
PRESSURE RELEASE: Quick
AIR CRISP: 20 minutes

---

INGREDIENT INFO: Brisket
is a tough, fibrous cut of
beef that is notoriously
difficult to cook well. The
Foodi Pressure Cooker is
the perfect tool for cooking
meats like beef brisket—the
meat is tenderized quickly
and the crisping lid adds
that crave-able texture
to finish.

**3 pounds beef brisket, some (but not all) fat trimmed**

**¼ cup barbecue spice rub**

**1 cup water**

**2 cups barbecue sauce**

1. Season the brisket liberally and evenly with the barbecue spice rub.

2. Add the water, then place the brisket in the pot. Assemble pressure lid, making sure the pressure release valve is in the SEAL position.

3. Select PRESSURE and set to HI. Set time to 1 hour, 30 minutes. Select START/STOP to begin.

4. When pressure cooking is complete, quick release the pressure by moving the pressure release valve to the VENT position. Carefully remove lid when unit has finished releasing pressure.

5. Carefully remove the brisket from the pot and place on a cutting board. Let cool at room temperature for 10 minutes, or until brisket can be easily handled.

6. Cut the brisket into 2-inch chunks. Drain the cooking liquid from the pot. Place the brisket chunks in the pot. Add the barbecue sauce and stir gently so the brisket chunks are coated. Close crisping lid.

7. Select AIR CRISP, set temperature to 360°F, and set time to 20 minutes (for more charred-like results, set time to 23 minutes). Select START/STOP to begin.

8. When cooking is complete, open lid and serve.

*Per serving: Calories: 449; Total Fat: 14g; Saturated Fat: 0g; Cholesterol: 0mg; Sodium: 933mg; Carbohydrates: 32g; Fiber: 1g; Protein: 48g*

# Cheese and Pepperoni Calzones

**SERVES 4**

*Calzones are a baked Italian sandwich of sorts that originated as a folded piece of pizza. Typically, they're made from bread dough stuffed with salami, ham, vegetables, and cheese—lots of cheese. For this version I use a premade pizza dough to keep things simple.*

NUT-FREE, UNDER 30 MINUTES, FAMILY FAVORITE

**PREP TIME:** 10 minutes
**TOTAL COOK TIME:** 18 minutes

**AIR CRISP:** 18 minutes

**ACCESSORIES:** Cook & Crisp Basket

**HACK IT:** Make a double batch and freeze half of the calzones for quick dinners or lunch emergencies. Thaw to room temperature then reheat in the microwave or Foodi Pressure Cooker at 300°F until heated through.

All-purpose flour, for dusting

16 ounces store-bought pizza dough

1 egg, beaten

2 cups shredded mozzarella cheese

1 cup ricotta cheese

½ cup grated Parmesan cheese

½ cup sliced pepperoni

Cooking spray

Pizza sauce, for dipping

1. Dust a clean work surface with the flour. Divide the pizza dough into four equal pieces. Place the dough on the floured surface and roll each piece into an 8-inch round of even thickness. Dust your rolling pin and work surface with additional flour, as needed, to ensure the dough does not stick. Brush egg wash around the edges of each round.

2. Place Cook & Crisp Basket in pot. Close crisping lid. Select AIR CRISP, set temperature to 390°F, and set time to 5 minutes. Select START/STOP to begin preheating.

3. In a medium bowl, combine the mozzarella, ricotta, and Parmesan cheese. Fold in the pepperoni.

4. Spoon one-quarter of the cheese mixture onto one side of each dough round. Fold the other half over the filling and press firmly to seal the edges together. Brush each calzone all over with the egg wash.

5. Once unit is preheated, open lid and coat the basket with cooking spray. Place two calzones in the basket in a single layer. Close crisping lid.

6. Select AIR CRISP, set temperature to 390°F, and set time to 9 minutes. Select START/STOP to begin.

7. After 7 minutes, open lid to check for doneness. If desired, cook for up to 2 minutes more, until golden brown.

8. When cooking is complete, remove calzone from basket. Repeat steps 5 and 6 with the remaining calzones. Serve warm.

*Per serving: Calories: 593; Total Fat: 29g; Saturated Fat: 15g; Cholesterol: 122mg; Sodium: 1253mg; Carbohydrates: 51g; Fiber: 4g; Protein: 37g*

# Flank Steak Tacos by Meg Jordan

*Chef says:* *Flank steak is one of the healthiest beef cuts you can buy. Overall, it has fewer calories and more protein than a rib eye or porterhouse, which makes it great as a base for tacos. Once you add toppings, tacos can become quite high in calories. But since flank is a fairly lean cut, I can top these tacos with guacamole and not worry about the extra fat.*

**DAIRY-FREE, NUT-FREE, UNDER 30 MINUTES, FAMILY FAVORITE**

**PREP TIME:** 5 minutes, plus 30 minutes to marinate
**TOTAL COOK TIME:** 16 minutes

**SEAR/SAUTÉ:** 16 minutes

**HACK IT:** Use bottled lime juice from the store to cut down on prep time.

- 2 pounds flank steak, cut into ¼-inch strips
- ¼ cup freshly squeezed lime juice
- 3 tablespoons grated garlic
- 3 tablespoons extra-virgin olive oil
- 2 teaspoons kosher salt
- 2 teaspoons freshly ground black pepper
- 2 tablespoons canola oil
- 12 (8-inch) flour tortillas

1. Place the steak, lime juice, garlic, olive oil, salt, and pepper in a large resealable plastic bag. Refrigerate and marinate for a minimum of 30 minutes or up to 3 hours.

2. Select SEAR/SAUTÉ and set to MD:HI. Select START/STOP to begin. Let preheat for 5 minutes.

3. Add the canola oil and heat for 1 minute. Working in batches, place the steak in the pot and cook, stirring frequently, until the steak is browned, about 8 minutes per batch.

4. Divide the steak slices evenly between the tortillas. Add desired toppings, such as guacamole or sliced avocado, sour cream, pineapple chunks, salsa, and cilantro, and serve immediately.

*Per serving: Calories: 981; Total Fat: 47g; Saturated Fat: 5g; Cholesterol: 0mg; Sodium: 1497mg; Carbohydrates: 75g; Fiber: 3g; Protein: 62g*

# Spicy Thai Basil Beef by Caroline Schliep

**SERVES 8**

**Chef says:** *Thai basil beef, also known as* pad kha paow, *is a traditional Thai dish that is perfect for a quick weeknight meal. I learned to make this easy meal while I was studying abroad in Thailand. And don't let its simplicity fool you; it definitely packs a punch. Every time I make this dish it brings me back the wonderful time I spent at Dhara Dhevi Resort cooking in their open-air kitchens.*

**DAIRY-FREE, NUT-FREE, UNDER 30 MINUTES**

**PREP TIME:** 10 minutes
**TOTAL COOK TIME:** 20 minutes

**SEAR/SAUTÉ:** 13 minutes

**SUBSTITUTION TIP:** If you can't find Thai basil in your grocery store, regular basil will do the trick.

2 pounds ground beef

2 tablespoons sriracha

4 tablespoons fish sauce

3 tablespoons soy sauce

Zest of 2 limes

Juice of 2 limes

3 tablespoons brown sugar

2 shallots, diced

2 tablespoons minced garlic

1 red bell pepper, diced

1 bunch Thai basil leaves

6 scallions, sliced

1. Select SEAR/SAUTÉ and set temperature to HI. Select START/STOP to begin. Let preheat for 5 minutes.

2. Add the ground beef. Cook, stirring occasionally, until the beef is fully cooked, 3 to 5 minutes.

3. In a small bowl, whisk together the sriracha, fish sauce, soy sauce, lime zest and juice, and brown sugar.

4. Once the beef is cooked, add the shallot and garlic and cook until soft, about 2 minutes.

5. Add sauce mixture and stir. Let boil until reduced slightly, about 5 minutes.

6. Add the bell pepper and basil. Cook just until the basil wilts, about 1 minute.

7. When cooking is complete, garnish with the scallions and serve over rice, if desired.

*Per serving: Calories: 269; Total Fat: 17g; Saturated Fat: 7g; Cholesterol: 75mg; Sodium: 1137mg; Carbohydrates: 6g; Fiber: 0g; Protein: 22g*

# Beef Brisket

by Doug Malvo, Ninja® Foodi™ Family Member

**SERVES 4**

*Kenzie says:* The Ninja Foodi Pressure Cooker makes quick work of tough cuts of meat, such as brisket. This recipe makes irresistibly delicious and tender beef brisket with just a few simple ingredients. Not only is this the easiest and quickest brisket recipe, but it is sure to become one of your favorite ways to use the Ninja Foodi Pressure Cooker!

DAIRY-FREE, NUT-FREE

**PREP TIME:** 5 minutes
**TOTAL COOK TIME:** 1 hour, 10 minutes

**SEAR/SAUTÉ:** 10 minutes
**PRESSURE COOK:** 60 minutes
**APPROX. PRESSURE BUILD:** 10 minutes
**PRESSURE RELEASE:** 20 minutes, then Quick

**HACK IT:** Use the leftovers from this recipe to make a quick and easy Brisket Chili Verde (page 287).

**Find Doug on Facebook: Foodi Nation**

**3 pounds beef brisket, quartered**
**1 onion, cut into quarters**
**2 cups beef broth**
**Splash Worcestershire sauce**
**1 teaspoon kosher salt**

1. Select SEAR/SAUTÉ and set temperature to MD:HI. Select START/STOP to begin and allow to preheat for 5 minutes.

2. Add the brisket (fat side down) into the cooking pot and sear for 5 minutes. Using tongs, carefully flip the brisket over and sear on the other side for an additional 5 minutes.

3. In the cooking pot, combine the onion, beef broth, Worcestershire sauce, and salt.

4. Assemble the pressure lid, making sure the pressure release valve is in the SEAL position.

5. Select PRESSURE and set to HI. Set the time to 60 minutes. Select START/STOP to begin.

6. When pressure cooking is complete, allow the pressure to naturally release for 20 minutes. After 20 minutes, quick release any remaining pressure by moving the pressure release valve to the VENT position. Carefully remove lid when unit has finished releasing pressure.

7. Shred or slice the meat, as desired for serving.

Per serving: *Calories: 486; Total Fat: 20g; Saturated Fat: 0g; Cholesterol: 382mg; Sodium: 782mg; Carbohydrates: 3g; Fiber:1 g; Protein: 72g*

# Spicy Pork Grain Bowl

**SERVES 4**

*Grain bowls, which combine a grain, protein, and toppings for a complete meal, have become a big trend. I used quinoa in this recipe for an extra dose of protein, but any grain can be used. With optional toppings, picky eaters in the family can build a bowl to their own liking.*

**DAIRY-FREE, GLUTEN-FREE, NUT-FREE, 360 MEAL, UNDER 30 MINUTES**

**PREP TIME:** 5 minutes
**TOTAL COOK TIME:** 17 minutes

**APPROX. PRESSURE BUILD:** 10 minutes
**PRESSURE COOK:** 2 minutes
**PRESSURE RELEASE:** 10 minutes, then Quick
**AIR CRISP:** 15 minutes

**ACCESSORIES:** Reversible Rack

**HACK IT:** Buy precut fruit at the grocery store for the toppings to save time on prep.

Per serving: *Calories: 499; Total Fat: 14g; Saturated Fat: 4g; Cholesterol: 33mg; Sodium: 1255mg; Carbohydrates: 65g; Fiber: 9g; Protein: 31g*

- ¼ cup smoked paprika
- 2 tablespoons ground cumin
- ½ teaspoon cayenne pepper
- 2 tablespoons dark brown sugar
- 3 tablespoons kosher salt, divided
- 2 teaspoons freshly ground black pepper
- 2 (6-ounce) boneless pork chops
- 2 cups quinoa
- 3 cups chicken stock

1. In a small bowl, mix together the paprika, cumin, cayenne pepper, sugar, salt, and pepper.

2. Pat the pork chops dry with a paper towel, then rub the spice mixture over the meat ensuring that it's fully covered.

3. Place the quinoa, chicken stock, and salt into the pot. Assemble pressure lid, making sure the pressure release valve is in the SEAL position.

4. Select PRESSURE and set to HI. Set time to 2 minutes. Select START/STOP to begin.

5. When pressure cooking is complete, allow pressure to naturally release for 10 minutes. After 10 minutes, quick release remaining pressure by turning the pressure release valve to the VENT position. Carefully remove lid when unit has finished releasing pressure.

6. Place Reversible Rack in pot in the higher position. Place the pork on the rack. Close crisping lid.

7. Select AIR CRISP, set temperature to 375ºF, and set time to 15 minutes. Select START/STOP to begin.

8. After 8 minutes, open lid, and using tongs, flip the pork chops. Close lid and continue cooking until the pork chops have reached an internal temperature of 165ºF.

9. When cooking is complete, remove the pork and rice from the pot. Slice the pork and serve in bowls over the rice with desired toppings, such as mint, avocado, mango, blueberries, sprouts, or grape tomatoes.

# Sweet-and-Sour Rack of Ribs

**SERVES 4**

*These ribs are great for a game-day party, weeknight dinner, or summer cookout. Serve with all your barbecue favorites—try my Caprese Pasta Salad (page 168), Barbecue Baked Beans (page 315), or Cheesy Biscuits (page 321).*

**DAIRY-FREE, NUT-FREE**

**PREP TIME:** 10 minutes
**TOTAL COOK TIME:**
29 minutes

**APPROX. PRESSURE BUILD:**
10 minutes
**PRESSURE COOK:**
19 minutes
**PRESSURE RELEASE:** Quick
**AIR CRISP:** 20 minutes

**ACCESSORIES:** Cook & Crisp Basket

Per serving: *Calories: 869; Total Fat: 41g; Saturated Fat: 15g; Cholesterol: 255mg; Sodium: 1269mg; Carbohydrates: 75g; Fiber: 4g; Protein: 54g*

1 (3-pound) rack St. Louis ribs, cut in thirds
1 teaspoon sea salt
½ teaspoon freshly ground black pepper
½ cup water
¼ cup apple cider vinegar
½ cup tomato ketchup
1 (8-ounce) can crushed pineapple
3 tablespoons brown sugar
2 tablespoons cornstarch
1 tablespoon soy sauce

1. Season the ribs with salt and pepper.

2. Pour the water into the pot. Place the ribs in the Cook & Crisp Basket and insert basket in pot. Assemble pressure lid, making sure the pressure release valve is in the SEAL position.

3. Select PRESSURE and set to HI. Set time to 19 minutes. Select START/STOP to begin.

4. Add the vinegar, ketchup, pineapple, brown sugar, cornstarch, and soy sauce to a blender and blend under high speed until well combined.

5. When pressure cooking is complete, quick release the pressure by turning the pressure release valve to the VENT position. Carefully remove pressure lid when unit has finished releasing pressure.

6. Liberally brush the ribs with the sauce. Close crisping lid.

7. Select AIR CRISP, set temperature to 400°F, and set time to 20 minutes. Select START/STOP to begin.

8. After 10 minutes, open lid and liberally brush ribs with additional sauce. Flip the ribs and brush the other side. Close lid and continue cooking. Add additional time and basting as desired for crispier results.

9. When cooking is complete, the internal temperature of the meat should read at least 185°F on a meat thermometer. Remove basket and ribs and serve.

# Asian-Glazed Pork Shoulder by Sam Ferguson

*Chef says:* As a restaurant chef, late nights eating and drinking in Chinatown are a rite of passage—and this dish reminds me of those nights. I will always cherish those moments of sitting down at a lazy Susan table with 8 or 10 of my coworkers to share an elaborate spread of classic Chinese dishes, everyone spinning the table to get their hands on their favorite dish before it was all gone. This dish is an homage to those memories.

**DAIRY-FREE, GLUTEN-FREE, NUT-FREE, 5 INGREDIENT**

**PREP TIME:** 5 minutes, plus time to marinate
**TOTAL COOK TIME:** 1 hour, 5 minutes

**APPROX. PRESSURE BUILD:** 10 minutes
**PRESSURE COOK:** 45 minutes
**PRESSURE RELEASE:** Quick
**AIR CRISP:** 20 minutes

**ACCESSORIES:** Cook & Crisp Basket

**INGREDIENT INFO:** Hoisin-garlic sauce is a prepared food staple that packs a ton of flavor. These types of sauces are readily available at most grocery stores and are a fast and convenient way to create a lot of flavor in your dishes. They work great on meat, fish, and vegetables—stock up your pantry with these items and you'll never need to make your own marinade or sauce again.

1 boneless pork shoulder, between 2½ and 3 pounds

2½ cups garlic-hoisin sauce, divided, plus additional for glazing

¾ cups water

1 head broccoli, cut into 2-inch florets

1 tablespoon canola oil

Kosher salt

Freshly ground black pepper

1. Place the pork shoulder and 1½ cups of hoisin sauce in large, resealable plastic bag. Move contents to ensure that all pork has been coated with the sauce and seal bag. Refrigerate and let marinate for at least 10 minutes and up to 4 hours.

2. Place Cook & Crisp Basket in pot. Place the water in the pot. Place the pork in the basket. Assemble pressure lid, making sure the pressure release valve is in the SEAL position.

3. Select PRESSURE and set to HI. Set time to 45 minutes. Select START/STOP to begin.

4. Combine the broccoli, oil, ½ cup of hoisin sauce, and salt and pepper in a large bowl. Mix well to coat broccoli with sauce and seasonings.

5. When pressure cooking is complete, quick release the pressure by moving the pressure release valve to the VENT position. Carefully remove lid when unit has finished releasing pressure.

6. Move the pork to one side of the basket and place broccoli in the other side. Brush the remaining ½ cup of hoisin sauce over the pork. Close crisping lid.

7. Select AIR CRISP, set temperature to 390°F, and set time to 20 minutes. Select START/STOP to begin.

8. Every 5 minutes or so, open lid and glaze pork with additional hoisin sauce. Close lid and continue cooking. Begin

checking pork for desired crispiness after 15 minutes, cooking for up to an additional 5 minutes if desired.

9. When cooking is complete, remove pork and broccoli and serve in a family-style dish. If desired, pour some of the cooking liquid over the top of pork and broccoli for even more flavor.

*Per serving: Calories: 1139; Total Fat: 67g; Saturated Fat: 21g; Cholesterol: 205mg; Sodium: 2802mg; Carbohydrates: 77g; Fiber: 7g; Protein: 55g*

# Crispy Korean-Style Ribs

**SERVES 4**

*These ribs are super easy—simply mix the ingredients and marinate. Because the ribs are pressure cooked to tenderize and pack in flavor before crisping, you only need to marinate them for about 30 minutes. Korean barbecue ribs are typically made with beef short ribs, but I use baby back ribs in this version.*

**DAIRY-FREE, NUT-FREE**

**PREP TIME:** 10 minutes, plus 30 minutes to marinate
**TOTAL COOK TIME:** 25 minutes

**APPROX. PRESSURE BUILD:** 10 minutes
**PRESSURE COOK:** 10 minutes
**PRESSURE RELEASE:** Quick
**AIR CRISP:** 15 minutes

**ACCESSORIES:** Cook & Crisp Basket

**VARIATION TIP:** Using St. Louis-style ribs? Increase the pressure cook time to 18 minutes.

½ **cup soy sauce**
2 **tablespoons rice vinegar**
2 **tablespoons sesame oil**
1 **tablespoon cayenne pepper**
8 **garlic cloves, minced**
1 **tablespoon grated fresh ginger**
1 **small onion, minced**
1 **(3-pound) rack baby back ribs, cut into quarters**
½ **cup water**
¼ **cup honey**
**Sesame seeds, for garnish**

1. In a mixing bowl, combine the soy sauce, rice vinegar, sesame oil, cayenne pepper, garlic, ginger, and onion. Pour the mixture over the ribs, cover, and let marinate in the refrigerator for 30 minutes.

2. Place the ribs in the Cook & Crisp Basket, reserving the remaining marinade. Pour the water in the pot and place basket in pot. Assemble pressure lid, making sure the pressure release valve is in the SEAL position.

3. Select PRESURE and set to HI. Set time to 10 minutes. Select START/STOP to begin.

4. When pressure cooking is complete, quick release the pressure by turning the pressure release valve to the VENT position. Carefully remove lid when pressure has finished releasing.

5. Pour the remaining marinade over the ribs. Close lid.

6. Select AIR CRISP, set temperature to 400°F, and set time to 15 minutes. Select START/STOP to begin.

7. After 10 minutes, open lid and liberally brush the ribs with the honey. Close lid and continue cooking.

8. When cooking is complete, open lid and remove the ribs. Cut them into individual ribs. Sprinkle with the sesame seeds and serve.

*Per serving: Calories: 1133; Total Fat: 88g; Saturated Fat: 31g; Cholesterol: 270mg; Sodium: 2055mg; Carbohydrates: 25g; Fiber: 1g; Protein: 57g*

# Pork Chops with Green Beans and Scalloped Potatoes by Caroline Schliep

**SERVES 2**

***Chef says:*** *Perfectly cooked pork chops paired with layers of cheesy potatoes and green beans, this dish was one of my favorite dinners growing up. But, at the end of the meal, I was always stuck doing the dishes, and when made traditionally, this meal takes quite a few pots and pans. Now with the Ninja® Foodi™ Pressure Cooker, the whole meal can be made in one dish for easy cleanup.*

GLUTEN-FREE, NUT-FREE, 360 MEAL

---

**PREP TIME:** 15 minutes
**TOTAL COOK TIME:**
45 minutes

---

**APPROX. PRESSURE BUILD:**
10 minutes
**PRESSURE COOK:**
25 minutes
**PRESSURE RELEASE:**
25 minutes, then Quick
**BROIL:** 20 minutes

---

**HACK IT:** For a quicker prep time, use instant scalloped potatoes instead of making them from scratch.

1½ cups chicken broth

2 cups half-and-half

¼ cup cornstarch

2 teaspoons garlic powder

Kosher salt

Freshly ground black pepper

4 Russet potatoes, sliced ¼-inch thick

4 cups shredded Cheddar cheese, divided

2 bone-in pork chops

½ pound green beans, ends trimmed

1 teaspoon minced garlic

1 teaspoon extra-virgin olive oil

1. In a medium bowl, whisk together the chicken broth, half-and-half, cornstarch, garlic powder, salt, and pepper. Pour just enough broth mixture to cover the bottom of the pot.

2. Layer half of the sliced potatoes in the bottom of the pot. Cover the potatoes with 1 cup of cheese, then layer the remaining potatoes over the cheese. Cover the second layer of potatoes with 1 cup of cheese, then pour in the remaining broth mixture to cover potatoes. Assemble pressure lid, making sure the pressure release valve is in the SEAL position.

3. Select PRESSURE and set to HI. Set time to 25 minutes. Select START/STOP to begin.

4. When pressure cooking is complete, allow pressure to release naturally for 25 minutes. After 25 minutes, quick release remaining pressure by moving the pressure release valve to the VENT position. Carefully remove lid when unit has finished releasing pressure.

5. Cover the potatoes with remaining 2 cups of cheese. Place the Reversible Rack in the broil position in the pot. Close crisping lid.

CONTINUED ▶

# Pork Chops with Green Beans and Scalloped Potatoes continued

6. Select BROIL and set time to 20 minutes. Select START/ STOP to begin.

7. Season the pork chops with salt and pepper.

8. After 4 minutes, open lid. Place the pork chops on the rack. Close the lid and continue cooking for another 12 minutes.

9. In a large bowl, toss the green beans with the garlic and oil, and season with salt and pepper.

10. After 12 minutes, open lid and add the green beans to the rack with the pork chops. Close lid and continue cooking for the remaining 4 minutes.

11. When cooking is complete, open lid and serve.

Per serving: *Calories: 1916; Total Fat: 118g; Saturated Fat: 70g; Cholesterol: 412mg; Sodium: 3116mg; Carbohydrates: 107g; Fiber: 15g; Protein: 105g*

# Pork Tenderloin with Warm Balsamic and Apple Chutney by Caroline Schliep

*Chef says: Pork has always lent itself wonderfully to fruity flavors. For this recipe, I wanted to pair this delectable herb-crusted tenderloin with a sweet yet tangy apple chutney. It will surely fill your soul with autumn flavors and leave your guests thinking you are a top chef. It's also perfect for a date night or a cozy fall evening. The real secret is the Ninja® Foodi™ Pressure Cooker does the hard work for you, coming together all in one pot.*

**GLUTEN-FREE, NUT-FREE, UNDER 30 MINUTES**

**PREP TIME:** 10 minutes
**TOTAL COOK TIME:**
23 minutes

**SEAR/SAUTÉ:** 8 minutes
**APPROX. PRESSURE BUILD:**
10 minutes
**PRESSURE COOK:** 7 minutes
**PRESSURE RELEASE:**
14 minutes, then Quick

**VARIATION TIP:** Swap apple with another fruit like cranberries, pears, peaches, or mango.

- 1 pound pork tenderloin
- 2½ tablespoons minced rosemary, divided
- 2½ tablespoons minced thyme, divided
- Kosher salt
- Freshly ground black pepper
- 2 tablespoons extra-virgin olive oil
- 1 small white onion
- 1 tablespoon minced garlic
- ¾ cup apple juice
- 2 apples, cut into ½-inch cubes
- 2½ tablespoons balsamic vinegar
- 1 tablespoon honey
- 2½ teaspoons cornstarch
- 3 tablespoons unsalted butter, cubed

1. Select SEAR/SAUTÉ and set to HI. Select START/STOP to begin. Let preheat for 5 minutes.

2. Season the pork with 1 tablespoon of rosemary, 1 tablespoon of thyme, salt, and pepper.

3. Once unit is preheated, add the olive oil. Once hot, add the pork and sear for 3 minutes on each side. Once seared, place the pork on a plate and set aside.

4. Add the onion, garlic, and apple juice. Stir, scraping the bottom of the pot to remove any brown bits. Add apples and vinegar and stir. Return the pork to the pot, nestling it in the apple mixture. Assemble pressure lid, making sure the pressure release valve is in the SEAL position.

5. Select PRESSURE and set to HI. Set time to 7 minutes. Select START/STOP to begin.

6. When pressure cooking is complete, allow pressure to naturally release for 14 minutes. After 14 minutes, quick release the pressure by turning the pressure release valve

CONTINUED ▶

# Pork Tenderloin with Warm Balsamic and Apple Chutney continued

to the VENT position. Carefully remove lid when unit has finished releasing pressure.

7. Remove the pork from the pot, place it on a plate, and cover with aluminum foil.

8. Slightly mash the apples with a potato masher. Stir the honey into the mixture.

9. Remove ¼ cup of cooking liquid from the pot and mix it with the cornstarch until smooth. Pour this mixture into the pot and stir until thickened. Add the butter, 1 tablespoon of rosemary, and 1 tablespoon of thyme and stir until the butter is melted.

10. Slice the pork and serve it with the chutney. Garnish with the remaining ½ tablespoon of rosemary and ½ tablespoon of thyme.

Per serving: *Calories: 406; Total Fat: 20g; Saturated Fat: 8g; Cholesterol: 98mg; Sodium: 107mg; Carbohydrates: 33g; Fiber: 3g; Protein: 24g*

# Asian-Style Meatballs by Caroline Schliep

**Chef says:** *Coated in a sweet and tangy sauce, wrapped in fresh lettuce, and topped with crunchy peanuts, sliced scallions, and sesame seeds, these meatballs make for a perfect bite any day of the week or as a show-stopping appetizer for the big game. And if you plan on having any leftovers for yourself, you better plan on making a double recipe because they will be gone in no time.*

**DAIRY-FREE, NUT-FREE, UNDER 30 MINUTES**

**PREP TIME:** 10 minutes
**TOTAL COOK TIME:**
20 minutes

**APPROX. PRESSURE BUILD:**
10 minutes
**PRESSURE COOK:**
20 minutes
**PRESSURE RELEASE:** Quick

**MAKE MORE, MAKE LESS:**
Double the recipe to feed a bigger crowd.

1 pound frozen
  beef meatballs
1¼ cups garlic-hoisin sauce
¼ cup soy sauce
½ cup rice vinegar
2 tablespoons brown sugar

½ tablespoon sriracha
2 tablespoons freshly
  squeezed lime juice
2 tablespoons cornstarch
2 tablespoons water
1 head butter lettuce

1. Place the meatballs, hoisin sauce, soy sauce, rice vinegar, brown sugar, sriracha, and lime juice in the pot and stir. Assemble pressure lid, making sure the pressure release valve is in the SEAL position.

2. Select PRESSURE and set to HI. Set the time to 20 minutes. Select START/STOP to begin.

3. When pressure cooking is complete, quick release the pressure by turning the pressure release valve to the VENT position. Carefully remove the lid when the unit has finished releasing pressure.

4. Transfer the meatballs to a serving bowl.

5. In a small bowl, mix together the cornstarch and water until smooth. Pour this mixture into the pot, whisking it into the sauce. Once sauce has thickened, pour it over the meatballs.

6. Serve the meatballs in lettuce cups with the toppings of your choice, such as sesame seeds, sliced scallions, chopped peanuts, and julienned cucumber.

*Per serving: Calories: 337; Total Fat: 18g; Saturated Fat: 5g; Cholesterol: 25mg; Sodium: 2070mg; Carbohydrates: 41g; Fiber: 1g; Protein: 9g*

# Korean-Style Barbecue Meatloaf by Craig White

***Chef says:*** *This dish uses one of my favorite ingredients, gochujang. This Korean paste is a mixture of chili, glutinous rice, and soybean powder. It's savory, spicy, sweet, and everything you need to add a layer of depth to a dish that will keep your guests guessing. Add it to soups, rice, beans, barbecue sauces, and marinades to step up your flavor game.*

**NUT-FREE, UNDER 30 MINUTES**

**PREP TIME:** 15 minutes
**TOTAL COOK TIME:** 30 minutes

**APPROX. PRESSURE BUILD:** 10 minutes
**PRESSURE COOK:** 15 minutes
**PRESSURE RELEASE:** Quick
**BAKE/ROAST:** 15 minutes

**ACCESSORIES:** Ninja Loaf Pan, Reversible Rack

**VARIATION TIP:** Tired of "living your best loaf"? Just roll this meat mix into meatballs. Grab a ¼ cup measuring cup and portion them out. You could even substitute ground chicken or turkey for the meatloaf mix. As long as you're having fun, I have done my job here.

- 1 pound beef, pork, and veal meatloaf mix
- 1 large egg
- 1 cup panko bread crumbs
- ½ cup whole milk
- ⅓ cup minced onion
- ¼ cup chopped cilantro
- 1 garlic clove, grated
- 1 tablespoon grated fresh ginger
- ½ tablespoon fish sauce
- 1½ teaspoons sesame oil
- 1 tablespoon, plus 1 teaspoon soy sauce
- ¼ cup, plus 1 tablespoon gochujang
- 1 cup water
- 1 tablespoon honey

1. In a large bowl, stir together the beef, egg, bread crumbs, milk, onion, cilantro, garlic, ginger, fish sauce, sesame oil, 1 teaspoon of soy sauce, and 1 tablespoon of gochujang.

2. Place the meat mixture in the Ninja Loaf Pan or an 8½-inch loaf pan and cover tightly with aluminum foil.

3. Pour the water into the pot. Place the loaf pan on the Reversible Rack, making sure the rack is in the lower position. Place the rack with pan in the pot. Assemble pressure lid, making sure the pressure release valve is in the SEAL position.

4. Select PRESSURE and set to HI. Set time to 15 minutes. Select START/STOP to begin.

5. When pressure cooking is complete, quick release the pressure by moving the pressure release valve to the VENT position. Carefully remove lid when unit has finished releasing pressure.

6. Carefully remove the foil from the pan. Close crisping lid.

7. Select BAKE/ROAST, set temperature to 360ºF, and set time to 15 minutes. Select START/STOP to begin.

8.  In a small bowl stir together the remaining ¼ cup of gochujang, 1 tablespoon of soy sauce, and honey.

9.  After 7 minutes, open lid and top the meatloaf with the gochujang barbecue mixture. Close lid and continue cooking.

10. When cooking is complete, open lid and remove meatloaf from the pot. Let cool for 10 minutes before serving.

*Per serving: Calories: 389; Total Fat: 22g; Saturated Fat: 7g; Cholesterol: 129mg; Sodium: 887mg; Carbohydrates: 24g; Fiber: 3g; Protein: 31g*

# Pork and Ricotta Meatballs with Cheesy Grits by Sam Ferguson

SERVES 8 TO 10

*Chef says:* *During my time working in restaurants, I quickly learned that adding cheese to the meatball mix is a great way to create tons of moisture and flavor in the food. The obvious example of this is Parmesan, but one ingredient that people tend to be less familiar with is ricotta cheese. Ricotta is a perfect addition—rich, velvety, and smooth.*

**NUT-FREE, FAMILY FAVORITE, UNDER 30 MINUTES**

**PREP TIME:** 15 minutes
**TOTAL COOK TIME:** 26 minutes

**SEAR/SAUTÉ:** 12 minutes
**APPROX. PRESSURE BUILD:** 10 minutes
**PRESSURE COOK:** 6 minutes
**PRESSURE RELEASE:** Quick
**BROIL:** 8 minutes

**VARIATION TIP:** Many grocery stores offer a meatball/meatloaf ground meat blend—this is a great alternative to strictly a ground pork meatball. If you see this, buy it! It typically has equal parts ground pork, ground veal, and ground beef.

- 2 pounds ground pork
- 1 cup whole milk ricotta cheese
- 2 eggs
- 1 cup panko bread crumbs
- 4 garlic cloves, minced
- ¼ cup parsley, minced, plus more for garnishing
- 1½ cups grated Parmesan cheese, divided
- 2 tablespoons kosher salt, divided
- 1 teaspoon freshly ground black pepper
- 2 tablespoons canola oil
- 4 cups whole milk
- 1 cup coarse ground grits

1. In a large bowl, combine the pork, ricotta, eggs, bread crumbs, garlic, parsley, ½ cup of Parmesan, 1 tablespoon of salt, and pepper. Use your hands or a sturdy spatula to mix well.

2. Use a 3-ounce ice cream scoop to portion the mixture into individual meatballs. Use your hands to gently form them into balls.

3. Select SEAR/SAUTÉ and set to HI. Select START/STOP to begin. Let preheat for 5 minutes.

4. Add the oil. Add half the meatballs and sear for 6 minutes, flipping them after 3 minutes. Remove from the pot and repeat with the remaining meatballs. Remove the second batch of meatballs from the pot.

5. Add the milk, grits, and remaining 1 tablespoon of salt and stir. Gently place meatballs back in the pot. They will sink slightly when placed in the milk. Assemble pressure lid, making sure pressure release valve is in the SEAL position.

6. Select PRESSURE and set to HI. Set time to 6 minutes. Select START/STOP to begin.

CONTINUED ▶

# Pork and Ricotta Meatballs with Cheesy Grits continued

7. When pressure cooking is complete, quick release the pressure by moving the pressure release valve to the VENT position. Carefully remove lid when unit has finished releasing pressure.

8. Sprinkle the remaining 1 cup of Parmesan cheese over the top of the grits and meatballs. Close crisping lid.

9. Select BROIL and set time to 8 minutes. Select START/ STOP to begin.

10. When cooking is complete, serve immediately.

*Per serving: Calories: 544; Total Fat: 32g; Saturated Fat: 13g; Cholesterol: 151mg; Sodium: 763mg; Carbohydrates: 28g; Fiber: 1g; Protein: 37g*

# Brisket Chili Verde

**by CJ Volkmann, Ninja® Foodi™ Family Member**

**SERVES 4**

*CJ says:* For a quick, easy brisket chili verde, try this versatile dish in the Ninja Foodi Pressure Cooker. This recipe works with beef, pork, or chicken.

---

**DAIRY-FREE, GLUTEN-FREE, NUT-FREE, UNDER 30 MINUTES**

**PREP TIME:** 10 minutes
**TOTAL COOK TIME:** 19 minutes

**SEAR/SAUTÉ:** 4 minutes
**PRESSURE COOK:** 15 minutes
**APPROX. PRESSURE BUILD:** 10 minutes
**PRESSURE RELEASE:** Quick

**HACK IT:** Try the Beef Brisket on page 269 and use the leftovers for this quick and easy Brisket Chili Verde.

**Find CJ on Facebook & YouTube: Cooking with CJ**

---

1 tablespoon vegetable oil
½ white onion, diced
1 jalapeño pepper, diced
1 teaspoon garlic, minced
1 pound brisket, cooked
1 (19-ounce) can green chile enchilada sauce
1 (4-ounce) can fire-roasted diced green chiles
Juice of 1 lime
1 teaspoon seasoning salt
½ teaspoon ground chipotle pepper

1. Select SEAR/SAUTÉ and set temperature to HI. Select START/STOP to begin and allow to preheat for 5 minutes.

2. Add oil to the pot and allow to heat for 1 minute. Add the onion, jalapeño, and garlic. Sauté for 3 minutes or until onion is translucent.

3. Add the brisket, enchilada sauce, green chiles, lime juice, salt, and chipotle powder. Mix well.

4. Assemble the pressure lid, making sure the pressure release valve is in the SEAL position.

5. Select PRESSURE and set to HI. Set the time to 15 minutes. Select START/STOP to begin.

6. When cooking is complete, quick release the pressure by turning the pressure release valve to the VENT position. Carefully remove the lid when the unit has finished releasing pressure.

---

Per serving: *Calories: 427; Total Fat: 16g; Saturated Fat: 4g; Cholesterol: 78mg; Sodium: 1323mg; Carbohydrates: 30g; Fiber: 9g; Protein:41g*

# Pork Pie by Chelven Randolph

**SERVES 8**

**Chef says:** *My partner Amy says I love Mexican food more than any other cuisine, and she may be correct. I love the depth of flavor and flavor profiles of all Mexican food. There is an inherent labor of love associated with Mexican cuisine that I naturally gravitate toward. This is a version of a dish I ate in Los Angeles from a small Mexican restaurant close to my job. No one spoke English, and everything was prepared by two Mexican woman every day. Traditionally it is made with a masa dough and braised for hours.*

NUT-FREE, 360 MEAL, FAMILY FAVORITE

**PREP TIME:** 10 minutes
**TOTAL COOK TIME:** 45 minutes

**SEAR/SAUTÉ:** 15 minutes
**BAKE/ROAST:** 25 minutes

- 2 tablespoons extra-virgin olive oil
- 1 pound ground pork
- 1 yellow onion, diced
- 1 (12-ounce) can black beans, drained
- 1 cup frozen corn kernels
- 1 (4-ounce) can green chiles
- 2 tablespoons chili powder
- 1 box cornbread mix
- 1½ cups milk
- 1 cup shredded Cheddar cheese

1. Select SEAR/SAUTÉ and set temperature to MED. Select START/STOP to begin. Let preheat for 3 minutes.

2. Add the olive oil, pork, and onion. Brown the pork, stirring frequently to break the meat into smaller pieces, until cooked through, about 5 minutes.

3. Add the beans, corn, chiles, and chili powder and stir. Simmer, stirring frequently, about 10 minutes.

4. In a medium bowl, combine the cornbread mix, milk, and cheese. Pour it over simmering mixture in an even layer. Close crisping lid.

5. Select BAKE/ROAST, set temperature to 360°F, and set time for 25 minutes. Select START/STOP to begin.

6. After 20 minutes, use wooden toothpick to check if corn-bread is done. If the toothpick inserted into the cornbread does not come out clean, close lid and cook for the remaining 5 minutes.

7. When cooking is complete, open lid. Let cool for 10 minutes before slicing and serving.

*Per serving: Calories: 491; Total Fat: 24g; Saturated Fat: 9g; Cholesterol: 91mg; Sodium: 667mg; Carbohydrates: 47g; Fiber: 6g; Protein: 24g*

# Ropa Vieja by Kelly Gray

*Chef says:* *Ropa Vieja is traditional Cuban dish that I encountered on my first trip to Havana. Tender beef, vibrant vegetables, and bold spices combine in this one pot meal for an easy weeknight dinner with some Latin flair. One bite of this pressure cooker Ropa Vieja and I'm transported back to Cuba's buzzing streets filled with salsa music and brightly colored vintage cars. Try it on its own or a lo Cubano—paired with rice and beans and fried plantains—to experience a taste of Havana for yourself.*

**DAIRY-FREE, GLUTEN-FREE, NUT-FREE, FAMILY FAVORITE**

**PREP TIME:** 15 minutes
**TOTAL COOK TIME:** 1 hour, 25 minutes

**SEAR/SAUTÉ:** 42 minutes
**APPROX. PRESSURE BUILD:** 10 minutes
**PRESSURE COOK:** 40 minutes
**PRESSURE RELEASE:** Quick

**VARIATION TIP:** Substitute beef with a pork roast or chicken thighs for an equally delicious and traditional version of the meal. Cubans use whatever is available so don't be afraid to improvise. Simply adjust the pressure-cooking times based on the charts provided (see page 366).

- 2 tablespoons canola oil, divided
- 1 red bell pepper, thinly sliced
- 1 yellow bell pepper, thinly sliced
- 1 green bell pepper, thinly sliced
- 1 large onion, thinly sliced
- 4 garlic cloves, minced
- Kosher salt
- Freshly ground black pepper
- 2½ pounds chuck roast, cut in half
- 1 cup beef stock
- 2 bay leaves
- ½ cup dry white wine
- 1 tablespoon white vinegar
- 1 (16-ounce) can crushed tomatoes
- 1 (8-ounce) can tomato paste
- 2 teaspoons dried oregano
- 1½ teaspoons ground cumin
- 1 teaspoon paprika
- ⅛ teaspoon ground allspice
- 1 cup green olives with pimentos
- Cilantro, for garnish
- Lime wedges, for garnish

1. Select SEAR/SAUTÉ and set to HI. Select START/STOP to begin. Let preheat for 5 minutes.

2. Add 1 tablespoon of oil, the bell peppers, onions, and garlic, and season with salt and pepper. Cook, stirring occasionally, for about 5 minutes, or until vegetables have softened and are fragrant.

3. Liberally season the chuck with salt and pepper.

4. When the vegetables are cooked, remove and set aside.

5. Add the remaining 1 tablespoon of oil and meat. Sear the roast on both sides so that a dark crust forms, about 5 minutes per side.

6. Add the beef stock and bay leaves. Scrape the bottom of the pot with a rubber or wooden spoon to release any browned bits stuck to it. Assemble pressure lid, making sure the pressure release valve is in the SEAL position.

CONTINUED ▶

# Ropa Vieja continued

7. Select PRESSURE and set to HI. Set time to 40 minutes. Select START/STOP to begin.

8. When pressure cooking is complete, quick release the pressure by turning the pressure release valve to the VENT position. Carefully remove lid when unit has finished releasing pressure.

9. Carefully shred the beef in the pot using two forks.

10. Select SEAR/SAUTÉ and set to MED. Select START/STOP to begin. Add the vegetables, wine, vinegar, crushed tomatoes, tomato paste, oregano, cumin, paprika, and all-spice and stir with a rubber or wooden spoon, being sure to scrape the bottom of the pot. Simmer, stirring occasionally, for about 25 minutes or until sauce has reduced and thickened.

11. Add the olives and continue cooking for 2 minutes. Serve, garnished with cilantro and lime wedges.

Per serving: *Calories: 479; Total Fat: 23g; Saturated Fat: 7g; Cholesterol: 132mg; Sodium: 624mg; Carbohydrates: 21g; Fiber: 6g; Protein: 44g*

# Bunless Burgers

**by Nick Martinez, Ninja® Foodi™ Family Member**

**SERVES 4**

***Nick says:*** *No grill? Raining? Snowing? No problem! Burgers in the Foodi are simple, and the flavor is delicious! Bunless burgers are a keto staple and using the Foodi makes them even easier to prepare. We cook these in the Cook & Crisp Basket, but you can also use the Reversible Rack. Crisp some bacon alongside the burgers, add a few slices of avocado and enjoy! Want to add a bun? Place them on the reversible rack and broil for 2 minutes.*

DAIRY-FREE, GLUTEN-FREE, NUT-FREE, UNDER 30 MINUTES, 5 INGREDIENT

**PREP TIME:** 5 minutes
**TOTAL COOK TIME:** 10 minutes

**AIR CRISP:** 10 minutes

**ACCESSORIES:** Cook & Crisp Basket

**Find Nick @theketodadlife / Facebook: The Keto Dad**

¼ **teaspoon onion powder**
¼ **teaspoon garlic powder**
¼ **teaspoon Italian seasoning**
**Dash Himalayan pink salt**
**1 pound ground beef**

1. Place the Cook & Crisp Basket into the cooking pot. Select AIR CRISP, set the temperature to 375ºF, and set the time to 5 minutes to preheat. Select START/STOP to begin.

2. In a small bowl, stir together the onion powder, garlic powder, Italian seasoning, and salt.

3. Divide the ground beef into 4 equal portions and shape each into a patty. Season both side of the patties with the seasoning mix and place them on a sheet of parchment paper.

4. Once the unit is preheated, add the burgers to the basket, working in batches as needed. Close the crisping lid.

5. Select AIR CRISP, set the temperature to 375ºF, and set the time to 8 to 10 minutes. Select START/STOP to begin. Cook the burgers until cooking is complete; no need to flip the burgers!

*Per serving: Calories: 172; Total Fat: 8g; Saturated Fat: 3g; Cholesterol: 65mg; Sodium: 82mg; Carbohydrates: 0g; Fiber: 0g; Protein: 23g*

# Beef Stroganoff by Chelven Randolph

| SERVES 6 |

***Chef says:*** *Beef stroganoff was not a dish I grew up eating, but all my friends did. Whenever I went to my Russian friend's house, I would pray that his mom made stroganoff. Traditional stroganoff is made with a mustard and beef broth and contains no onions or mushrooms. But my version is the amalgamation of all the different styles I've had over the years. I've seen it served over white rice or spaghetti and made with tomato paste as well. But the one I always come back to is this one.*

**NUT-FREE**

**PREP TIME:** 20 minutes
**TOTAL COOK TIME:**
55 minutes

**SEAR/SAUTÉ:** 8 minutes
**APPROX. PRESSURE BUILD:**
10 minutes
**PRESSURE COOK:**
10, plus 5 minutes
**PRESSURE RELEASE:** Quick
**AIR CRISP:** 15 minutes

**VARIATION TIP:** If you want to save considerable time, you can always substitute ground beef for the stew meat. That way you can just brown the meat in the bottom of the pan instead of pressure cooking!

- 2 tablespoons unsalted butter
- 1 yellow onion, diced
- 4 cups cremini mushrooms, sliced
- 2 pounds beef stew meat, cut in 1- to 2-inch cubes
- 2 teaspoons freshly ground black pepper
- 2 sprigs fresh thyme
- 2 tablespoons soy sauce
- 2 cups chicken stock
- 1 (16-ounce) package egg noodles
- 2 tablespoons cornstarch
- 2 tablespoons water
- ½ cup sour cream

1. Select SEAR/SAUTÉ and set to MED. Select START/STOP to begin. Let preheat for 3 minutes.

2. Add the butter, onion, and mushrooms and sauté for 5 minutes.

3. Add the beef, black pepper, thyme, soy sauce, and chicken stock. Simmer for 2 to 3 minutes. Assemble pressure lid, making sure the pressure release valve is in the SEAL position.

4. Select PRESSURE and set to HI. Set time to 10 minutes. Select START/STOP to begin.

5. When pressure cooking is complete, quick release the pressure by turning the pressure release valve to the VENT position. Carefully remove lid when unit has finished releasing pressure.

6. Add the egg noodles. Stir well. Assemble pressure lid, making sure the pressure release valve is in the SEAL position.

7. Select PRESSURE and set to HI. Set time to 5 minutes. Select START/STOP to begin.

8. In a small bowl, mix the cornstarch and water until smooth.

9. When pressure cooking is complete, quick release the pressure by turning the pressure release valve to the VENT position. Carefully remove lid when unit has finished releasing pressure.

10. Stir in cornstarch until incorporated. Stir in the sour cream. Serve immediately.

*Per serving: Calories: 448; Total Fat: 16g; Saturated Fat: 6g; Cholesterol: 55mg; Sodium: 605mg; Carbohydrates: 35g; Fiber: 2g; Protein: 41g*

# Lamb Tagine by Chelven Randolph

SERVES 8

**Chef says:** *Tagine is a traditional Moroccan dish. The name refers to the clay pot in which it is traditionally cooked. Also known as a* marqa, *the dish is synonymous with Middle Eastern and Northern African cuisine. The stew is typically made with various proteins like mutton or poultry and a mix of earthy spices, nuts, and dried fruit. The entire dish is braised for hours in a tagine pot, with little to no water. The cone shape of the tagine lid allows condensation to build and ultimately act as the moisture. This version is made in the Ninja® Foodi™ Pressure Cooker.*

DAIRY-FREE, GLUTEN-FREE, 360 MEAL

PREP TIME: 15 minutes
TOTAL COOK TIME: 55 minutes

APPROX. PRESSURE BUILD: 10 minutes
PRESSURE COOK: 5 minutes, plus 30 minutes
PRESSURE RELEASE: Quick
SEAR/SAUTÉ: 20 minutes

VARIATION TIP: Lamb stew meat is typically the shoulder or boneless shank portion. If you cannot find either, try ground lamb meat. If you're not a fan of lamb, chicken works just as well. If you are going to use chicken, I recommend using boneless, skinless chicken thighs and omit the pressure-cooking portion in step 8.

1 cup couscous

2 cups water

3 tablespoons extra-virgin olive oil, divided

2 yellow onions, diced

3 garlic cloves, minced

2 pounds lamb stew meat, cut into 1- to 2-inch cubes

1 cup dried apricots, sliced

2 cups chicken stock

2 tablespoons ras el hanout seasoning

1 (14.5-ounce) can chickpeas, drained

Kosher salt

Freshly ground black pepper

1 cup toasted almonds, for garnish

1. Place the couscous in the pot and pour in the water. Assemble pressure lid, making sure the pressure release valve is in the SEAL position.

2. Select PRESSURE and set to HI. Set time to 5 minutes. Select START/STOP to begin.

3. When pressure cooking is complete, quick release the pressure by turning the pressure release valve to the VENT position. Carefully remove lid when unit has finished releasing pressure.

4. Stir 1 tablespoon of oil into the couscous, then transfer the couscous to a bowl.

5. Select SEAR/SAUTÉ and set to MD:HI. Select START/STOP to begin. Let preheat for 3 minutes

6. Add the remaining 2 tablespoons of oil, onion, garlic, and lamb. Sauté for 7 to 10 minutes, stirring frequently.

7. Add the apricots, chicken stock, and ras el hanout. Stir to combine. Assemble pressure lid, making sure the pressure release valve is in the SEAL position.

8. Select PRESSURE and set to HI. Set time to 30 minutes. Select START/STOP to begin.

9. When pressure cooking is complete, quick release the pressure by turning the pressure release valve to the VENT position. Carefully remove lid when unit has finished releasing pressure.

10. Stir in the chickpeas.

11. Select SEAR/SAUTÉ and set to MD:LO. Select START/STOP to begin. Let the mixture simmer for 10 minutes. Season with salt and pepper.

12. When cooking is complete, ladle the tagine over the couscous. Garnish with the toasted almonds.

Per serving: *Calories: 596; Total Fat: 21g; Saturated Fat: 4g; Cholesterol: 74mg; Sodium: 354mg; Carbohydrates: 65g; Fiber: 14g; Protein: 39g*

# Spiced Lamb Meatballs by Craig White

SERVES 8

**Chef says:** *Growing up I didn't eat much lamb. And the "thanks for mutton" Seinfeld episode really scared me into not wanting to eat it. It wasn't until I started working in restaurants and producing charcuterie that I fell in love with it. Its flavor can hold up to aggressive seasonings, marinades, and spices. Serve these meatballs with a harissa-spiked tomato sauce, tzatziki, or use them in my Italian Pasta Potpie (page 259).*

**DAIRY-FREE, NUT-FREE, UNDER 30 MINUTES**

**PREP TIME:** 20 minutes
**TOTAL COOK TIME:** 29 minutes

**AIR CRISP:** 29 minutes

**ACCESSORIES:** Cook & Crisp Basket

**SUBSTITUTION TIP:** You can substitute beef, pork, or a meatloaf mix for the lamb in this recipe.

2 pounds ground lamb
¼ cup bread crumbs
2 large eggs, beaten
3 garlic cloves, minced
2 teaspoons ground cumin
1 teaspoon smoked paprika
½ teaspoon cinnamon
½ teaspoon chili flakes
¼ cup minced onion
¼ cup chopped parsley
Kosher salt
Freshly ground black pepper
Cooking spray

1. In a large bowl, add the lamb, bread crumbs, eggs, garlic, cumin, paprika, cinnamon, chili flakes, onion, parsley, salt, and pepper. Using your hands, mix together until combined and sticky.

2. Using a ¼ cup measuring cup, measure out the mixture and roll into meatballs by hand.

3. Insert Cook & Crisp Basket into pot. Close crisping lid. Select AIR CRISP, set temperature to 390°F, and set time to 29 minutes. Select START/STOP to begin. Let preheat for 5 minutes.

4. Open lid and place half the meatballs into the basket. Spray them with the cooking spray. Close lid and cook for 12 minutes.

5. Open lid and place the cooked meatballs in a bowl. Add the remaining meatballs to the basket and coat them with the cooking spray. Close lid and cook for the remaining 12 minutes.

6. When cooking is complete, open lid and serve.

*Per serving: Calories: 329; Total Fat: 16g; Saturated Fat: 9g; Cholesterol: 127mg; Sodium: 129mg; Carbohydrates: 4g; Fiber: 1g; Protein: 21g*

# Lamb Chops with Garlic Butter Sauce and Roasted Carrots by Meg Jordan

**SERVES 3**

***Chef says:*** *This is a modified version of my dad's classic recipe, which he made often when I was growing up. He likes to tell anyone he comes across that I accidentally dumped too much dried parsley in his stovetop version over 20 years ago! I thought making lamb was tedious and needed to be done in an oven, but the Ninja® Foodi™ Pressure Cooker proves that you can make elevated cuts of meat without needing to wait for your oven to heat up.*

**GLUTEN-FREE, NUT-FREE**

**PREP TIME:** 5 minutes
**TOTAL COOK TIME:**
43 minutes

**SEAR/SAUTÉ:** 8 minutes
**BAKE/ROAST:** 20 minutes
**BROIL:** 10 minutes

**ACCESSORIES:**
Reversible Rack

4 tablespoons
  unsalted butter

1 tablespoon
  balsamic vinegar

2 teaspoons dried parsley

2 teaspoons kosher
  salt, divided

2 teaspoons freshly ground
  black pepper, divided

5 garlic cloves, minced

1 (32-ounce) bag
  baby carrots

2 tablespoons canola
  oil, divided

6 lamb chops

1. Select SEAR/SAUTÉ and set temperature to MD:LO. Select START/STOP to begin. Let preheat for 5 minutes.

2. Add the butter, vinegar, parsley, 1 teaspoon of salt, and 1 teaspoon of pepper. Mix together and cook until the butter is bubbling, about 8 minutes.

3. Add the garlic and stir until fragrant. Transfer the mixture to a small bowl and cover to keep warm. Wipe the pot clean and return to unit.

4. In a medium bowl, toss the carrots with 1 tablespoon of canola oil and the remaining 1 teaspoon each of salt and pepper. Place the carrots in the pot. Close crisping lid.

5. Select BAKE/ROAST, set temperature to 390°F, and set time to 20 minutes.

6. Pat the lamb chop dry with a paper towel. Coat them with the remaining 1 tablespoon of oil, and season with salt and pepper.

7. After 10 minutes, open lid and stir the carrots. Close lid and continue cooking.

CONTINUED ▶

# Lamb Chops with Garlic Butter Sauce and Roasted Carrots continued

8. When cooking is complete, open lid. Place Reversible Rack in pot, making sure it is in the higher position. Place the lamb chops on the rack and close crisping lid.

9. Select BROIL and set time to 10 minutes. Select START/ STOP to begin.

10. After 5 minutes, open lid and flip the lamb chops. Close lid and continue cooking until chops have reached internal temperature of at least 145°F.

11. Serve the chops with garlic butter sauce drizzled on top along with the roasted carrots.

Per serving: Calories: 774; Total Fat: 61g; Saturated Fat: 30g; Cholesterol: 140mg; Sodium: 658mg; Carbohydrates: 28g; Fiber: 9g; Protein: 28g

# Braised Lamb Shanks by Sam Ferguson

**SERVES 4**

**Chef says:** *I chose this recipe because slow cooking is similar to the French cooking style of braising—one of the first cooking techniques I properly learned as a scabby young line cook in Boston. The aromas during cooking will draw anyone in the room to the Foodi™ Pressure Cooker, and the flavors of this dish will keep you coming back to cook it time and time again.*

DAIRY-FREE, GLUTEN-FREE, NUT-FREE, 360 MEAL

---

**PREP TIME:** 15 minutes
**TOTAL COOK TIME:** 4 hours 15 minutes

---

**SEAR/SAUTÉ:** 15 minutes
**SLOW COOK:** 4 hours

---

**HACK IT:** Don't have 4 hours? It is simple to convert this from slow cooking to pressure cooking—just pressure cook on HI for 45 minutes in step 6.

2 bone-in lamb shanks, 2 to 2½ pounds each

Kosher salt

Freshly ground black pepper

2 tablespoons canola oil

2 Yukon gold potatoes, cut into 1-inch pieces

2 carrots, cut into 2-inch pieces

2 parsnips, peeled and cut into 2-inch pieces

1 (14-ounce) bag frozen pearl onions

1 bottle (750 mL) red wine

1 cup chicken stock

1 tablespoon chopped fresh rosemary

1. Select SEAR/SAUTÉ and set to HI. Select START/STOP to begin. Let preheat for 5 minutes.

2. Season the lamb shanks with salt and pepper.

3. Add the oil and lamb. Cook for 5 minutes on one side, then turn and cook for an additional 5 minutes. Remove the lamb and set aside.

4. Add the potatoes, carrots, parsnips, and pearl onions. Cook for 5 minutes, stirring occasionally.

5. Stir in the red wine, chicken stock, and rosemary. Add the lamb back to the pot and press down on the shanks to ensure they are mostly submerged in liquid. Assemble pressure lid, making sure the pressure release valve is in the VENT position.

6. Select SLOW COOK and set to HI. Set time to 4 hours. Select START/STOP to begin.

7. When cooking is complete, remove lid and serve.

---

**Per serving:** *Calories: 791; Total Fat: 34g; Saturated Fat: 13g; Cholesterol: 150mg; Sodium: 591mg; Carbohydrates: 47g; Fiber: 9g; Protein: 51g*

# 10
# Staples

# Crispy Bacon

**MAKES 1 POUND BACON**

*I'm a believer that bacon should only be served when crispy—and the Foodi™ Pressure Cooker's design makes it easy to get a consistent crunch all over. By cooking the bacon in the Cook & Crisp Basket, you get super-heated air circulating around all parts of the bacon slices, helping give it a crispy, even result.*

**DAIRY-FREE, GLUTEN-FREE, NUT-FREE, UNDER 30 MINUTES, 5 INGREDIENT**

**PREP TIME:** 2 minutes
**TOTAL COOK TIME:** 25 minutes

**AIR CRISP:** 25 minutes

**ACCESSORIES:** Cook & Crisp Basket

**1 pound bacon**

1. Place Cook & Crisp Basket in pot. Place the bacon in the basket (arrange in a single layer if you prefer flat bacon, but this isn't necessary). Close crisping lid.

2. Select AIR CRISP, set temperature to 390ºF, and set time to 25 minutes. Select START/STOP to begin.

3. After 8 minutes, open lid and stir to separate the bacon slides. Close lid and continue cooking. After another 8 minutes, open lid and separate the bacon to ensure the strips are cooked evenly. Close lid and continue cooking.

4. When cooking is complete, open lid and remove bacon. Serve.

*Per serving (¼ pound): Calories: 472; Total Fat: 45g; Saturated Fat: 15g; Cholesterol: 77mg; Sodium: 750mg; Carbohydrates: 2g; Fiber: 0g; Protein: 14g*

# Hard-Boiled Eggs

*Hard-boiled eggs are so incredibly versatile—and the Ninja® Foodi™ makes it so easy to make anywhere from a few to a whole dozen in no time. Pack two for a quick breakfast on the go or slice them up on top of a salad. The options are endless.*

**DAIRY-FREE, GLUTEN-FREE, NUT-FREE, VEGETARIAN, UNDER 30 MINUTES, FAMILY FAVORITE, 5 INGREDIENT**

**PREP TIME:** 2 minutes
**TOTAL COOK TIME:** 15 minutes

**APPROX. PRESSURE BUILD:** 7 minutes
**PRESSURE COOK:** 8 minutes
**PRESSURE RELEASE:** Quick

**ACCESSORIES:** Reversible Rack

**1 cup water**                    **2 to 12 eggs**

1. Place Reversible Rack in pot, making sure it is in the lower position. Add the water to the pot. Arrange the eggs on the rack in a single layer. Assemble pressure lid, making sure the pressure release valve is in the SEAL position.

2. Select PRESSURE and set to LO. Set time to 8 minutes. Select START/STOP to begin.

3. Prepare a large bowl of ice water.

4. When pressure cooking is complete, quick release the pressure by moving the pressure release valve to the VENT position. Carefully remove lid when unit has finished releasing pressure.

5. Using a slotted spoon, immediately transfer the eggs to the ice water bath and let cool for 5 minutes.

Per serving (1 egg): *Calories: 72; Total Fat: 5g; Saturated Fat: 2g; Cholesterol: 186mg; Sodium: 70mg; Carbohydrates: 0g; Fiber: 0g; Protein: 6g*

# Simple Strawberry Jam

*There are so many options for jams and jellies at your local market—but why not try your hand at making your own? It's remarkably easy and the Foodi™ Pressure Cooker makes it even easier. Try this version on toast, as a pancake topping, or stirred into your favorite yogurt for a delicious semi-homemade breakfast.*

DAIRY-FREE, GLUTEN-FREE, NUT-FREE, VEGAN, 5 INGREDIENT

PREP TIME: 10 minutes
TOTAL COOK TIME: 42 minutes

APPROX. PRESSURE BUILD: 10 minutes
PRESSURE COOK: 1 minute
PRESSURE RELEASE: 10 minutes, then Quick
SEAR/SAUTÉ: 20 minutes

ACCESSORIES: Silicone Potato Masher

VARIATION TIP: Add raspberries or blueberries to turn this into a mixed berry jam.

2 pounds strawberries, hulled and halved

Juice of 2 lemons

1½ cups granulated sugar

1. Place ingredients in the pot. Using a silicone potato masher, mash together to begin to release the strawberry juices. Assemble pressure lid, making sure the pressure release valve is in the SEAL position.

2. Select PRESSURE and set to HI. Set time to 1 minute. Select START/STOP to begin.

3. When pressure cooking is complete, allow pressure to naturally release for 10 minutes. After 10 minutes, quick release remaining pressure by moving the pressure release valve to the VENT position. Cover the vent with a cloth in case of any spraying. Carefully remove lid when pressure has finished releasing.

4. Select SEAR/SAUTÉ and set to MD:HI. Select START/STOP to begin. Let the jam reduce for 10 to 20 minutes, stirring frequently, until it tightens.

5. When cooking is complete, mash the strawberries together using the silicone potato masher for a textured jam, or transfer the strawberry mixture to a food processor and purée for a smooth consistency. Let the jam cool, pour it into a glass jar with a tight-fitting lid, and refrigerate for up to 2 weeks.

*Per serving (2 tablespoons): Calories: 120; Total Fat: 0g; Saturated Fat: 0g; Cholesterol: 0mg; Sodium: 2mg; Carbohydrates: 31g; Fiber: 2g; Protein: 1g*

# Applesauce

*Here in New England we love to go apple picking in the fall. My husband and I love heading out of the city on a nice cool weekend to wander the beautiful orchards in Massachusetts. We always end up coming home with way more apples than we know what to do with. Making applesauce is an easy way to transform those leftover apples into a perfectly sweet treat.*

DAIRY-FREE, GLUTEN-FREE, NUT-FREE, VEGETARIAN, UNDER 30 MINUTES, FAMILY FAVORITE, 5 INGREDIENT

PREP TIME: 5 minutes
TOTAL COOK TIME: 8 minutes

APPROX. PRESSURE BUILD: 10 minutes
PRESSURE COOK: 8 minutes
PRESSURE RELEASE: Quick

VARIATION TIP: Add other fruit, like cut peaches or blueberries, to the pot during step 1 to customize your applesauce.

**6 apples, peeled, cored, and chopped**

**2 tablespoons maple syrup**

**1 tablespoon brown sugar**

**¼ cup apple cider**

**½ teaspoon cinnamon**

1.  Place all the ingredients in the pot. Assemble pressure lid, making sure the pressure release valve is in the SEAL position.

2.  Select PRESSURE and set to HI. Set time for 8 minutes. Select START/STOP to begin.

3.  When pressure cooking is complete, quick release the pressure by moving the pressure release valve to the VENT position. Carefully remove lid when unit has finished releasing pressure.

4.  Use a wooden spoon to stir and break any remaining chunks of apple into smaller pieces.

5.  Serve warm or cool to room temperature. Store in an airtight container in the refrigerator.

*Per serving: Calories: 144; Total Fat: 0g; Saturated Fat: 0g; Cholesterol: 0mg; Sodium: 3mg; Carbohydrates: 38g; Fiber: 6g; Protein: 1g*

# Fluffy Quinoa

**SERVES 6**

*If you're looking to add a good source of protein to round out your meal, look no further than quinoa. High in fiber and ultra-versatile, quinoa fits perfectly in your salads, alongside roasted vegetables, or as the base to a grain bowl.*

**DAIRY-FREE, NUT-FREE, VEGAN, UNDER 30 MINUTES, 5 INGREDIENT**

**PREP TIME:** 1 minute
**TOTAL COOK TIME:** 8 minutes

**APPROX. PRESSURE BUILD:** 10 minutes
**PRESSURE COOK:** 8 minutes
**PRESSURE RELEASE:** Quick

**VARIATION TIP:** Looking to change up the flavor of your quinoa? Try pressure cooking it in chicken stock or vegetable broth instead of water.

**1 cup quinoa, rinsed**          **1½ cups water**

1. Place the quinoa and water in the pot. Assemble pressure lid, making sure the pressure release valve is in the SEAL position.

2. Select PRESSURE and set to HI. Set time for 8 minutes. Select START/STOP to begin.

3. When pressure cooking is complete, quick release the pressure by moving the pressure release valve to the VENT position. Carefully remove lid when unit has finished releasing pressure.

4. Serve hot, or store in an airtight container in the refrigerator to use throughout the week.

**Per serving:** *Calories: 104; Total Fat: 2g; Saturated Fat: 0g; Cholesterol: 0mg; Sodium: 2mg; Carbohydrates: 18g; Fiber: 2g; Protein: 4g*

# Chicken Stock

*Chicken stock is a pantry staple that can be used in so many recipes, from braising greens and cooking grains to making sauces and soups. Try your hand at this home-made version, which packs a ton of flavor and gives you full control of the ingredients you're using.*

**DAIRY-FREE, GLUTEN-FREE, NUT-FREE**

**PREP TIME:** 5 minutes
**TOTAL COOK TIME:**
45 minutes

**APPROX. PRESSURE BUILD:**
10 minutes
**PRESSURE COOK:**
45 minutes
**PRESSURE RELEASE:**
25 minutes, then Quick

**SUBSTITUTION TIP:**
Planning to make the Garlic-Herb Roasted Chicken (page 214)? Save the chicken carcass and use it in this recipe in place of the chicken wings.

**3 pounds chicken wings**
**1 carrot, peeled**
**2 ribs celery, halved**
**1 large onion, halved**
**1 head garlic, halved**
**4 sprigs fresh thyme**
**2 bay leaves**
**1 teaspoon black peppercorns**
**1 teaspoon kosher salt**

1. Place all the ingredients in the pot. Cover with enough water to reach the max fill line. Assemble pressure lid, making sure the pressure release valve is in the SEAL position.

2. Select PRESSURE and set to HI. Set time for 45 minutes. Select START/STOP to begin.

3. When pressure cooking is complete, allow pressure to naturally release for 25 minutes. After 25 minutes, quick release any remaining pressure by moving the pressure release valve to the VENT position. Carefully remove lid when unit has finished releasing pressure.

4. Strain the chicken stock through a fine-mesh sieve and discard the solid pieces. Use a spoon to skim any remaining fat from surface and discard. Let cool, then transfer to airtight containers. The stock can last in the freezer for up to 3 months.

*Per serving (1 cup): Calories: 60; Total Fat: 2g; Saturated Fat: 1g; Cholesterol: 7mg; Sodium: 142mg; Carbohydrates: 4g; Fiber: 0g; Protein: 4g*

# Barbecue Baked Beans by Sam Ferguson

**SERVES 8**

***Chef says:*** *Baked beans make a great addition to a potluck dinner, a family get together, or a weekend barbecue—and with the Ninja® Foodi™ Pressure Cooker there is no time commitment of having to slow cook them for hours on end before they're ready to enjoy.*

**GLUTEN-FREE, UNDER 30 MINUTES**

**PREP TIME:** 15 minutes
**TOTAL COOK TIME:**
25 minutes

**SEAR/SAUTÉ:** 10 minutes
**APPROX. PRESSURE BUILD:**
7 minutes
**PRESSURE COOK:**
15 minutes
**PRESSURE RELEASE:** Quick

**VARIATION TIP:** To transform this recipe into an easy and complete weeknight meal, add 6 chopped hot dogs or prepared sausages to the pot in step 3.

**5 bacon strips, thinly sliced**

**2 green bell peppers, chopped**

**1 white onion, chopped**

**2 cups barbecue sauce**

**½ cup molasses**

**½ cup dark brown sugar**

**½ cup apple cider vinegar**

**1 (15-ounce) can kidney beans, rinsed and drained**

**2 (15-ounce) cans cannellini beans, rinsed and drained**

**1 (15-ounce) can black beans, rinsed and drained**

1. Select SEAR/SAUTÉ and set to HI. Select START/STOP to begin. Let preheat for 5 minutes.

2. Add the bacon and cook for 5 minutes, stirring frequently. Add the bell peppers and onion and cook for an additional 5 minutes, stirring occasionally.

3. Add the barbecue sauce, molasses, brown sugar, vinegar, kidney beans, cannellini beans, and black beans and stir well. Assemble pressure lid, making sure the pressure release valve is in the SEAL position.

4. Select PRESSURE and set to LO. Set time to 15 minutes. Select START/STOP to begin.

5. When pressure cooking is complete, quick release the pressure by moving the pressure release valve to the VENT position. Carefully remove lid when unit has finished releasing pressure.

6. Serve.

*Per serving: Calories: 439; Total Fat: 6g; Saturated Fat: 2g; Cholesterol: 13mg; Sodium: 988mg; Carbohydrates: 81g; Fiber: 11g; Protein: 16g*

# Black Beans

*You can easily customize black beans with a variety of spices and flavors in your Ninja® Foodi™ Pressure Cooker to add to your next salad or eat as a side dish—and cooking them yourself from dry gives you so much more bang for your buck.*

DAIRY-FREE, GLUTEN-FREE, NUT-FREE, VEGAN, UNDER 30 MINUTES, 5 INGREDIENT

**PREP TIME:** 2 minutes
**TOTAL COOK TIME:** 25 minutes

**APPROX. PRESSURE BUILD:** 10 minutes
**PRESSURE COOK:** 25 minutes
**PRESSURE RELEASE:** 20 minutes, then Quick

**VARIATION TIP:** This simple recipe is intentionally unseasoned so you can use the black beans in anything from soup to grain bowls to dessert! Add salt and other spices if you choose in step 1 if you plan on eating these as a standalone side dish.

**2 cups dry black beans**          **6 cups water**

1. Place the beans and water in the pot. Assemble pressure lid, making sure the pressure release valve is in the SEAL position.

2. Select PRESSURE and set to HI. Set time for 25 minutes. Select START/STOP to begin.

3. When pressure cooking is complete, allow pressure to naturally release for 20 minutes. After 20 minutes, quick release remaining pressure by moving the pressure release valve to the VENT position. Carefully remove lid when unit has finished releasing pressure.

4. Drain the beans and store them in an airtight container until ready to use.

Per serving (½ cup): *Calories: 110; Total Fat: 1g; Saturated Fat: 0g; Cholesterol: 0mg; Sodium: 2mg; Carbohydrates: 20g; Fiber: 5g; Protein: 7g*

# Baked Sweet Potato

**SERVES 4**

*Whether you enjoy them plain and simple with a little butter, or topped with your favorite chili, sweet potatoes are versatile and—even better—full of vitamin C. Bake them right in your Ninja® Foodi™ Pressure Cooker for a fork-tender result that cooks much faster than in a traditional oven.*

**DAIRY-FREE, GLUTEN-FREE, NUT-FREE, VEGAN, 5 INGREDIENT**

**PREP TIME:** 1 minute
**TOTAL COOK TIME:** 35 minutes

**AIR CRISP:** 35 minutes

**ACCESSORIES:** Cook & Crisp Basket

**4 whole sweet potatoes**
**½ teaspoon sea salt**
**½ teaspoon freshly ground black pepper**

1. Place Cook & Crisp Basket in pot. Close crisping lid. Select AIR CRISP, set temperature to 390°F, and set time to 5 minutes. Select START/STOP to begin to begin preheating.

2. Pierce each sweet potato with a fork three times.

3. Once unit is preheated, place the sweet potatoes in the basket and season them with salt and pepper. Close crisping lid.

4. Select AIR CRISP, set temperature to 400°F, and set time to 35 minutes. Select START/STOP to begin.

5. When cooking is complete, check that the sweet potatoes are fork-tender and use tongs to remove them from the basket. Serve immediately.

*Per serving: Calories: 112; Total Fat: 0g; Saturated Fat: 0g; Cholesterol: 0mg; Sodium: 306mg; Carbohydrates: 26g; Fiber: 4g; Protein: 2g*

# Simple Steamed Artichokes

**SERVES 2**

*They might look complicated, but don't let those complex layers fool you—artichokes can be prepared in a cinch. From the flesh in the leaves to the tender heart, there is so much flavor to be found in these fun-to-eat beauties. Pick them up the next time you see them at your local market during springtime when they are apt to be the ripest.*

**DAIRY-FREE, GLUTEN-FREE, NUT-FREE, VEGAN, UNDER 30 MINUTES, 5 INGREDIENT**

**PREP TIME:** 5 minutes
**TOTAL COOK TIME:** 20 minutes

**APPROX. PRESSURE BUILD:** 10 minutes
**PRESSURE COOK:** 10 minutes
**PRESSURE RELEASE:** Quick

**ACCESSORIES:** Cook & Crisp Basket

**VARIATION TIP:** Drizzle your favorite sauce over the artichokes when serving, like the mustard cream sauce from my Charred Broccoli with Mustard Cream Sauce (see page 101).

1 cup water
4 garlic cloves
1 bay leaf

½ lemon
2 large artichokes, trimmed

1. Place the water, garlic cloves, and bay leaf in the pot.

2. Rub the cut lemon on the outside of the artichokes, then add them to the water mixture.

3. Place Cook & Crisp Basket in pot. Place the artichokes in the basket. Assemble pressure lid, making sure the pressure release valve is in the SEAL position.

4. Select PRESSURE and set to HI. Set time for 10 minutes. Select START/STOP to begin.

5. When pressure cooking is complete, quick release the pressure by moving the pressure release valve to the VENT position. Carefully remove lid when unit has finished releasing pressure.

6. Remove the artichokes from the pot and serve immediately.

*Per serving: Calories: 89; Total Fat: 0g; Saturated Fat: 0g; Cholesterol: 0mg; Sodium: 154mg; Carbohydrates: 20g; Fiber: 9g; Protein: 6g*

# Cheesy Biscuits

**MAKES 8**

*These no-frills cheesy "drop biscuits" are easy to pull together—which is a good thing because your dinner guests won't be able to get enough of them. The secret is to use cold butter to get a flaky and crumbly interior.*

NUT-FREE, VEGETARIAN, UNDER 30 MINUTES, FAMILY FAVORITE

PREP TIME: 4 minutes
TOTAL COOK TIME: 12 minutes

AIR CRISP: 12 minutes

ACCESSORIES: Cook & Crisp Basket

2 cups pancake and baking mix
½ teaspoon garlic powder
½ teaspoon onion powder
½ teaspoon sea salt
4 tablespoons cold unsalted butter, cut into ½ tablespoon-sized pieces
¼ cup water
¼ cup milk
½ cup shredded Cheddar cheese

1. Place Cook & Crisp Basket in pot. Close crisping lid. Select AIR CRISP, set temperature to 400°F, and set time to 5 minutes. Select START/STOP to begin preheating.

2. Combine the baking mix, garlic powder, onion powder, and salt in a large bowl. Add the butter and, using a pastry cutter or two forks, cut the butter into the mixture so that pea-size pieces are coated in the flour mixture. Add the water, milk, and cheese, and stir until well combined. Form 8 biscuits from the dough mixture.

3. Once unit has preheated, open lid and place 4 biscuits in the basket. Close crisping lid.

4. Select AIR CRISP, set temperature to 400°F, and set time to 6 minutes. Select START/STOP to begin.

5. When cooking is complete, carefully remove the biscuits and set aside to cool. Place the remaining uncooked biscuits in the basket and repeat step 4.

Per serving: *Calories: 186; Total Fat: 11g; Saturated Fat: 6g; Cholesterol: 21mg; Sodium: 489mg; Carbohydrates: 19g; Fiber: 1g; Protein: 4g*

# Boston Brown Bread by Sam Ferguson

***Chef says:*** *The inspiration for this recipe is twofold. First, Boston Brown Bread's heritage is deeply rooted in New England history—the original recipe used molasses produced in Boston and was eaten overwhelmingly by the city's swelling Irish immigrant population. Second, my great-aunt Ginny would make this recipe when I was a kid and always gave me a spoonful of molasses as a reward for being good. Pro tip—griddle slices of this bread in butter using SEAR/SAUTÉ right in your Foodi™!*

**NUT-FREE, VEGETARIAN**

**PREP TIME:** 10 minutes
**TOTAL COOK TIME:**
40 minutes

**APPROX. PRESSURE BUILD:**
10 minutes
**PRESSURE COOK:**
25 minutes
**PRESSURE RELEASE:** Quick
**BAKE/ROAST:** 15 minutes

**ACCESSORIES:** Ninja Loaf Pan, Reversible Rack

**VARIATION TIP:** Swap in any dried fruit on hand for the currants in step 1. This bread typically calls for currants but feel free to use whatever dried fruit you'd like to experiment with.

½ cup whole-wheat flour
½ cup whole-grain rye flour
½ cup stone-ground yellow cornmeal
1 teaspoon kosher salt
1 teaspoon baking soda
1 cup whole milk
⅓ cup blackstrap molasses
½ cup dried currants
1 tablespoon unsalted butter, at room temperature
1 cup water
Cooking spray

1. In a medium bowl, combine the whole-wheat flour, whole-grain rye flour, cornmeal, salt, and baking soda. Use a rubber spatula to mix well. Add the milk, molasses, and currants, then stir well until just combined.

2. Grease the inside of Ninja Loaf Pan or 7-inch rectangular loaf pan with the butter. Add the dough to the pan and use spatula to ensure it lays even and flat. Wrap the loaf pan tightly with plastic wrap.

3. Place Reversible Rack in pot, making sure it is in the lower steam position. Pour the water into the pot. Place the pan on the rack. Assemble pressure lid, making sure pressure release valve is in the SEAL position.

4. Select PRESSURE and set to HI. Set time to 25 minutes. Select START/STOP to begin.

5. When pressure cooking is complete, quick release pressure by moving the pressure release valve to the VENT position. Carefully remove lid when unit has finished releasing pressure.

6. Remove Ninja Loaf Pan from pot and remove plastic wrap. Place pan back on the rack. Close crisping lid.

7. Select BAKE/ROAST, set temperature to 350ºF, and set time to 15 minutes. Select START/STOP to begin.

8. After 10 minutes, open lid and spray the bread with a light, even coating of cooking spray. Close lid and continue cooking.

9. When cooking is complete, open lid and remove rack with the pan. Let the bread to cool in the pan on the rack at room temperature for at least 30 minutes before serving.

**Per serving:** *Calories: 182; Total Fat: 3g; Saturated Fat: 2g; Cholesterol: 2mg; Sodium: 263mg; Carbohydrates: 38g; Fiber: 4g; Protein: 4g*

# Herb Scones

MAKES 4

*When some people think of scones, their minds immediately default to something with berries or cinnamon that you might see on a brunch or breakfast menu. I love a good savory scone in place of bread at the dinner table, and these herb-filled ones are a great complement to poultry or red meat.*

NUT-FREE, VEGETARIAN, UNDER 30 MINUTES, 5 INGREDIENT

PREP TIME: 2 minutes
TOTAL COOK TIME:
8 minutes

AIR CRISP: 8 minutes

ACCESSORIES: Cook & Crisp Basket

VARIATION TIP: Looking for even more herb flavor in your scones? Add some garlic powder or thyme during step 2.

1 cup pancake and baking mix

1 teaspoon chopped fresh rosemary

1 teaspoon chopped fresh parsley

¼ teaspoon sea salt

¼ cup milk

¼ cup (½ stick) cold butter, cut into small pieces

1. Place Cook & Crisp Basket in pot. Close crisping lid. Select AIR CRISP, set temperature to 400°F, and set time to 5 minutes. Select START/STOP to begin preheating.

2. Combine pancake mix, rosemary, parsley, salt, and milk in a medium bowl, stirring until well blended. Cut in butter, using your hands to mix until the dough has a sandy texture. Form 4 scones from the dough mixture.

3. Once unit has preheated, place the scones in the basket. Close crisping lid.

4. Select AIR CRISP, set temperature to 400°F, and set time to 8 minutes. Select START/STOP to begin.

5. When cooking is complete, carefully remove the scones and set aside to cool.

Per serving: *Calories: 240; Total Fat: 17g; Saturated Fat: 8g; Cholesterol: 32mg; Sodium: 579mg; Carbohydrates: 22g; Fiber: 0g; Protein: 3g*

# Cheesy Mashed Potatoes

**SERVES 4**

*Mashed potatoes are my favorite comfort food—they're creamy and fluffy all at the same time. Here I've added some cream cheese to make them super luxurious and cut the cooking time down in a big way using pressure, meaning they're ready to share with friends and family at dinner in only a few minutes.*

**GLUTEN-FREE, VEGETARIAN, UNDER 30 MINUTES, FAMILY FAVORITE, 5 INGREDIENT**

**PREP TIME:** 5 minutes
**TOTAL COOK TIME:**
8 minutes

**APPROX. PRESSURE BUILD:**
10 minutes
**PRESSURE COOK:** 8 minutes
**PRESSURE RELEASE:** Quick

**HACK IT:** Sprinkle some shredded Cheddar cheese over the top and broil using the crisping lid for an even cheesier dish.

2 pounds potatoes, peeled and chopped
5 garlic cloves, minced
½ cup Chicken Stock (page 312)
½ teaspoon sea salt
2½ tablespoons unsalted butter, divided
½ cup cream cheese

1. Add the potatoes, garlic, chicken stock, salt, and ½ tablespoon of butter. Assemble pressure lid, making sure the pressure release valve is in the SEAL position.

2. Select PRESSURE and set to HI. Set time for 8 minutes. Select START/STOP to begin.

3. When pressure cooking is complete, quick release the pressure by moving the pressure release valve to the VENT position. Carefully remove lid when unit has finished releasing pressure.

4. Use a potato masher to mash the potatoes. Add the remaining 2 tablespoons of butter and cream cheese and stir.

*Per serving: Calories: 328; Total Fat: 18g; Saturated Fat: 11g; Cholesterol: 51mg; Sodium: 413mg; Carbohydrates: 38g; Fiber: 6g; Protein: 6g*

# Candied Bacon by Meg Jordan

**SERVES 6**

**Chef says:** *Growing up with a butcher grandfather, I ate meat quite often. I was introduced to bacon at an early age and have been obsessed with it ever since. This recipe is like candy for adults—the saltiness of the bacon combined with the sweetness of the sugar is so good, you can't eat just one. These are also great crumbled on top of a salad for a nice crunch.*

DAIRY-FREE, GLUTEN-FREE, NUT-FREE, UNDER 30 MINUTES, 5 INGREDIENT

PREP TIME: 5 minutes
TOTAL COOK TIME:
16 minutes

AIR CRISP: 16 minutes

ACCESSORIES: Cook & Crisp Basket

VARIATION TIP: Don't have dark brown sugar? Light brown sugar works as well.

1 cup dark brown sugar
2 teaspoons smoked paprika

½ teaspoon freshly ground black pepper
1 pound bacon

1. In a large bowl, mix together the sugar, smoked paprika, and pepper. Add the bacon and toss thoroughly to coat the bacon strips.

2. Place Cook & Crisp Basket in pot. Lay the prepared bacon slices evenly over the edge of the basket. Close crisping lid.

3. Select AIR CRISP, set temperature to 330°F, and set time to 16 minutes. Select START/STOP to begin.

4. After 10 minutes, open lid to check on the bacon. If further crisping is desired, close the lid to continue cooking.

*Per serving: Calories: 409; Total Fat: 30g; Saturated Fat: 10g; Cholesterol: 51mg; Sodium: 507mg; Carbohydrates: 25g; Fiber: 0g; Protein: 10g*

# Dehydrated Strawberries

**by Aurelia McCollom, Ninja® Foodi™ Family Member**

**MAKES 1 CUP**

***Aurelia says:*** *So crisp and refreshing! A wonderful flavor.*

DAIRY-FREE, FAMILY FAVORITE, GLUTEN-FREE, NUT-FREE, VEGAN, 5 INGREDIENT

PREP TIME: 20 minutes
TOTAL COOK TIME: 8 hours

DEHYDRATE: 8 hours

ACCESSORIES: Cook & Crisp Basket

INGREDIENT TIP: Very juicy strawberries will require more time. The least amount of time for proper drying is 8 hours. The most has been 12 hours.

**Find Aurelia on Facebook: Ninja Foodi & All Ninja Multi-Cooker Systems+Recipes— since 2013!**

**2 pounds fresh strawberries, hulled and cut into ⅛-inch-thick slices**

1. Place the strawberries in a single layer in the Cook & Crisp Basket, and onto the layered rack insert.

2. Select DEHYDRATE, set the temperature to 135ºF, and set the time to 8 hours. Select START/STOP to begin.

3. If you feel you need more time, set it for another hour and check the strawberries during the dehydrating time. When crisp, they are done.

Per serving (½ pound): Calories: 145; Total Fat: 1g; Saturated Fat: 0g; Cholesterol: 0mg; Sodium: 5mg; Carbohydrates: 35g; Fiber: 9g; Protein: 3g

# 11

# Desserts

# Sugar Cookie Pizza by Caroline Schliep

**Chef says:** *I have such fond memories of baking in the kitchen with my mother from a very young age. We would always be baking something, whether it be Christmas cookies, birthday cakes, or cupcakes. This recipe in particular was something we would always make because it's no fuss and is fun for all ages. I mean who doesn't love a sugar cookie that is smothered with cream cheese frosting and decorated with a rainbow of fresh fruit?*

**NUT-FREE, VEGETARIAN, 5 INGREDIENT**

**PREP TIME:** 10 minutes
**TOTAL COOK TIME:** 35 minutes
**CHILL TIME:** 1 hour

**BAKE/ROAST:** 40 minutes

**ACCESSORIES:** Ninja Multi-Purpose Pan, Reversible Rack

**VARIATION TIP:** Sugar cookie dough is interchangeable for any cookie dough of your choice!

22 ounces premade sugar cookie dough

5 tablespoons unsalted butter, at room temperature

1 (8-ounce) package cream cheese, at room temperature

2 cups confectioners' sugar

1 teaspoon vanilla extract

1. Select BAKE/ROAST, set temperature to 325°F, and set time to 40 minutes. Select START/STOP to begin. Let preheat for 5 minutes.

2. Press the cookie dough into the Ninja Multi-Purpose Pan in an even layer.

3. Once unit is preheated, place the pan on the Reversible Rack and place rack in the pot. Close crisping lid and cook for 35 minutes.

4. Once cooking is complete, remove the pan from the pot. Let cool in the refrigerator for 30 minutes.

5. In a large bowl, whisk together the butter, cream cheese, confectioners' sugar, and vanilla.

6. Once the cookie is chilled, carefully remove it from the pan. Using a spatula, spread the cream cheese mixture over cookie. Chill in the refrigerator for another 30 minutes.

7. Decorate with toppings of choice, such as sliced strawberries, raspberries, blueberries, blackberries, sliced kiwi, sliced mango, or sliced pineapple. Cut and serve.

*Per serving: Calories: 791; Total Fat: 44g; Saturated Fat: 20g; Cholesterol: 97mg; Sodium: 551mg; Carbohydrates: 92g; Fiber: 1g; Protein: 7g*

# Sweet and Salty Bars by Caroline Schliep

SERVES 12

**Chef says:** *I have always loved playing with sweet and savory combinations. For this recipe, potato chips and pretzels are tossed in a sticky mixture of marshmallows and peanut butter and topped with chocolate. All of which comes together to create a dessert with the ultimate balance of sweet and salty. It will cure even the toughest of sweet tooths. And I can guarantee it will have your taste buds doing backflips and your stomach asking for more.*

**VEGETARIAN, UNDER 30 MINUTES**

**PREP TIME:** 5 minutes
**TOTAL COOK TIME:** 10 minutes

**SEAR/SAUTÉ:** 3 minutes

**SUBSTITUTION TIP:** You can swap the corn syrup for honey, agave, maple syrup, or molasses.

- 1 cup light corn syrup
- 1 cup granulated sugar
- 1 teaspoon vanilla extract
- 1 (10-ounce) bag mini marshmallows
- 1 cup crunchy peanut butter
- 1 (9-ounce) bag potato chips with ridges, slightly crushed
- 1 cup pretzels, slightly crushed
- 1 (10-ounce) bag hard-shelled candy-coated chocolates

1. Select SEAR/SAUTÉ and set temperature to MD:HI. Select START/STOP to begin. Let preheat for 5 minutes.

2. Add the corn syrup, sugar, and vanilla and stir until the sugar is melted.

3. Add the marshmallows and peanut butter and stir until the marshmallows are melted.

4. Add the potato chips and pretzels and stir until everything is evenly coated in the marshmallow mixture.

5. Pour the mixture into a 9-by-13-inch pan and place the chocolate candies on top, slightly pressing them in. Let cool, then cut into squares and serve.

Per serving: *Calories: 585; Total Fat: 21g; Saturated Fat: 6g; Cholesterol: 5mg; Sodium: 403mg; Carbohydrates: 96g; Fiber: 3g; Protein: 9g*

# Coconut Rice Pudding by Craig White

**Chef says:** *I am not a pastry chef, and these are the kinds of desserts I make—super simple, rich, and can be prepared relatively quickly. I like serving dishes like this when I'm entertaining because it gives me more time with my guests. Set up a topping station with fresh mango, toasted coconut, and nuts to really elevate this rice pudding to the next level and let your guests customize their dessert.*

GLUTEN-FREE, NUT-FREE, VEGETARIAN, UNDER 30 MINUTES, 5 INGREDIENT

PREP TIME: 5 minutes
TOTAL COOK TIME: 8 minutes

APPROX. PRESSURE BUILD: 10 minutes
PRESSURE COOK: 8 minutes
PRESSURE RELEASE: 10 minutes, then Quick

INGREDIENT INFO: If you have ever had risotto before, chances are it was made with arborio rice. Arborio rice is a great grain for rice pudding as it has good chew and is creamier than other rice because of its high starch content.

¾ cup arborio rice
1 (15-ounce) can unsweetened full-fat coconut milk
1 cup milk
1 cup water
¾ cup granulated sugar
½ teaspoon vanilla extract

1. Rinse the rice under cold running water in a fine-mesh strainer.

2. Place the rice, coconut milk, milk, water, sugar, and vanilla in the pot and stir. Assemble pressure lid, making sure the pressure release valve is in the SEAL position.

3. Select PRESSURE and set to HI. Set time to 8 minutes. Select START/STOP to begin.

4. When pressure cooking is complete, allow pressure to naturally release for 10 minutes. After 10 minutes, quick release remaining pressure by moving the pressure release valve to the VENT position. Carefully remove lid when unit has finished releasing pressure.

5. Press a layer of plastic wrap directly on top of the rice (it should be touching) to prevent a skin from forming on top of the pudding. Let pudding cool to room temperature, then refrigerate overnight to set.

*Per serving: Calories: 363; Total Fat: 18g; Saturated Fat: 16g; Cholesterol: 3mg; Sodium: 31mg; Carbohydrates: 50g; Fiber: 2g; Protein: 5g*

# Cheese Babka by Craig White

SERVES 8

**Chef says:** *I was introduced to babka by my girlfriend Michelle. Being Polish and a trained pastry chef, she makes a legit babka. I solicited her expertise in the ancient art of babka baking, and she guided me in the right direction. Having tasted my first attempt, she recommended cutting it like cinnamon buns, and it completely transformed this recipe. It allows more heat transfer with the filling and creates a beautiful crust. You can enjoy this babka for breakfast, dessert, or just a midday snack with a cup of tea or coffee.*

NUT-FREE, VEGETARIAN, UNDER 30 MINUTES, FAMILY FAVORITE

**PREP TIME:** 25 minutes
**TOTAL COOK TIME:** 30 minutes

**BAKE/ROAST:** 25 minutes

**ACCESSORIES:** Ninja Multi-Purpose Pan, Reversible Rack

**VARIATION TIP:** You can also make this recipe without the cheese filling or turn it into a swirled chocolate babka by adding a chocolate filling instead of the cheese.

## FOR THE DOUGH

1 (.31-ounce) packet dry active yeast

¼ cup water, warmed to 110°F

¼ cup, plus ¼ teaspoon granulated sugar, divided

2 cups all-purpose flour

2 large eggs, divided

½ teaspoon kosher salt

3 tablespoons unsalted butter, at room temperature

¼ cup milk

## FOR THE FILLING

8 ounces cream cheese

¼ cup granulated sugar

1 tablespoon sour cream

1 tablespoon all-purpose flour

½ teaspoon vanilla extract

Zest of 1 lemon

Cooking spray

All-purpose flour, for dusting

3 tablespoons water

### TO MAKE THE DOUGH

1. In a small bowl, combine the yeast, warm water, and ¼ teaspoon of sugar. Let sit 10 minutes until foamy.

2. Place the flour, yeast mixture, remaining ¼ cup of sugar, 1 egg, salt, butter, and milk into the bowl of stand mixer. Using the dough hook attachment, mix on medium-low speed until the dough is smooth and elastic, about 10 minutes.

### TO MAKE THE FILLING

In a medium bowl, whisk together all the filling ingredients until smooth.

### TO MAKE THE BABKA

1. Spray the cooking pot with the cooking spray. Place the dough in the pot. Cover the dough with plastic wrap and let it rise in a warm place until doubled in size, about 1 hour.

CONTINUED ▶

# Cheese Babka continued

2. Spray the Ninja Multi-Purpose Pan or 8-inch baking pan with cooking spray.

3. Turn the dough out onto a floured work surface. Punch down the dough. Using a rolling pin, roll it out into a 10-by-12-inch rectangle. Spread the cheese filling evenly on top of the dough. From the longer edge of the dough, roll it up like a jelly roll.

4. Cut the roll evenly into 12 pieces. Place each piece cut-side up in the prepared pan. The rolls should be touching but with visible gaps in between.

5. Beat the remaining egg with 1 teaspoon of water. Gently brush the tops of the rolls with this egg wash.

6. Place the remaining 3 tablespoons of water in the pot. Place the pan on the Reversible Rack, making sure the rack is in the lower position. Then place the rack with pan in the pot.

7. Select SEAR/SAUTÉ and set to LO. Select START/STOP to begin.

8. After 5 minutes, select START/STOP to turn off the heat. Let the rolls rise for another 15 minutes in the warm pot.

9. Remove the rack and pan from the pot. Close crisping lid.

10. Select BAKE/ROAST, set temperature to 325ºF, and set time to 30 minutes. Select START/STOP to begin. Let preheat for 5 minutes.

11. Place the rack with pan in the pot. Close lid and cook for 25 minutes.

12. Once cooking is complete, open lid and remove rack and pan. Let the babka completely cool before serving.

Per serving: Calories: 325; Total Fat: 16g; Saturated Fat: 10g; Cholesterol: 90mg; Sodium: 286mg; Carbohydrates: 38g; Fiber: 1g; Protein: 7g

# Coconut Cream "Custard" Bars by Kelly Gray

**SERVES 8**

***Chef says:*** *I love creamy, custardy desserts like crème brûlée and flan, but making them from scratch can be both intimidating and time consuming. This recipe was developed after a third failed attempt at making coconut crème brûlée for my Hawaii-bound friend's going-away party. Strapped for time, I decided to dress up a box of vanilla pudding with cream and some leftover ingredients, put it on a cookie crust, and called it a day. To my delight, the result was just as creamy, crunchy, and satisfying as I had imagined my custard would be. I think you'd be hard-pressed to find somebody who wouldn't agree.*

**VEGETARIAN, UNDER 30 MINUTES**

**PREP TIME:** 8 minutes
**TOTAL COOK TIME:** 20 minutes

**BAKE/ROAST:** 10 minutes
**AIR CRISP:** 10 minutes

**ACCESSORIES:** Ninja Multi-Purpose Pan, Reversible Rack, Ninja Loaf Pan

**VARIATION TIP:** Add ½ teaspoon each of almond and coconut extract in step 9 for amplified flavor.

**NOTE:** Amount of liquid may vary depending on pudding brand. Just be sure that the total volume of milk and cream matches the total amount of liquid called for on the instruction label of the instant pudding mix.

- 1¼ cups all-purpose flour
- 6 tablespoons unsalted butter, melted
- 2 tablespoons granulated sugar
- ½ cup unsweetened shredded coconut, divided
- ½ cup chopped almonds, divided
- Cooking spray
- 1 package instant vanilla pudding
- 1 cup milk
- 1 cup heavy (whipping) cream
- 4 tablespoons finely chopped dark chocolate, divided

1. Select BAKE/ROAST, set temperature to 375ºF, and set time to 15 minutes. Select START/STOP to begin. Let preheat for 5 minutes.

2. To make the crust, combine the flour, butter, sugar, ¼ cup of coconut, and ¼ cup of almonds in a large bowl and stir until a crumbly dough forms.

3. Grease the Ninja Multi-Purpose Pan or an 8-inch round baking dish with cooking spray. Place the dough in the pan and press it into an even layer covering the bottom.

4. Once unit has preheated, place pan on Reversible Rack, making sure the rack is in the lower position. Open lid and place rack in pot. Close crisping lid. Reduce temperature to 325ºF.

5. Place remaining ¼ cup each of almonds and coconut in a Ninja Loaf Pan or any small loaf pan and set aside.

6. When cooking is complete, remove rack with pan and let cool for 10 minutes.

CONTINUED ▶

7. Quickly place the loaf pan with coconut and almonds in the bottom of the pot. Close crisping lid.

8. Select AIR CRISP, set temperature to 350°F, and set time to 10 minutes. Select START/STOP to begin.

9. While the nuts and coconut toast, whisk together the instant pudding with the milk, cream, and 3 tablespoons of chocolate.

10. After 5 minutes, open lid and stir the coconut and almonds. Close lid and continue cooking for another 5 minutes.

11. When cooking is complete, open lid and remove pan from pot. Add the almonds and coconut to the pudding. Stir until fully incorporated. Pour this in a smooth, even layer on top of the crust.

12. Refrigerate for about 10 minutes. Garnish with the remaining 1 tablespoon of chocolate, cut into wedges, and serve.

Per serving: *Calories: 476; Total Fat: 33g; Saturated Fat: 21g; Cholesterol: 67mg; Sodium: 215mg; Carbohydrates: 39g; Fiber: 4g; Protein: 6g*

# Rhubarb, Raspberry, and Peach Cobbler by Kelly Gray

**SERVES 6**

***Chef says:*** *I remember helping my grandmother harvest fresh strawberries and rhubarb from the garden for her pies and preserves. Rhubarb is a stalky, pink vegetable that is extremely tart and unassuming. I was therefore shocked as a child when she proposed that we use it in a pie. But grandma knew best. Rhubarb's tartness is the perfect complement to sweet strawberries, or any seasonal fruit for that matter. This recipe, a twist on my childhood favorite, is for my grandmother. Rhubarb, peaches, and raspberries offer a bright and balanced fruit filling topped with a crunchy oat crumble. This easy, rustic dessert takes me back to summer in my grandmother's garden. Enjoy warm with vanilla ice cream or with fresh whipped cream.*

**VEGETARIAN, FAMILY FAVORITE**

**PREP TIME:** 20 minutes
**TOTAL COOK TIME:** 40 minutes

**BAKE/ROAST:** 40 minutes

**ACCESSORIES:** Ninja Multi-Purpose Pan, Reversible Rack

**VARIATION TIP:** Rhubarb out of season? Just add extra raspberries or peaches or even a chopped apple or two. Add 2 tablespoons of freshly squeezed lemon juice to brighten up the fruit flavors and replace the tartness of the rhubarb.

- 1 cup all-purpose flour, divided
- ¾ cup granulated sugar
- ½ teaspoon kosher salt, divided
- 2½ cups diced fresh rhubarb
- 2½ cups fresh raspberries
- 2½ cups fresh peaches, peeled and sliced into ¾-inch pieces
- Cooking spray
- ¾ cup brown sugar
- ½ cup oat flakes (oatmeal)
- 1 teaspoon cinnamon
- Pinch ground nutmeg
- 6 tablespoons unsalted butter, sliced, at room temperature
- ½ cup chopped pecans or walnuts

1. Select BAKE/ROAST, set temperature to 400°F, and set time to 30 minutes. Select START/STOP to begin. Let preheat for 5 minutes.

2. In a large bowl, whisk together ¼ cup of flour, granulated sugar, and ¼ teaspoon of salt. Add the rhubarb, raspberries, and peach and mix until evenly coated.

3. Grease a Ninja Multi-Purpose Pan or a 1½-quart round ceramic baking dish with cooking spray. Add the fruit mixture to the pan.

4. Place pan on Reversible Rack, making sure the rack is in the lower position. Cover pan with aluminum foil.

5. Once unit has preheated, place rack in pot. Close crisping lid and adjust temperature to 375°F. Cook for 25 minutes.

CONTINUED ▶

# Rhubarb, Raspberry, and Peach Cobbler continued

6.  In a medium bowl, combine the remaining ¾ cup of flour, brown sugar, oat flakes, cinnamon, remaining ¼ teaspoon of salt, nutmeg, butter, and pecans. Mix well.

7.  When cooking is complete, open lid. Remove the foil and stir the fruit. Spread the topping evenly over the fruit. Close crisping lid.

8.  Select BAKE/ROAST, set temperature to 400°F, and set time to 15 minutes. Select START/STOP to begin. Cook until the topping is browned and the fruit is bubbling.

9.  When cooking is complete, remove rack with pan from pot and serve.

*Per serving: Calories: 476; Total Fat: 19g; Saturated Fat: 8g; Cholesterol: 21mg; Sodium: 204mg; Carbohydrates: 76g; Fiber: 7g; Protein: 6g*

# Apple Crisp

*Apple Crisp is a quick and easy alternative to apple pie, but it packs all of the warm cinnamon, spiced apple, and buttery crumble crust you crave. Most crisps and crumbles are easy enough to make, but with the Foodi™ Pressure Cooker, it's even quicker—no need to bake the apples for hours to soften. Use pressure to tenderize, top with the crumble, and Air Crisp to finish. Enjoy with a scoop of vanilla ice cream and a drizzle of caramel sauce.*

**NUT-FREE, VEGETARIAN, UNDER 30 MINUTES**

**PREP TIME:** 15 minutes
**TOTAL COOK TIME:** 20 minutes

**APPROX. PRESSURE BUILD:** 10 minutes
**PRESSURE TIME:** 0 minutes
**PRESSURE RELEASE:** 10 minutes, then Quick
**AIR CRISP:** 10 minutes

**ACCESSORIES:** Ninja Multi-Purpose Pan, Reversible Rack

**VARIATION TIP:** Use this formula to make a variety of delicious crisps and crumbles. Simply swap the apples for fresh strawberries, blueberries, or peaches.

**4 to 5 Granny Smith apples, peeled and cut into 1-inch cubes**
**1 tablespoon cornstarch**
**½ cup, plus 1 tablespoon water**
**2 teaspoons cinnamon, divided**
**1 teaspoon freshly squeezed lemon juice**
**5 tablespoons granulated sugar, divided**
**½ cup all-purpose flour**
**½ cup rolled oats**
**⅔ cup brown sugar**
**⅓ cup unsalted butter, melted**

1. Place the apples in the Ninja Multi-Purpose Pan or a 1½-quart round ceramic baking dish.

2. In a small bowl, stir together the cornstarch, 1 tablespoon of water, 1 teaspoon of cinnamon, lemon juice, and 3 tablespoons of granulated sugar. Pour this mixture over the apples.

3. Place pan on Reversible Rack, making sure the rack is in the lower position. Cover the pan with aluminum foil. Pour the remaining ½ cup of water into the pot. Insert rack with pan in pot. Assemble pressure lid, making sure the pressure release valve is in the SEAL position.

4. Select PRESSURE and set to HI. Set time to 0 minutes. Select START/STOP to begin.

5. In a medium bowl, combine the flour, oats, brown sugar, butter, remaining 1 teaspoon of cinnamon, and remaining 2 tablespoons of granulated sugar until a crumble forms.

6. When pressure cooking is complete, allow the pressure to naturally release for 10 minutes. After 10 minutes, quick release remaining pressure by moving the pressure release

CONTINUED ▶

# Apple Crisp  continued

valve to the VENT position. Carefully remove lid when pressure has finished releasing.

7. Remove the foil and stir the fruit mixture. Evenly spread the crumble topping over the apples. Close crisping lid.

8. Select AIR CRISP, set temperature to 375°F, and set time to 10 minutes. Select START/STOP to begin.

9. Cooking is complete when the top is browned and the fruit is bubbling. Remove rack with the pan from the pot and serve.

*Per serving: Calories: 261; Total Fat: 9g; Saturated Fat: 6g; Cholesterol: 23mg; Sodium: 6mg; Carbohydrates: 46g; Fiber: 4g; Protein: 2g*

# Brownie Bites

by Tony Turner, Ninja® Foodi™ Family Member

**SERVES 10**

**Tony says:** *I created these brownie bites out of necessity—all we had was a box of brownie mix, so I made up the batter, put the brownies into my silicone mold, and pressure cooked them. I can't believe how incredibly delicious they turned out—nice and fudgy with no crumbs. We added a little chocolate and caramel syrup, topped them with some confectioners' sugar—and boom! The ultimate dessert.*

DAIRY-FREE, NUT-FREE, VEGETARIAN

PREP TIME: 5 minutes
TOTAL COOK TIME:
45 minutes

APPROX. PRESSURE BUILD:
10 minutes
PRESSURE COOK:
45 minutes
PRESSURE RELEASE:
10 minutes, then Quick

ACCESSORIES:
Reversible Rack

**Find Tony on YouTube:
Live From the Camper
/ Facebook Group:
Ninja Foodi & Instant
Pot Universe**

Cooking spray

1 (18-ounce) box brownie mix, prepared to package instructions

Confectioners' sugar, for garnish

Carmel sauce, for garnish

1. Coat a silicone egg mold with nonstick cooking spray and set aside.

2. In a large bowl, prepare the brownie mix according to package instructions. Using a cookie scoop, transfer the batter to the prepared mold.

3. Place 1 cup water in the pot. Place the filled molds onto the Reversible Rack in the lower steam position, and lower into the pot.

4. Assemble the pressure lid, making sure the pressure release valve is in the SEAL position.

5. Select PRESSURE and set to HI. Set the time to 45 minutes. Select START/STOP to begin.

6. When pressure cooking is complete, allow the pressure to naturally release for 10 minutes. After 10 minutes, quick release any remaining pressure by moving the pressure release valve to the VENT position. Carefully remove the lid when the unit has finished releasing pressure.

7. Carefully remove the mold from the cooker and let cool for 5 minutes.

8. Flip the brownie onto a plate and garnish with confectioners' sugar and caramel sauce.

*Per serving: Calories: 288; Total Fat: 5g; Saturated Fat: 1g; Cholesterol: 0mg; Sodium: 168mg; Carbohydrates: 43g; Fiber: 1g; Protein: 2g*

# Bacon Blondies by Meg Jordan

**SERVES 6**

*Chef says:* As you can probably tell from my various recipes in this book, I am a huge fan of bacon. In addition to my bacon obsession, I also have a very bad sweet tooth. Combine those two and you have the ultimate dessert recipe with these Bacon Blondies. I love to serve these with some vanilla ice cream on top as an extra contrast to the bacon.

**NUT-FREE, FAMILY FAVORITE, 5 INGREDIENT**

**PREP TIME:** 15 minutes
**TOTAL COOK TIME:** 35 minutes

**SEAR/SAUTÉ:** 5 minutes
**BAKE/ROAST:** 25 minutes

**ACCESSORIES:** Ninja Multi-Purpose Pan, Reversible Rack

**HACK IT:** Buy precooked bacon at the grocery store to cut down on overall cook time.

6 slices uncooked bacon, cut into ¼ slices

1½ cups unsalted butter, at room temperature, plus additional for greasing

1 cup dark brown sugar

2 cups all-purpose flour

Ice cream, for serving

1. Grease the Ninja Multi-Purpose Pan with butter.

2. Select SEAR/SAUTÉ and set to HI. Select START/STOP to begin. Let preheat for 5 minutes.

3. Place the bacon in the pot. Cook, stirring frequently, for about 5 minutes, or until the fat is rendered and bacon starts to brown. Transfer the bacon to a paper towel-lined plate to drain. Wipe the pot clean of any remaining fat and return to unit.

4. In a medium bowl, beat the butter and brown sugar with a hand mixer until well incorporated. Slowly add in the flour and continue to beat until the flour is fully combined and a soft dough forms. Next, fold the cooked bacon into the dough.

5. Press the dough into the prepared pan. Place pan on Reversible Rack, ensuring it is in the lower position. Lower rack into pot. Close crisping lid.

6. Select BAKE/ROAST, set temperature to 350°F, and set time to 25 minutes. Select START/STOP to begin.

7. After 20 minutes, open lid and check for doneness by sticking a toothpick through the center of the dough. If it comes out clean, remove rack and pan from unit. If not, close lid and continue cooking.

8. When cooking is complete, remove rack and pan from unit. Let the blondies cool for about 30 minutes before serving with ice cream, if desired.

*Per serving: Calories: 771; Total Fat: 54g; Saturated Fat: 32g; Cholesterol: 143mg; Sodium: 453mg; Carbohydrates: 60g; Fiber: 1g; Protein: 12g*

# Peanut Butter Pie by Chelven Randolph

SERVES 8

**Chef says:** *This is one of my absolute favorite desserts of all time. The combination of chocolate and peanut butter is a game changer. Whether you are going to a holiday party, summer cookout, or company potluck, this dessert will go over well.*

**VEGETARIAN, UNDER 30 MINUTES**

---

**PREP TIME:** 10 minutes
**TOTAL COOK TIME:**
30 minutes
**CHILL TIME:** 3 hours

---

**APPROX. PRESSURE BUILD:**
10 minutes
**PRESSURE COOK:**
25 minutes
**PRESSURE RELEASE:**
15 minutes, then Quick

---

**ACCESSORIES:** Ninja Multi-Purpose Pan, Reversible Rack

---

**SUBSTITUTION TIP:** Have a peanut allergy? No worries, you can use chocolate cookie crumbs and Nutella instead of peanut butter!

10 peanut butter cookies, crushed

3 tablespoons unsalted butter, melted

2 (8-ounces) packages cream cheese, at room temperature

¾ cup granulated sugar

2 eggs

⅓ cup creamy peanut butter

10 chocolate peanut butter cups, chopped

2 cups water

1 (14-ounce) tub whipped cream topping

1. In a small bowl, mix together peanut butter cookie crumbs and melted butter. Press the mixture into the bottom of the Ninja Multi-Purpose Pan or 8-inch baking dish.

2. In a medium bowl, use an electric hand mixer to combine the cream cheese, sugar, eggs, and peanut butter. Mix on medium speed for 5 minutes.

3. Place the chopped chocolate peanut butter cups evenly on top of crust in the pan. Pour the batter on top. Cover tightly with aluminum foil.

4. Place the water in the pot. Insert Reversible Rack into pot, making sure it is on the lower position. Place covered multipurpose pan onto rack. Assemble pressure lid, making sure the pressure release valve is in the SEAL position.

5. Select PRESSURE and set to HI. Set time to 25 minutes. Press START/STOP to begin.

6. When pressure cooking is complete, allow pressure to naturally release for 15 minutes. After 15 minutes, quick release remaining pressure by moving the pressure release valve to the VENT position. Carefully remove lid when unit has finished releasing pressure.

7. Remove the pan and chill in the refrigerator for at least 3 hours or overnight before serving topped with whipped cream.

*Per serving: Calories: 645; Total Fat: 47g; Saturated Fat: 27g; Cholesterol: 134mg; Sodium: 383mg; Carbohydrates: 48g; Fiber: 1g; Protein: 13g*

# Chocolate Peanut Butter and Jelly Puffs by Sam Ferguson

**SERVES 4**

***Chef says:*** *This recipe is dedicated to my great-aunt Ginny. She was constantly trying new recipes she found in her favorite magazines. She was never intimidated to try something new—at least that's the way it seemed to me. She had a raspberry patch in her backyard and whenever I visited, she'd take me out to pick fresh raspberries for jam or pie. I love raspberries—and cooking—because of her.*

VEGETARIAN, UNDER 30 MINUTES, FAMILY FAVORITE

**PREP TIME:** 25 minutes
**TOTAL COOK TIME:** 15 minutes

**AIR CRISP:** 15 minutes

**ACCESSORIES:** Cook & Crisp Basket

**MAKE MORE, MAKE LESS:** While a little heavy on the upfront labor, these PBJ puffs freeze well and are super easy to make in large batches. After you have made a batch through step 4, place uncooked dough balls on a greased baking sheet and freeze. Once frozen, consolidate them into a zip-top bag for easier storing. When you want a quick treat, remove the desired amount and let sit at room temperature for 15 minutes before cooking.

1 (16-ounce) tube prepared flaky biscuit dough
2 (1½-ounce) milk chocolate bars
Cooking spray
16 teaspoons (about ⅓ cup) creamy peanut butter
1 cup confectioners' sugar
1 tablespoon whole milk
¼ cup raspberry jam

1. Remove biscuits from tube. There is a natural width-wise separation in each biscuit. Gently peel each biscuit in half using this separation.

2. Break the chocolate into 16 small pieces.

3. Spray a baking sheet with cooking spray.

4. Using your hands, stretch a biscuit half until it is about 3-inches in diameter. Place a teaspoon of peanut butter in center of each biscuit half, then place piece of chocolate on top. Pull an edge of dough over the top of the chocolate and pinch together to seal. Continue pulling the dough over the top of the chocolate and pinching until the chocolate is completely covered. The dough is pliable, so gently form it into a ball with your hands. Place on the prepared baking sheet. Repeat this step with the remaining biscuit dough, peanut butter, and chocolate.

5. Place the baking sheet in the refrigerator for 5 minutes.

6. Place Cook & Crisp Basket in pot. Close crisping lid. Select AIR CRISP, set temperature to 360°F, and set time to 20 minutes. Select START/STOP to begin. Let preheat for 5 minutes.

7. Remove the biscuits from the refrigerator and spray the tops with cooking spray. Open lid and spray the basket with cooking spray. Place 5 biscuit balls in the basket. Close lid and cook for 5 minutes.

CONTINUED ▶

# Chocolate Peanut Butter and Jelly Puffs continued

8. When cooking is complete, remove the biscuit balls from the basket. Repeat step 7 two more times with remaining biscuit balls.

9. Mix together the confectioners' sugar, milk, and jam in a small bowl to make a frosting.

10. When the cooked biscuit balls are cool enough to handle, dunk the top of each into the frosting. As frosting is beginning to set, garnish with any toppings desired, such as sprinkles, crushed toffee or candy, or mini marshmallows.

Per serving: *Calories: 663; Total Fat: 25g; Saturated Fat: 8g; Cholesterol: 5mg; Sodium: 1094mg; Carbohydrates: 101g; Fiber: 3g; Protein: 14g*

# Red Velvet Cheesecake by Chelven Randolph

**SERVES 8**

***Chef says:*** *My mom was known for many dishes, but her red velvet cheesecake brought people from far and wide. Although I have never been a sweets person, I would always have a slice of her red velvet cake. I made this recipe because I am not a good baker or a pastry chef by any means, but this is as foolproof as a cheesecake can be. Red velvet is one of the most common Southern desserts, and this dish is sure to get everyone asking for the recipe.*

**NUT-FREE, VEGETARIAN, FAMILY FAVORITE**

**PREP TIME:** 10 minutes
**TOTAL COOK TIME:** 25 minutes
**CHILL TIME:** 3 hours

**APPROX. PRESSURE BUILD:** 10 minutes
**PRESSURE COOK:** 25 minutes
**PRESSURE RELEASE:** 15 minutes, then Quick

**ACCESSORIES:** Ninja Multi-Purpose Pan, Reversible Rack

**VARIATION TIP:** Top with vanilla frosting and crushed pecans to really get the Southern flair! For a traditional-style cheesecake, make the crust with crushed graham crackers.

2 cups Oreo cookie crumbs

3 tablespoons unsalted butter, melted

2 (8-ounce) packages cream cheese, at room temperature

½ cup granulated sugar

½ cup buttermilk

2 tablespoons unsweetened cocoa powder

1 teaspoon vanilla extract

2 tablespoons red food coloring

½ teaspoon white vinegar

1 cup water

1. In a small bowl, combine the cookie crumbs and butter. Press this mixture into the bottom of the Ninja Multi-Purpose Pan or 8-inch baking pan.

2. In a large bowl, use an electric hand mixer to combine the cream cheese, sugar, buttermilk, cocoa powder, vanilla, food coloring, and vinegar for 3 minutes. Pour this over the cookie crust. Cover the pan tightly with aluminum foil.

3. Place the water in the pot. Insert Reversible Rack into pot, making sure it is in the lower position. Place the covered multi-purpose pan onto the rack. Assemble pressure lid, making sure the pressure release valve is in the SEAL position.

4. Select PRESSURE on HI. Set time to 25 minutes. Press START/STOP to begin.

5. When pressure cooking is complete, allow pressure to naturally release for 15 minutes. After 15 minutes, quick release remaining pressure by moving the pressure release valve to the VENT position. Carefully remove lid when unit has finished releasing pressure.

6. Remove cheesecake from the pot. Refrigerate for 3 hours, or overnight if possible before serving.

*Per serving: Calories: 437; Total Fat: 31g; Saturated Fat: 18g; Cholesterol: 74mg; Sodium: 338mg; Carbohydrates: 36g; Fiber: 3g; Protein: 7g*

# Hazelnut Cheesecake by Meg Jordan

**SERVES 8**

***Chef says:*** *I'm typically not a fan of cheesecake. However, once I tried a version with hazelnut spread, I loved it. Premade graham cracker crust cuts down on the prep time and need for other kitchen accessories. With the rich flavor of hazelnut, I keep the toppings simple and serve either alone or with whipped cream.*

**VEGETARIAN, FAMILY FAVORITE, 5 INGREDIENT**

**PREP TIME:** 15 minutes
**TOTAL COOK TIME:** 25 minutes

**APPROX. PRESSURE BUILD:** 10 minutes
**PRESSURE COOK:** 25 minutes
**PRESSURE RELEASE:** 10 minutes, then Quick

**ACCESSORIES:** Ninja Multi-Purpose Pan, Reversible Rack

**VARIATION TIP:** Replace the hazelnut spread with peanut butter for a new variation on cheesecake.

Unsalted butter, for greasing

1 store-bought premade graham cracker crust

2 (8-ounce) packages cream cheese, at room temperature

¼ cup confectioners' sugar, sifted

2 eggs

1 (13-ounce) jar hazelnut spread

1 cup water

1. Grease the Ninja Multi-Purpose Pan with butter. Place the crust in the pan, crumbling as necessary to fit.

2. In a medium bowl, beat together the cream cheese, sugar, and eggs with a hand mixer until well incorporated. Add the hazelnut spread and beat until well combined. Add the cream cheese mixture over the crust.

3. Pour the water into the pot. Place Reversible Rack in pot, making sure it is in the lower position. Place pan on rack. Assemble pressure lid, making sure the pressure release valve is in the SEAL position.

4. Select PRESSURE and set to HI. Set time to 25 minutes. Select START/STOP to begin.

5. When pressure cooking is complete, allow pressure to naturally release for 10 minutes. After 10 minutes, quick release remaining pressure by moving the pressure release valve to the VENT position. Carefully remove lid when unit has finished releasing pressure.

6. Remove rack and pan from pot. Gently dab the top of the cheesecake with a paper towel to remove excess moisture. Refrigerate for at least 2 hours before serving.

*Per serving: Calories: 676; Total Fat: 47g; Saturated Fat: 29g; Cholesterol: 66mg; Sodium: 375mg; Carbohydrates: 57g; Fiber: 3g; Protein: 9g*

# Cherry Cheesecake by Sam Ferguson

**Chef says:** *Cheesecake has been my favorite dessert ever since Diddy made Da Band walk from Manhattan to Brooklyn to pick him up a slice for dessert. I remember watching that episode and thinking, "What is cheesecake and why does Puffy love it so much?" Well, now I know—it's the perfect end to a meal and sometimes you just gotta have it, even when filming a reality TV show.*

**NUT-FREE, FAMILY FAVORITE, UNDER 30 MINUTES**

---

**PREP TIME:** 15 minutes
**TOTAL COOK TIME:** 30 minutes
**CHILL TIME:** 4 hours

---

**APPROX. PRESSURE BUILD:** 10 minutes
**PRESSURE COOK:** 30 minutes
**PRESSURE RELEASE:** 10 minutes, then Quick

---

**ACCESSORIES:** Ninja Multi-Purpose Pan, Reversible Rack

---

**SUBSTITUTION TIP:** Don't have graham crackers? You can substitute any cookies or cereal you have kicking around—the sweeter the better.

4 (8-ounce) packages cream cheese, at room temperature

1 cup granulated sugar

3 tablespoons cornstarch

3 whole eggs

2 egg yolks

¼ cup heavy (whipping) cream

1 teaspoon kosher salt

1½ cups crushed graham crackers

½ cup (1 stick) unsalted butter, melted

1 cup water

1 (14-ounce) can cherries in syrup

1. In a large bowl, combine the cream cheese, sugar, cornstarch, eggs, egg yolks, cream, and salt. Use an electric mixer to mix until smooth and velvety.

2. In a medium bowl, combine the graham crackers and melted butter until it resembles wet sand.

3. Line the inside of the Ninja Multi-Purpose Pan or another 9-inch round baking dish with plastic wrap. Ensure the wrap is flush to the bottom of the dish and comes fully up the sides of the pan.

4. Place the graham cracker mixture in the center of the dish. Use a silicone-tipped spatula to press the mix outward. The mix should lay completely and evenly across the bottom of the dish.

5. Pour the cheesecake batter over the crust, then use the spatula to evenly smooth it out. Tightly wrap the top of the baking dish with a new piece of plastic wrap so that the cheesecake is completely covered.

6. Place the cheesecake on Reversible Rack, making sure it is in the lower steam position. Place rack with pan in pot. Pour the water into the pot. Assemble pressure lid, making sure the pressure release valve is in the SEAL position.

CONTINUED ▶

# Cherry Cheesecake continued

7. Select PRESSURE and set to HI. Set time to 30 minutes. Select START/STOP to begin.

8. When pressure cooking is complete, allow pressure to naturally release for 10 minutes. After 10 minutes, quick release remaining pressure by moving the pressure release valve to the VENT position. Carefully remove lid when unit has finished releasing pressure.

9. Remove top layer of plastic wrap from the cheesecake. Refrigerate the cheesecake to completely cool, at least 4 hours.

10. When ready to serve, remove the cheesecake from the refrigerator and place on a serving dish or cutting board. Use top edges of the remaining plastic wrap to remove cheesecake from the pan. Pull the plastic wrap out from underneath cheesecake. Top the cheesecake with the cherries in syrup as desired and serve.

Per serving: *Calories: 789; Total Fat: 58g; Saturated Fat: 35g; Cholesterol: 279mg; Sodium: 760mg; Carbohydrates: 57g; Fiber: 1g; Protein: 13g*

# Tres Leches Cake by Kelly Gray

**SERVES 8**

***Chef says:*** *Tres leches cake is a simple dessert that transforms a common yellow sponge cake into a moist, mouthwatering, masterpiece by soaking it in a creamy three-milk blend and topping it with a cloud of whipped cream. With origins in Latin America, this decadent dessert is commonplace at all gatherings, holidays, and birthday parties south of the border. It was love at first bite when I tasted the sweet, creamy goodness at a Mexican friend's backyard barbecue, and it's been a staple in my house ever since.*

**NUT-FREE, FAMILY FAVORITE, 5 INGREDIENT**

**PREP TIME:** 10 minutes
**TOTAL COOK TIME:** 38 minutes

**BAKE/ROAST:** 38 minutes

**ACCESSORIES:** Ninja Multi-Purpose Pan, Reversible Rack

**VARIATION TIP:** Add a drop of coconut extract to the milk mixture and top cake with toasted coconut for a delicious twist on this classic dessert.

1 box of yellow cake mix

Cooking spray

1 (16-ounce) can evaporated milk

1 (16-ounce) can sweetened condensed milk

1 cup heavy (whipping) cream

1. Close crisping lid. Select BAKE/ROAST, set temperature to 400°F, and set time to 43 minutes. Select START/STOP to begin. Let preheat for 5 minutes.

2. Prepare the cake batter according to the box instructions.

3. Grease a Ninja Multi-Purpose Pan or a 1½-quart round baking dish with cooking spray. Pour the batter into the pan. Place the pan on Reversible Rack, making sure rack is in the lower position.

4. Once unit has preheated, open lid and place rack with pan in pot. Close lid, and reduce temperature to 315°F. Cook for 38 minutes.

5. In a medium bowl whisk together the evaporated milk, condensed milk, and heavy cream.

6. When cooking is complete, remove rack with pan from pot and let cool for 10 minutes.

7. Remove pan from the rack. Using a long-pronged fork, poke holes every inch or so across the surface of the cake. Slowly pour the milk mixture over the cake. Refrigerate for 1 hour.

8. Once the cake has cooled and absorbed the milk mixture, slice and serve. If desired, top with whipped cream and strawberries.

*Per serving: Calories: 644; Total Fat: 28g; Saturated Fat: 14g; Cholesterol: 78mg; Sodium: 574mg; Carbohydrates: 89g; Fiber: 1g; Protein: 12g*

# Churro Bites

by Lauren Cardona, Ninja® Foodi™ Family Member

**SERVES 7**

*Lauren says:* Who doesn't love eating churros dipped in delicious sauces at fairs throughout the summer? Now you can have the sugary cinnamon-y goodness all year-round—in just a matter of minutes. I love to get creative with dipping sauces, too! From chocolate to strawberry to marshmallow, you just can't go wrong.

FAMILY FAVORITE, NUT-FREE, VEGETARIAN, UNDER 30 MINUTES

PREP TIME: 5 minutes
TOTAL COOK TIME:
12 minutes

APPROX. PRESSURE BUILD:
10 minutes
PRESSURE COOK:
12 minutes
PRESSURE RELEASE:
10 minutes, then Quick

ACCESSORIES:
Ninja Silicone Mold,
Reversible Rack

COOKING TIP: To make a DIY foil sling: Take about 18 inches of foil and fold it half lengthwise and then, lengthwise, in half again. You will end up with a 3-inch strip of foil. Lay the strip on your counter and place the egg bite molds on top of the foil (in the center) and then carefully lift the foil from the ends. The foil acts as a "sling" and will make it much easier to get the egg molds in and out of the Foodi.

Cooking spray

1 (21-ounce) box cinnamon swirl crumb cake and muffin mix, brown sugar mix packet removed and reserved

2 large eggs

1 cup buttermilk

1 teaspoon ground cinnamon, divided

¼ cup packed light brown sugar

1½ cups water

1 tablespoon granulated sugar

Chocolate sauce, for serving (optional)

Caramel sauce, for serving (optional)

Strawberry sauce, for serving (optional)

Whipped topping, for serving (optional)

Peanut butter, for serving (optional)

1. Lightly coat 2 egg bite molds with cooking spray and set aside.

2. In a large bowl, combine the cake mix, brown sugar mix packet, eggs, buttermilk, and ½ teaspoon of cinnamon. Mix until evenly combined.

3. Using a cookie scoop, transfer the batter to the prepared mold, filling each three-quarters full. Tightly cover the molds with aluminum foil, or with the silicone cover that came with the egg molds.

4. Pour the water into the cooking pot. Place the egg molds onto the Reversible Rack in the lower steam position and lower into the pot.

5. If using a foil sling (see TIP), ensure the foil cover is tight enough to support the egg mold that will sit on top. Rotate the top egg mold slightly to ensure that the molds do not press into one another.

6. Assemble the pressure lid, making sure the pressure release valve is in the SEAL position.

7. Select PRESSURE and set to HI. Set the time to 12 minutes. Select START/STOP to begin.

8. When pressure cooking is complete, allow the pressure to naturally release for 10 minutes. After 10 minutes, quick release any remaining pressure by moving the pressure release valve to the VENT position. Carefully remove the lid when the unit has finished releasing pressure.

9. In a small bowl, stir together the brown sugar, granulated sugar, and remaining ½ teaspoon of cinnamon. Set aside.

10. Using the sling, remove the egg molds from the pot and let cool for 5 minutes.

11. One at a time, place a plate over the egg mold and flip the mold over. Gently press on the mold to release the churro bites.

12. Roll the warm churro bites in the brown sugar mixture, and sprinkle any remaining brown sugar on top. Serve with your favorite dipping sauce.

**Find Lauren at TheTastyTravelers.com / Facebook: The Tasty Travelers & The Ninja Community**

*Per serving (2 bites): Calories: 427; Total Fat: 11g; Saturated Fat: 3g; Cholesterol: 55mg; Sodium: 532mg; Carbohydrates: 77g; Fiber: 1g; Protein: 4g*

# Fried Oreos

*When the Ninja® Foodi™ Pressure Cooker first launched, I was blown away by the online communities that formed seemingly overnight. I love seeing the support and inspiration and was inspired myself to try things I hadn't even thought to make. Case in point are these fried Oreos. Crisp on the outside with a cookie and cream center, they are the perfect sweet treat.*

**NUT-FREE, VEGETARIAN, UNDER 30 MINUTES, 5 INGREDIENT**

**PREP TIME:** 5 minutes
**TOTAL COOK TIME:** 8 minutes

**AIR CRISP:** 8 minutes

**ACCESSORIES:** Cook & Crisp Basket

**½ cup complete pancake mix**
**⅓ cup water**
**Cooking spray**

**9 Oreo cookies**
**1 tablespoon confectioners' sugar**

1. Close crisping lid. Select AIR CRISP, set temperature to 400°F, and set time to 5 minutes. Select START/STOP to begin preheating.

2. In a medium bowl, combine the pancake mix and water until combined.

3. Spray the Cook & Crisp Basket with cooking spray.

4. Dip each cookie into the pancake batter and then arrange them in the basket in a single layer so they are not touching each other. Cook in batches if needed.

5. When unit has preheated, open lid and insert basket into pot. Close crisping lid.

6. Select AIR CRISP, set temperature to 400°F, and set time to 8 minutes. Select START/STOP to begin.

7. After 4 minutes, open lid and flip the cookies. Close lid and continue cooking.

8. When cooking is complete, check for desired crispness. Remove basket and sprinkle the cookies with confectioners' sugar. Serve.

*Per serving: Calories: 83; Total Fat: 2g; Saturated Fat: 1g; Cholesterol: 1mg; Sodium: 158mg; Carbohydrates: 14g; Fiber: 1g; Protein: 1g*

# Coffee Cake

*This recipe is adapted from my mother-in-law's award-winning, semi-homemade coffee cake recipe. This version is easy to whip up for your next brunch or to pair with coffee at the end of a dinner party. The Foodi™ Pressure Cooker preheats faster than the oven, so the whole thing comes together in under 30 minutes.*

**DAIRY-FREE, NUT-FREE, VEGETARIAN, UNDER 30 MINUTES**

**PREP TIME:** 15 minutes
**TOTAL COOK TIME:** 30 minutes

**BAKE/ROAST:** 30 minutes

**ACCESSORIES:** Ninja Tube Pan, Reversible Rack

**VARIATION TIP:** To make a denser cake that tastes more homemade than from a box, use whole milk instead of water when preparing the cake mix. You can also switch things up by stirring chocolate chips into the batter, or swapping out the yellow cake mix for chocolate.

**Cooking spray**
**1 box yellow cake mix**
**1 cup water**
**⅓ cup vegetable oil**
**3 large eggs**
**4 cups all-purpose flour**
**1 cup granulated sugar**
**3 tablespoons cinnamon**
**2 cups unsalted butter, melted**
**Confectioners' sugar, for garnish**

1. Grease a Ninja Tube Pan or a 7-inch Bundt pan with cooking spray.

2. Close crisping lid. Select BAKE/ROAST, set temperature to 325°F, and set time to 5 minutes. Select START/STOP to begin preheating.

3. In a large bowl, mix together the cake mix, water, oil, and eggs until combined. Pour the batter into the prepared pan.

4. When unit has preheated, place pan on Reversible Rack, making sure the rack is in the lower position. Open lid and place rack with pan in pot. Close crisping lid.

5. Select BAKE/ROAST, set temperature to 325°F, and set time to 30 minutes. Select START/STOP to begin.

6. In another large bowl, combine the flour, sugar, and cinnamon. Add the butter and mix until well combined and the mixture is a crumble.

7. After 25 minutes, open lid and check for doneness. If a toothpick inserted into the cake comes out clean, the cake is done. If necessary, close lid and continue baking.

8. Open lid and spread the crumble topping on top of the cakes. Close lid and bake for an additional 4 to 5 minutes.

9. When cooking is complete, carefully remove pan from pot and place it on a cooling rack. Let cool. Using a fine mesh sieve, garnish the coffee cake with confectioners' sugar.

*Per serving: Calories: 1152; Total Fat: 65g; Saturated Fat: 32g; Cholesterol: 193mg; Sodium: 464mg; Carbohydrates: 132g; Fiber: 4g; Protein: 13g*

# Flourless Chocolate Cake

**SERVES 8**

*Flourless chocolate cake has always been a personal favorite of mine, not to mention it is inherently gluten-free, making it the perfect dessert for all types of diets. The fudgy, gooey center is rich and decadent. Top with whipped cream, chocolate ganache, fresh berries, or a scoop of vanilla ice cream. Perfect for special occasions or late nights when you have a sweet tooth craving.*

**GLUTEN-FREE, NUT-FREE, VEGETARIAN, FAMILY FAVORITE**

**PREP TIME:** 10 minutes
**TOTAL COOK TIME:** 40 minutes

**BAKE/ROAST:** 40 minutes

**ACCESSORIES:** Ninja Multi-Purpose Pan, Reversible Rack

**HACK IT:** This chocolate cake will be puffy with a crispy shell that will start to fall in on itself as it cools. Press a cutting board over the top of the cake pan to smooth the edges, then flip onto a cake plate and dust cocoa powder or confectioners' sugar over top to cover up imperfections.

Unsalted butter, at room temperature, for greasing the pan

9½ tablespoons unsalted butter, melted and cooled

4 large eggs, whites and yolks separated

1 cup granulated sugar, divided

½ cup unsweetened cocoa powder

¼ teaspoon vanilla extract

¼ teaspoon sea salt

1 cup plus 2 tablespoons semisweet chocolate chips, melted

**OPTIONAL TOPPINGS:**

Whipped cream

Fruit sauce

1. Grease a Ninja Multi-Purpose Pan or an 8-inch baking pan with butter and line the pan with a circle of parchment paper. Grease the parchment paper with butter.

2. Close crisping lid. Select BAKE/ROAST, set temperature to 350°F, and set time to 5 minutes. Select START/STOP to begin preheating.

3. In a large bowl, beat the melted butter and egg yolks. Add ½ cup of sugar, cocoa powder, vanilla extract, and salt. Slowly add the melted chocolate and stir.

4. In a medium bowl, beat the egg whites until soft peaks form. Add the remaining ½ cup of sugar and beat until stiff peaks form.

5. Gently fold the egg white mixture into the chocolate mixture. Pour the batter into the prepared pan.

6. When unit has preheated, place pan on Reversible Rack, making sure the rack is in the lower position. Open lid and place rack with pan in pot. Close crisping lid.

7. Select BAKE/ROAST, set temperature to 350°F, and set time to 40 minutes. Select START/STOP to begin.

CONTINUED ▶

# Flourless Chocolate Cake continued

8. After 30 minutes, check for doneness. If a toothpick inserted into the cake comes out clean, the cake is done. If not, close lid and continue baking until done.

9. When cooking is complete, carefully remove pan from pot and place it on a cooling rack for 5 minutes, then serve.

Per serving: *Calories: 437; Total Fat: 29g; Saturated Fat: 17g; Cholesterol: 137mg; Sodium: 109mg; Carbohydrates: 49g; Fiber: 4g; Protein: 7g*

# Ninja® Foodi™ Pressure Cooker
## COOKING TIME CHARTS
### Pressure Cook Chart

| INGREDIENT | WEIGHT | PREPARATION | WATER | |
|---|---|---|---|---|
| **POULTRY** | | | | |
| **Chicken breasts** | 2 lbs | Bone in | 1 cup | |
| | 6 small or 4 large (about 2 lbs) | Boneless | 1 cup | |
| **Chicken breasts (frozen)** | 4 large (2 lbs) | Boneless | 1 cup | |
| **Chicken thighs** | 8 thighs (4 lbs) | Bone in/skin on | 1 cup | |
| | 8 thighs (2 lbs) | Boneless | 1 cup | |
| **Chicken, whole** | 4–5 lbs | Bone in/legs tied | 1 cup | |
| **Turkey breast** | 1 breast (6–8 lbs) | Bone in | 1 cup | |
| **GROUND MEAT** | | | | |
| **Ground beef, pork, or turkey** | 1–2 lbs | Ground (not in patties) | ½ cup | |
| **Ground beef, pork, or turkey (frozen)** | 1–2 lbs | Frozen, ground (not in patties) | ½ cup | |
| **RIBS** | | | | |
| **Pork baby back** | 2½–3½ lbs | Cut in thirds | 1 cup | |
| **ROASTS** | | | | |
| **Beef brisket** | 3–4 lbs | Whole | 1 cup | |
| **Boneless beef chuck-eye roast** | 3–4 lbs | Whole | 1 cup | |
| **Boneless pork butt** | 4 lbs | Season as desired | 1 cup | |
| **Pork tenderloin** | 2 tenderloins (1–1½ lbs each) | Season as desired | 1 cup | |

| ACCESSORY | PRESSURE | TIME | RELEASE |
|---|---|---|---|
| N/A | High | 15 mins | Quick |
| N/A | High | 8–10 mins | Quick |
| N/A | High | 25 mins | Quick |
| N/A | High | 20 mins | Quick |
| N/A | High | 20 mins | Quick |
| Cook & Crisp™ Basket | High | 25–30 mins | Quick |
| N/A | High | 40–50 mins | Quick |
| N/A | High | 5 mins | Quick |
| N/A | High | 20–25 mins | Quick |
| N/A | High | 20 mins | Quick |
| N/A | High | 1½ hrs | Quick |
| N/A | High | 1½ hrs | Quick |
| N/A | High | 1½ hrs | Quick |
| N/A | High | 3–4 mins | Quick |

# Pressure Cook Chart

| INGREDIENT | WEIGHT | PREPARATION | WATER | |
|---|---|---|---|---|
| **STEW MEAT** | | | | |
| **Boneless beef short ribs** | 6 ribs (3 lbs) | Whole | 1 cup | |
| **Boneless leg of lamb** | 3 lbs | Cut in 1-inch pieces | 1 cup | |
| **Boneless pork butt** | 3 lbs | Cut in 1-inch pieces | 1 cup | |
| **Chuck roast, for stew** | 2 lbs | Cut in 1-inch pieces | 1 cup | |
| **HARD-BOILED EGGS** | | | | |
| **Eggs†** | 1–12 eggs | None | ½ cup | |
| **VEGETABLES** | | | | |
| **Beets** | 8 small or 4 large | Rinse well, trim tops and ends; cool and peel after cooking | ½ cup | |
| **Broccoli** | 1 head or 4 cups | Cut in 1-2-inch florets, remove stem | 1 cup | |
| **Brussels sprouts** | 1 lb | Cut in half | 1 cup | |
| **Butternut squash (cubed for side dish or salad)** | 20 oz | Peel, cut in 1-inch pieces, remove seeds | 1 cup | |
| **Butternut squash (for mashed, puree, or soup)** | 20 oz | Peel, cut in 1-inch pieces, remove seeds | 1 cup | |
| **Cabbage (braised)** | 1 head | Cut in half, slice in ½-inch strips, remove core | 1 cup | |
| **Cabbage (crisp)** | 1 head | Cut in half, slice in ½-inch strips, remove core | 1 cup | |
| **Carrots** | 1 lb | Peel, cut in ½-inch pieces | ½ cup | |

†Remove immediately when complete and place in ice bath.

| | ACCESSORY | PRESSURE | TIME | RELEASE |
|---|---|---|---|---|
| | N/A | High | 25 mins | Quick |
| | N/A | High | 30 mins | Quick |
| | N/A | High | 30 mins | Quick |
| | N/A | High | 25 mins | Quick |
| | N/A | High | 4 mins | Quick |
| | N/A | High | 15–20 mins | Quick |
| | Reversible rack in lower position | Low | 1 min | Quick |
| | Reversible rack in lower position | Low | 1 min | Quick |
| | N/A | Low | 2 mins | Quick |
| | Reversible rack in lower position | High | 2 mins | Quick |
| | N/A | Low | 3 mins | Quick |
| | Reversible rack in lower position | Low | 2 mins | Quick |
| | N/A | High | 2–3 mins | Quick |

# Pressure Cook Chart

| INGREDIENT | WEIGHT | PREPARATION | WATER | |
|---|---|---|---|---|
| **Cauliflower** | 1 head | Cut in 1–2-inch florets, remove stem | ½ cup | |
| **Collard greens** | 2 bunches or 1 bag (16 oz) | Remove stems, chop leaves | ½ cup | |
| **Green beans** | 1 bag (12 oz) | Whole | 1 cup | |
| **Kale leaves/greens** | 2 bunches or 1 bag (16 oz) | Remove stems, chop leaves | ½ cup | |
| **Potatoes, red (cubed for side dish or salad)** | 2 lbs | Scrub, cut in 1-inch cubes | ½ cup | |
| **Potatoes, red (for mashed)** | 2 lbs | Scrub, whole, large potatoes cut in half | ½ cup | |
| **Potatoes, Russet or Yukon (cubed for side dish or salad)** | 2 lbs | Peel, cut in 1-inch cubes | ½ cup | |
| **Potatoes, Russet or Yukon (for mashed)** | 2 lbs | Peel, cut in 1-inch thick slices | ½ cup | |
| **Potatoes, sweet (cubed for side dish or salad)** | 1 lb | Peel, cut in 1-inch cubes | ½ cup | |
| **Potatoes, sweet (for mashed)** | 1 lb | Peel, cut in 1-inch thick slices | ½ cup | |
| **DOUBLE-CAPACITY VEGETABLES** | | | | |
| **Broccoli** | 2 heads or 8 cups | Cut in 1–2-inch florets, remove stem | 1 cup | |
| **Brussels sprouts** | 2 lbs | Cut in half, remove stem | 1 cup | |
| **Butternut squash** | 48 oz | Peel, cut in 1-inch pieces | 1 cup | |
| **Cabbage** | 1½ heads | Cut in half, remove core | 1 cup | |
| **Green beans** | 2 bags (24 oz) | Whole | 1 cup | |

*The time the unit takes to pressurize is long enough to cook this food.

| ACCESSORY | PRESSURE | TIME | RELEASE |
|---|---|---|---|
| N/A | Low | 1 min | Quick |
| N/A | Low | 6 mins | Quick |
| Reversible rack in lower position | Low | 0 mins* | Quick |
| N/A | Low | 3 mins | Quick |
| N/A | High | 1–2 mins | Quick |
| N/A | High | 15–20 mins | Quick |
| N/A | High | 1–2 mins | Quick |
| N/A | High | 6 mins | Quick |
| N/A | High | 1–2 mins | Quick |
| N/A | High | 6 mins | Quick |
| | | | |
| Deluxe Reversible Rack (both layers) | Low | 1 min | Quick |
| Deluxe Reversible Rack (both layers) | Low | 1 min | Quick |
| Deluxe Reversible Rack (both layers) | High | 3 mins | Quick |
| Deluxe Reversible Rack (both layers) | Low | 5 mins | Quick |
| Deluxe Reversible Rack (both layers) | Low | 0 mins* | Quick |

# Pressure Cook Chart

| INGREDIENT | AMOUNT | WATER | |
|---|---|---|---|
| **GRAINS** | | | |
| **Arborio rice*** | 1 cup | 3 cups | |
| **Basmati rice** | 1 cup | 1 cup | |
| **Brown rice, short/medium or long grain** | 1 cup | 1¼ cups | |
| **Coarse grits/polenta*** | 1 cup | 3½ cups | |
| **Farro** | 1 cup | 2 cups | |
| **Jasmine rice** | 1 cup | 1 cup | |
| **Kamut** | 1 cup | 2 cups | |
| **Millet** | 1 cup | 2 cups | |
| **Pearl barley** | 1 cup | 2 cups | |
| **Quinoa** | 1 cup | 1½ cups | |
| **Quinoa, red** | 1 cup | 1½ cups | |
| **Spelt** | 1 cup | 2½ cups | |
| **Steel-cut oats*** | 1 cup | 3 cups | |
| **Sushi rice** | 1 cup | 1½ cups | |
| **Texmati® rice, brown**** | 1 cup | 1¼ cups | |
| **Texmati® rice, light brown**** | 1 cup | 1¼ cups | |
| **Texmati® rice, white**** | 1 cup | 1 cup | |
| **Wheat berries** | 1 cup | 3 cups | |
| **White rice, long grain** | 1 cup | 1 cup | |
| **White rice, medium grain** | 1 cup | 1 cup | |
| **Wild rice** | 1 cup | 1 cup | |

*After releasing pressure, stir for 30 seconds to 1 minute, then let sit for 5 minutes.

**TEXMATI is a registered trademark of Riviana Foods, Inc. Use of the TEXMATI trademark does not imply any affiliation with or endorsement by Riviana Foods, Inc.

TIP For best results, rinse rice and grains thoroughly before pressure cooking.

| | PRESSURE | TIME | RELEASE |
|---|---|---|---|
| | High | 7 mins | Natural (10 mins) then Quick |
| | High | 2 mins | Natural (10 mins) then Quick |
| | High | 15 mins | Natural (10 mins) then Quick |
| | High | 4 mins | Natural (10 mins) then Quick |
| | High | 10 mins | Natural (10 mins) then Quick |
| | High | 2–3 mins | Natural (10 mins) then Quick |
| | High | 30 mins | Natural (10 mins) then Quick |
| | High | 6 mins | Natural (10 mins) then Quick |
| | High | 22 mins | Natural (10 mins) then Quick |
| | High | 2 mins | Natural (10 mins) then Quick |
| | High | 2 mins | Natural (10 mins) then Quick |
| | High | 25 mins | Natural (10 mins) then Quick |
| | High | 11 mins | Natural (10 mins) then Quick |
| | High | 3 mins | Natural (10 mins) then Quick |
| | High | 5 mins | Natural (10 mins) then Quick |
| | High | 2 mins | Natural (10 mins) then Quick |
| | High | 2 mins | Natural (10 mins) then Quick |
| | High | 15 mins | Natural (10 mins) then Quick |
| | High | 2 mins | Natural (10 mins) then Quick |
| | High | 3 mins | Natural (10 mins) then Quick |
| | High | 22 mins | Natural (10 mins) then Quick |

# Pressure Cook Chart

| INGREDIENT | AMOUNT | WATER | |
|---|---|---|---|
| **LEGUMES** | | | |
| **All beans, except lentils, should be soaked 8–24 hours before cooking.** | | | |
| **Black beans** | 1 lb, soaked 8–24 hrs | 6 cups | |
| **Black-eyed peas** | 1 lb, soaked 8–24 hrs | 6 cups | |
| **Cannellini beans** | 1 lb, soaked 8–24 hrs | 6 cups | |
| **Cranberry beans** | 1 lb, soaked 8–24 hrs | 6 cups | |
| **Garbanzo beans (chickpeas)** | 1 lb, soaked 8–24 hrs | 6 cups | |
| **Great northern bean** | 1 lb, soaked 8–24 hrs | 6 cups | |
| **Lentils (green or brown)** | 1 cup dry | 2 cups | |
| **Lima beans** | 1 lb, soaked 8–24 hrs | 6 cups | |
| **Navy beans** | 1 lb, soaked 8–24 hrs | 6 cups | |
| **Pinto beans** | 1 lb, soaked 8–24 hrs | 6 cups | |
| **Red kidney beans** | 1 lb, soaked 8–24 hrs | 6 cups | |
| **This section does not require beans to be soaked.** | | | |
| **Black beans** | 2 lbs | 4 quarts (16 cups) | |
| **Black-eyed peas** | 2 lbs | 4 quarts (16 cups) | |
| **Cannellini beans** | 2 lbs | 4 quarts (16 cups) | |
| **Cranberry beans** | 2 lbs | 4 quarts (16 cups) | |
| **Garbanzo beans (chickpeas)** | 2 lbs | 4 quarts (16 cups) | |
| **Great northern bean** | 2 lbs | 4 quarts (16 cups) | |
| **Lima beans** | 2 lbs | 4 quarts (16 cups) | |
| **Navy beans** | 2 lbs | 4 quarts (16 cups) | |
| **Pinto beans** | 2 lbs | 4 quarts (16 cups) | |
| **Red kidney beans** | 2 lbs | 4 quarts (16 cups) | |

| | PRESSURE | TIME | RELEASE |
|---|---|---|---|
| | Low | 5 mins | Natural (10 mins) then Quick |
| | Low | 5 mins | Natural (10 mins) then Quick |
| | Low | 3 mins | Natural (10 mins) then Quick |
| | Low | 3 mins | Natural (10 mins) then Quick |
| | Low | 3 mins | Natural (10 mins) then Quick |
| | Low | 1 min | Natural (10 mins) then Quick |
| | Low | 5 mins | Natural (10 mins) then Quick |
| | Low | 1 min | Natural (10 mins) then Quick |
| | Low | 3 mins | Natural (10 mins) then Quick |
| | Low | 3 mins | Natural (10 mins) then Quick |
| | Low | 3 mins | Natural (10 mins) then Quick |
| | High | 25 mins | Natural (15 mins) then Quick |
| | High | 25 mins | Natural (15 mins) then Quick |
| | High | 40 mins | Natural (15 mins) then Quick |
| | High | 40 mins | Natural (15 mins) then Quick |
| | High | 40 mins | Natural (15 mins) then Quick |
| | High | 30 mins | Natural (15 mins) then Quick |
| | High | 30 mins | Natural (15 mins) then Quick |
| | High | 30 mins | Natural (15 mins) then Quick |
| | High | 30 mins | Natural (15 mins) then Quick |
| | High | 40 mins | Natural (15 mins) then Quick |

# Air Crisp Chart for the Cook & Crisp™ Basket

| INGREDIENT | AMOUNT | PREPARATION | |
|---|---|---|---|
| **VEGETABLES** | | | |
| **Asparagus** | 1 bunch | Cut in half, trim stems | |
| **Beets** | 6 small or 4 large (about 2 lbs) | Whole | |
| **Bell peppers (for roasting)** | 4 peppers | Whole | |
| **Broccoli** | 1 head | Cut in 1–2-inch florets | |
| **Brussels sprouts** | 1 lb | Cut in half, remove stems | |
| **Butternut squash** | 1–1½ lbs | Cut in 1–2-inch pieces | |
| **Carrots** | 1 lb | Peeled, cut in ½-inch pieces | |
| **Cauliflower** | 1 head | Cut in 1–2-inch florets | |
| **Corn on the cob** | 4 ears, cut in half | Whole, remove husks | |
| **Green beans** | 1 bag (12 oz) | Trimmed | |
| **Kale (for chips)** | 6 cups, packed | Tear in pieces, remove stems | |
| **Mushrooms** | 8 oz | Rinse, cut in quarters | |
| **Potatoes, Russet** | 1½ lbs | Cut in 1-inch wedges | |
| | 1 lb | Hand-cut fries, thin | |
| | 1 lb | Hand-cut fries, soak 30 mins in cold water then pat dry | |
| | 4 whole (6–8 oz) | Pierce with fork 3 times | |
| **Potatoes, sweet** | 2 lbs | Cut in 1-inch chunks | |
| | 4 whole (6–8 oz) | Pierce with fork 3 times | |
| **Zucchini** | 1 lb | Cut in quarters lengthwise, then cut in 1-inch pieces | |

| OIL | TEMP | COOK TIME |
|---|---|---|
| 2 tsp | 390°F | 8–10 mins |
| None | 390°F | 45–60 mins |
| None | 400°F | 25–30 mins |
| 1 Tbsp | 390°F | 10–13 mins |
| 1 Tbsp | 390°F | 15–18 mins |
| 1 Tbsp | 390°F | 20–25 mins |
| 1 Tbsp | 390°F | 14–16 mins |
| 2 Tbsp | 390°F | 15–20 mins |
| 1 Tbsp | 390°F | 12–15 mins |
| 1 Tbsp | 390°F | 7–10 mins |
| None | 300°F | 8–11 mins |
| 1 Tbsp | 390°F | 7–8 mins |
| 1 Tbsp | 390°F | 20–25 mins |
| ½–3 Tbsp canola | 390°F | 20–25 mins |
| ½–3 Tbsp canola | 390°F | 24–27 mins |
| None | 390°F | 35–40 mins |
| 1 Tbsp | 390°F | 15–20 mins |
| None | 390°F | 35–40 mins |
| 1 Tbsp | 390°F | 15–20 mins |

# Air Crisp Chart for the Cook & Crisp™ Basket

| INGREDIENT | AMOUNT | PREPARATION | |
|---|---|---|---|
| **POULTRY** | | | |
| **Chicken breasts** | 2 breasts (¾–1½ lbs each) | Bone in | |
| | 2 breasts (½–¾ lb each) | Boneless | |
| **Chicken thighs** | 4 thighs (6-10 oz each) | Bone in | |
| | 4 thighs (4-8 oz each) | Boneless | |
| **Chicken wings** | 2 lbs | Drumettes & flats | |
| **Chicken, whole** | 1 chicken (4-6 lbs) | Trussed | |
| **Chicken drumsticks** | 2 lbs | None | |
| **BEEF** | | | |
| **Burgers** | 4 quarter-pound patties, 80% lean | 1-inch thick | |
| **Steaks** | 2 steaks (8 oz each) | Whole | |
| **PORK & LAMB** | | | |
| **Bacon** | 1 strip to 1 (16 oz) package | Lay strips evenly over edge of basket | |
| **Pork chops** | 2 thick-cut, bone-in chops (10–12 oz each) | Bone in | |
| | 4 boneless chops (6-8 oz each) | Boneless | |
| **Pork tenderloins** | 2 tenderloins (1–1½ lbs each) | Whole | |
| **Sausages** | 4 sausages | Whole | |
| **FISH & SEAFOOD** | | | |
| **Crab cakes** | 2 cakes (6-8 oz each) | None | |
| **Lobster tails** | 4 tails (3-4 oz each) | Whole | |
| **Salmon fillets** | 2 fillets (4 oz each) | None | |
| **Shrimp** | 16 jumbo | Raw, whole, peel, keep tails on | |

| | OIL | TEMP | COOK TIME |
|---|---|---|---|
| | Brushed with oil | 375°F | 25–35 mins |
| | Brushed with oil | 375°F | 22–25 mins |
| | Brushed with oil | 390°F | 22–28 mins |
| | Brushed with oil | 390°F | 18–22 mins |
| | 1 Tbsp | 390°F | 24–28 mins |
| | Brushed with oil | 375°F | 55–75 mins |
| | 1 Tbsp | 390°F | 20–22 mins |
| | | | |
| | None | 375°F | 10–12 mins |
| | None | 390°F | 10–20 mins |
| | | | |
| | None | 330°F | 13–16 mins (no preheat) |
| | Brushed with oil | 375°F | 15–17 mins |
| | Brushed with oil | 375°F | 15–18 mins |
| | Brushed with oil | 375°F | 25–35 mins |
| | None | 390°F | 8–10 mins |
| | | | |
| | Brushed with oil | 350°F | 8–12 mins |
| | None | 375°F | 7–10 mins |
| | Brushed with oil | 390°F | 10–13 mins |
| | 1 Tbsp | 390°F | 7–10 mins |

# Air Crisp Chart for the Cook & Crisp™ Basket

| INGREDIENT | AMOUNT | PREPARATION | |
|------------|--------|-------------|---|
| **FROZEN FOODS** | | | |
| **Chicken nuggets** | 1 box (12 oz) | None | |
| **Fish fillets** | 1 box (6 fillets) | None | |
| **Fish sticks** | 1 box (14.8 oz) | None | |
| **French fries** | 1 lb | None | |
| | 2 lbs | None | |
| **Mozzarella sticks** | 1 box (11 oz) | None | |
| **Pot stickers** | 1 bag (10 count) | None | |
| **Pizza Rolls** | 1 bag (20 oz, 40 count) | None | |
| **Popcorn shrimp** | 1 box (16 oz) | None | |
| **Tater Tots** | 1 lb | None | |

| | OIL | TEMP | COOK TIME |
|---|---|---|---|
| | None | 390°F | 11–13 mins |
| | None | 390°F | 13–15 mins |
| | None | 390°F | 9–11 mins |
| | None | 360°F | 18–22 mins |
| | None | 360°F | 28–32 mins |
| | None | 375°F | 6–9 mins |
| | Toss with 1 tsp canola oil | 390°F | 11–14 mins |
| | None | 390°F | 12–15 mins |
| | None | 390°F | 8–10 mins |
| | None | 360°F | 19–22 mins |

# Steam Chart for the Deluxe Reversible Rack

| INGREDIENT | AMOUNT | |
|---|---|---|
| **VEGETABLES** | | |
| **Artichokes** | 4 | |
| **Asparagus** | 1 bunch | |
| **Broccoli** | 1 crown or 1 bag (12 oz) florets | |
| **Brussels sprouts** | 1 lb | |
| **Butternut squash** | 24 oz | |
| **Cabbage** | 1 head | |
| **Carrots** | 1 lb | |
| **Cauliflower** | 1 head | |
| **Corn on the cob** | 4 ears | |
| **Green beans** | 1 bag (12 oz) | |
| **Kale** | 1 bag (16 oz) | |
| **Potatoes** | 1 lb | |
| **Potatoes, new** | 1 lb | |
| **Potatoes, sweet** | 1 lb | |
| **Spinach** | 1 bag (16 oz) | |
| **Sugar snap peas** | 1 lb | |
| **Summer Squash** | 1 lb | |
| **Zucchini** | 1 lb | |
| **EGGS** | | |
| **Poached eggs** | 4 | |

| | PREPARATION | LIQUID | COOK TIME |
|---|---|---|---|
| | Whole | 4 cups | 25–42 mins |
| | Whole spears | 3 cups | 7–15 mins |
| | Cut in florets | 2 cups | 5–9 mins |
| | Whole, trimmed | 3 cups | 8–17 mins |
| | Peeled, cut in 1-inch cubes | 2 cups | 10–17 mins |
| | Cut in wedges | 2 cups | 6–12 mins |
| | Peeled, cut in 1-inch pieces | 2 cups | 7–12 mins |
| | Cut in florets | 2 cups | 5–12 mins |
| | Whole, husks removed | 2 cups | 4–9 mins |
| | Whole | 2 cups | 6–12 mins |
| | Trimmed | 2 cups | 5–10 mins |
| | Peeled, cut in 1-inch pieces | 2 cups | 12–17 mins |
| | Whole | 4 cups | 15–22 mins |
| | Cut in ½-inch cubes | 3 cups | 8–14 mins |
| | Whole leaves | 2 cups | 3–7 mins |
| | Whole pods, trimmed | 2 cups | 5–8 mins |
| | Cut in 1-inch slices | 2 cups | 5–10 mins |
| | Cut in 1-inch slices | 2 cups | 5–10 mins |
| | In ramekins or silicone cups | 1 cup | 3–6 mins |

## Steam Chart for the Deluxe Reversible Rack

| INGREDIENT | AMOUNT | |
|---|---|---|
| **VEGETABLES** | | |
| **Asparagus** | 2 bunches | |
| **Broccoli** | 2 heads or 2 bags (24 oz) | |
| **Brussels sprouts** | 2 lbs | |
| **Butternut squash** | 48 oz | |
| **Cabbage** | 1½ heads | |
| **Carrots** | 2 lbs | |
| **Cauliflower** | 2 heads | |
| **Corn on the cob** | 4 ears | |
| **Green beans** | 2 bags (24 oz) | |
| **Kale** | 2 bags (32 oz) | |
| **Potatoes** | 2 lbs | |
| **Potatoes, sweet** | 2 lbs | |
| **Spinach** | 2 bags (32 oz) | |
| **Sugar snap peas** | 2 lbs | |
| **Summer squash** | 2 lbs | |
| **Zucchini** | 2 lbs | |

| | PREPARATION | WATER | COOK TIME |
|---|---|---|---|
| | Whole, trim ends | 2 cups | 8–12 mins |
| | Cut in 1–2-inch florets | 2 cups | 7–10 mins |
| | Whole, trim ends | 2 cups | 10–12 mins |
| | Peel, cut into 1-inch cubes | 2 cups | 18–22 mins |
| | Cut in half, sliced in ½-inch strips, core removed | 2 cups | 20–22 mins |
| | Peeled, cut into 1-inch pieces | 2 cups | 15–18 mins |
| | Cut in 1–2-inch florets | 2 cups | 12–15 mins |
| | Whole, remove husks | 2 cups | 7–9 mins |
| | Whole | 2 cups | 12–15 mins |
| | Trim | 2 cups | 10–14 mins |
| | Peel, cut in 1-inch pieces | 2 cups | 16–18 mins |
| | Cut into 1-inch cubes | 2 cups | 18–22 mins |
| | Whole leaves | 2 cups | 8–12 mins |
| | Whole pods, trimmed | 2 cups | 10–12 mins |
| | Cut into 1-inch slices | 2 cups | 16–18 mins |
| | Cut into 1-inch slices | 2 cups | 14–16 mins |

# Dehydrate Chart for the Cook & Crisp™ Basket with the Cook & Crisp Layered Insert,* Dehydrating Rack** or Deluxe Reversible Rack

| INGREDIENT | PREPARATION | |
|---|---|---|
| **FROZEN FOODS** | | |
| **Apple chips** | Cut in ⅛-inch slices (remove core), rinse in lemon water, pat dry | |
| **Asparagus** | Cut in 1-inch pieces, blanch | |
| **Bananas** | Peel, cut in ⅜-inch slices | |
| **Beet chips** | Peel, cut in ⅛-inch slices | |
| **Eggplant** | Peel, cut in ¼-inch slices, blanch | |
| **Fresh herbs** | Rinse, pat dry, remove stems | |
| **Ginger root** | Cut in ⅜-inch slices | |
| **Mangoes** | Peel, cut in ⅜-inch slices, remove pits | |
| **Mushrooms** | Clean with soft brush (do not wash) | |
| **Pineapple** | Peel, cut in ⅜–½-inch slices, core removed | |
| **Strawberries** | Cut in half or in ½-inch slices | |
| **Tomatoes** | Cut in ⅜-inch slices or grate; steam if planning to rehydrate | |
| **JERKY - MEAT, POULTRY, FISH** | | |
| **Beef jerky** | Cut in ¼-inch slices, marinate overnight | |
| **Chicken jerky** | Cut in ¼-inch slices, marinate overnight | |
| **Turkey jerky** | Cut in ¼-inch slices, marinate overnight | |
| **Salmon jerky** | Cut in ¼-inch slices, marinate overnight | |

*If the Ninja Cook & Crisp Layered Insert is not included with your unit, it can be purchased on ninjaaccessories.com.
**The Ninja dehydrating rack is sold separately on ninjaaccessories.com.

TIP Most fruits and vegetables take between 6 and 8 hours (at 135°F) to dehydrate; meats take between 5 and 7 hours (at 150°F). The longer you dehydrate your ingredients, the crispier they will be.

| | TEMP | DEHYDRATE TIME |
|---|---|---|
| | 135°F | 7–8 hrs |
| | 135°F | 6–8 hrs |
| | 135°F | 8–10 hrs |
| | 135°F | 7–8 hrs |
| | 135°F | 6–8 hrs |
| | 135°F | 4–6 hrs |
| | 135°F | 6 hrs |
| | 135°F | 6–8 hrs |
| | 135°F | 6–8 hrs |
| | 135°F | 6–8 hrs |
| | 135°F | 6–8 hrs |
| | 135°F | 6–8 hrs |
| | 150°F | 5–7 hrs |
| | 150°F | 5–7 hrs |
| | 150°F | 5–7 hrs |
| | 165°F | 5–8 hrs |

# TenderCrisp™ Chart

| PROTEIN | AMOUNT | ACCESSORY | |
|---|---|---|---|
| **Whole chicken** | 1 chicken (6-7 lbs) | Cook & Crisp™ Basket | |
| **St. Louis ribs** | 1 rack, cut in quarters | Cook & Crisp Basket | |
| **Frozen chicken breasts** | 2 breasts (6-8 oz each) | Deluxe Reversible Rack, in higher broil position | |
| **Frozen New York strip steaks** | 2 steaks (12 oz each) | Deluxe Reversible Rack, in higher broil position | |
| | 2 steaks (14 oz each) | Deluxe Reversible Rack, in higher broil position | |
| | 2 steaks (16 oz each) | Deluxe Reversible Rack, in higher broil position | |
| **Frozen chicken wings** | 1 lb | Cook & Crisp Basket | |
| **Bone-in skin-on chicken thighs** | 4 thighs (6-8 oz each) | Cook & Crisp Basket | |
| **Frozen pork chops** | 4 chops (6-8 oz each) | Deluxe Reversible Rack, in higher broil position | |
| **Frozen jumbo shrimp** | 28 uncooked, peeled, deveined | Deluxe Reversible Rack, Deluxe Layer installed, place shrimp on both layers | |

| | WATER | PRESSURE COOK | PRESSURE RELEASE | CRISPING LID |
|---|---|---|---|---|
| | ½ cup | High for 40 mins | | Air Crisp at 400°F for 15 mins |
| | ½ cup | High for 19 mins | | Air Crisp at 400°F for 10–15 mins |
| | 1 cup | High for 10 mins | | Broil for 10 mins |
| | 1 cup | High for 1 min | Quick release pressure. | Broil for 8–10 mins |
| | 1 cup | High for 2 mins | Carefully remove lid. | Broil for 11–15 mins |
| | 1 cup | High for 3 mins | Pat protein dry with paper towel and brush with oil or sauce. | Broil for 11–15 mins |
| | ½ cup | High for 5 mins | | Air Crisp at 390°F for 15–20 mins |
| | ½ cup | High for 2 mins | | Air Crisp at 400°F for 10 mins |
| | 1 cup | High for 2 mins | | Air Crisp at 400°F for 8–12 mins |
| | 1 cup | High for 0 mins | | Air Crisp at 400°F for 5 mins |

# INDEX

# MEASUREMENT CONVERSIONS

## VOLUME EQUIVALENTS (LIQUID)

| US Standard | US Standard (ounces) | Metric (approximate) |
|---|---|---|
| 2 tablespoons | 1 fl. oz. | 30 mL |
| ¼ cup | 2 fl. oz. | 60 mL |
| ½ cup | 4 fl. oz. | 120 mL |
| 1 cup | 8 fl. oz. | 240 mL |
| 1½ cups | 12 fl. oz. | 355 mL |
| 2 cups or 1 pint | 16 fl. oz. | 475 mL |
| 4 cups or 1 quart | 32 fl. oz. | 1 L |
| 1 gallon | 128 fl. oz. | 4 L |

## VOLUME EQUIVALENTS (DRY)

| US Standard | Metric (approximate) |
|---|---|
| ⅛ teaspoon | 0.5 mL |
| ¼ teaspoon | 1 mL |
| ½ teaspoon | 2 mL |
| ¾ teaspoon | 4 mL |
| 1 teaspoon | 5 mL |
| 1 tablespoon | 15 mL |
| ¼ cup | 59 mL |
| ⅓ cup | 79 mL |
| ½ cup | 118 mL |
| ⅔ cup | 156 mL |
| ¾ cup | 177 mL |
| 1 cup | 235 mL |
| 2 cups or 1 pint | 475 mL |
| 3 cups | 700 mL |
| 4 cups or 1 quart | 1 L |

## OVEN TEMPERATURES

| Fahrenheit (F) | Celsius (C) (approximate) |
|---|---|
| 250°F | 120°C |
| 300°F | 150°C |
| 325°F | 165°C |
| 350°F | 180°C |
| 375°F | 190°C |
| 400°F | 200°C |
| 425°F | 220°C |
| 450°F | 230°C |

## WEIGHT EQUIVALENTS

| US Standard | Metric (approximate) |
|---|---|
| ½ ounce | 15 g |
| 1 ounce | 30 g |
| 2 ounces | 60 g |
| 4 ounces | 115 g |
| 8 ounces | 225 g |
| 12 ounces | 340 g |
| 16 ounces or 1 pound | 455 g |

# ACKNOWLEDGMENTS

**FIRST AND FOREMOST, THANK YOU TO JULIEN, MY BEST FRIEND, MY** faithful taste tester, my cameraman, and my husband. Thank you for supporting me and my crazy ideas, for caffeinating me during long days of recipe testing, and for feeding me during late nights of copywriting.

To my friends and family, thank you for your words of encouragement and for cheering me on throughout this journey. I am so thankful to have each and every one of you in my corner.

To my amazing Ninja® Test Kitchen team, Sam, Meg, Craig, Kelly, Chelven, and Caroline, thank you for inspiring me every day. Thank you for supporting my wild ideas, for making me look forward to coming to work, and for filling the world with flavorful recipes. I am so excited that the world gets to learn more about each of you and your recipes through this book.

To Bridget and my team at Callisto Media, thank you for joining me on this journey and for believing in the Foodi™ Pressure Cooker. I am so happy to be working with you again and am proud to be part of the Callisto Media family.

Last but never least, to my readers, thank you for trying my recipes and sharing them with your friends and loved ones. I know you will love the Ninja Foodi Pressure Cooker and these recipes as much as I do!

# ABOUT THE AUTHOR

**KENZIE SWANHART**

**Director, Culinary Innovation and Marketing
Head of Ninja® Test Kitchen**

Kenzie Swanhart is a home cook turned food blogger and cookbook author, providing her readers inspiration for in and out of the kitchen. With more than 250,000 copies of her cookbooks in print, Kenzie never wavers in her mission: creating and sharing easy yet flavorful recipes made with real ingredients with her readers.

As the head of culinary innovation and marketing for Ninja, a leading kitchen appliance company, Kenzie and her team provide a unique, food-first point of view for the development of new products and recipes to make consumers' lives easier and healthier. You'll also see her serving as the face of Ninja on the leading television home shopping network, where she shares tips, tricks, and recipes for the company's full line of products.

Kenzie lives in Boston with her husband Julien and their dog Charlie.

# ABOUT THE CHEFS

### MEG JORDAN
### Senior Culinary Recipe and Content Developer

Meg is an advertising agency professional turned culinary specialist after making a career change in 2017. After spending almost a decade working in media with Fortune 500 clients, Meg decided to pursue her lifelong passion of working in the culinary industry. A graduate of the Boston University Culinary Arts Certificate program, Meg studied under various high-profile chefs in the Boston culinary scene as well as chef Jacques Pepin. Meg joined the Ninja® Test Kitchen team in 2018, and in her spare time, she enjoys learning more about the art of charcuterie and whole animal butchery.

### SAM FERGUSON
### Culinary Manager

Sam Ferguson is a culinary innovation and marketing manager at Ninja, overseeing and leading the culinary product development of heated cooking appliances. After 10 fulfilling years in the restaurant industry, Sam was ready to step out of the grind of kitchen life and into something less stressful but equally rewarding. Enter Ninja! As a leader on the product development team, Sam strives to create high-quality, innovative, and truly useful cooking tools for all home chefs around the world. Sam lives in Boston with his wife Lily and his beagle Waylon.

### CRAIG WHITE
**Research Chef**

Craig's love for charcuterie and the craft of cooking can be traced back to when he was four years old and his mother caught him cooking hot dogs in the middle of the night. He attended culinary school at Le Cordon Bleu and was given his first chance in a kitchen by chef Jody Adams at Rialto, where he worked his way up the line. He has worked under James Beard Award-winning chefs Nancy Silverton of Mozza in Los Angeles and Frank McClelland of L'Espalier in Boston. He opened and owned Half Baked Cafe and Bakery in Beverly Farms and during this time was also charcutier for Matt Jennings at Townsman in Boston. After two years as chef de cuisine at Ledger in Salem, he joined Ninja® as a consultant and is now settled in as lead culinary developer for Ninja Motorized. And although through his cooking he has been "positively impacting people's lives every day," he is excited to do it "in every home around the world" with Ninja. Craig lives in Salem, Massachusetts. In his free time, he enjoys traveling and kayaking with his girlfriend Michelle, collecting cookbooks and tattoos, and playing guitar. He continues to consult for restaurants and is currently working on Consumed apparel, a culinary and pop-culture designed T-shirt company.

### KELLY GRAY
**Research Chef**

Kelly Gray is a food scientist and travel enthusiast with a cooking style influenced by childhood nostalgia and foreign cultures. Her experience spans many aspects of the food industry from restaurant work to baking mix formulation, and even shellfish farming. As an alumna of California State Polytechnic University, Pomona, with a degree in Food Science and Technology and Culinology®, Kelly's culinary approach is as analytical as it is creative—quite useful in her current role in the Ninja Test Kitchen. As a believer in the relationship between good food, community, and well-being, Kelly hopes to encourage people to come back into the kitchen with approachable recipes and state-of-the-art appliances that make cooking enjoyable and stress free. If not in the test kitchen or cooking for her friends and family, you can find Kelly enjoying the outdoors, salsa dancing, or daydreaming about a trip to someplace new.

**CHELVEN RANDOLPH**
### Research Chef

Cooking with love is the only way Chef Chelven Randolph knows how to cook. Raised in the kitchen by his mother, Linda McCoy, who was also a chef, Chelven fell in love with the idea of creating unique dishes as therapy. His family life was firmly rooted in the concept that breaking bread with friends and loved ones was a time to nourish the soul as well as the body. Born in Boston, Massachusetts, Chelven acquired his culinary skills in an array of award-winning kitchens like Castle Hill Inn in Newport, Rhode Island, and Fig & Olive in Beverly Hills, California. Most recently he was the sous chef at Coppa Enoteca in the South End of Boston operated by James Beard Award-winning chefs Ken Oringer and Jamie Bissonnette. Chelven brings fresh and unique ideas from his vast experience in kitchens around the country. Chelven lives in Bellingham, Massachusetts, with his partner Amy and their two children.

**CAROLINE SCHLIEP**
### Kitchen Manager

Caroline Schliep is a Midwest native turned New Englander who has had a passion for cooking since a young age. Her love of travel has led her to work at many restaurants around the country, even studying abroad in Singapore and Thailand with At-Sunrice GlobalChef Academy. She is an alumna of Johnson & Wales University in Providence, Rhode Island, where she earned an associate's degree in Culinary Arts and a bachelor's degree in Culinary Nutrition and Food Science. Nowadays you can find her in the Ninja® Test Kitchen where she takes on many roles, from recipe development and validation to food styling and monthly culinary trend reports.

# NOTES